A Garland Series

AMERICAN INDIAN ETHNOHISTORY

Indians of the Southwest

compiled and edited by

DAVID AGEE HORR
Brandeis University

Navajo Indians II

NAVAJO ACTIVITIES AFFECTING
THE ACOMA—LAGUNA AREA,
1746–1910

Myra Ellen Jenkins
Ward Alan Minge

THE NAVAJO INDIANS

Frank D. Reeve

Garland Publishing Inc., New York & London
1974

Library of Congress Cataloging in Publication Data

Jenkins, Myra Ellen.
    Navajo activities affecting the Acoma-Laguna area,
1746-1910.

    (Navajo Indians, 2) (American Indian ethnohistory:
Indians of the Southwest)
    M. E. Jenkins and W. A. Minge's report presented
before the Indian Claims Commission, joint exhibit
no. 530, docket no. 229; F. D. Reeve's report: exhibit
no. R-150, docket no. 229.
    Bibliography: p.
    1. Navaho Indians—History. 2. Laguna Indians—
History. 3. Acoma Indians—History. I. Minge, Ward
Alan, joint author. II. Reeve, Frank Driver, 1899-
The Navajo Indians. 1974. III. United States.
Indian Claims Commission. IV. Title. V. Series.
VI. Series: American Indian ethnohistory: Indians
of the Southwest.
E99.N3N338 no. 2   970.3s [970.3]   74-2380
ISBN 0-8240-0704-2

Printed in the United States of America

Contents*

5

*There are three volumes on the Navajo Indians in the Garland American Indian Ethnohistory Series. The prefatory material is in Volume I; the Commission Findings in Volume III.

**Garland Publishing has repaginated this work (at outside center) to facilitate scholarly use. However, original pagination has been retained for internal reference.

6

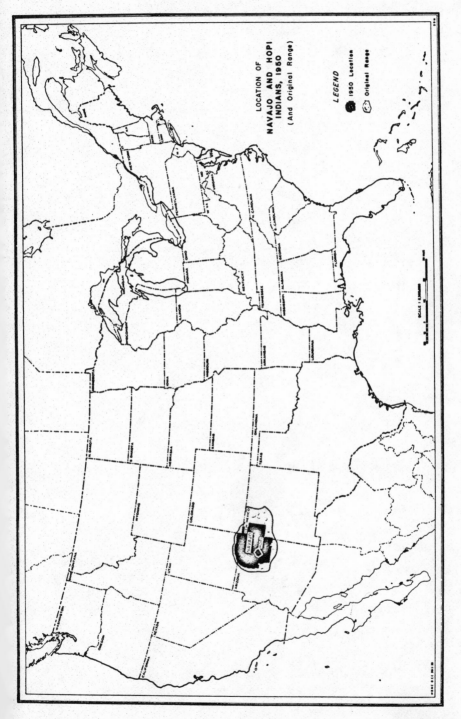

LOCATION OF
NAVAJO AND HOPI
INDIANS, 1950
(And Original Range)

LEGEND

● 1950 Location

⬡ Original Range

SCALE 1 2 SGMARD

7

8

RECORD OF NAVAJO ACTIVITIES AFFECTING THE ACOMA-LAGUNA AREA, 1746-1910

by

Myra Ellen Jenkins

Ward Alan Minge

9

Docket 229
Claim Ex 530

10

13

TABLE OF CONTENTS
_II_   Mexican Period, 1822-1846

14

INDEX TO MEXICAN PERIOD

-A-

-B-

16

17

18

19

21

22

TABLE OF CONTENTS
Territorial Period, 1846-1910

23

24

26

27

28

RECORD OF NAVAJO ACTIVITIES AFFECTING THE LAGUNA-ACOMA

AREA, SPANISH PERIOD, 1746-1821

by

Myra Ellen Jenkins

Ward Alan Minge

29

30

Navajo presence in the Ácoma-Laguna region dates from
the middle of the 18th century when the Navajos, fleeing
from the Utes,[1] permitted themselves to be settled at
Encinal, under Fray Juan Sanz de Lezaún, and at Cebolleta
under Fray Manuel Vermejo. These missions failed within two
years, however, because the Navajos refused to accept a
settled way of life or to adopt the Christian faith, and
hence Governor Tomás Veléz Cachupín sent the Ácomas to
Encinal and the Lagunas to Cebolleta to plant the fields and
build churches, which the Navajos refused to do.[2]

Veléz Cachupín, however, was apparently aware that
the mission at Encinal posed a threat to the prior rights of
Ácoma in that region and wrote to Fray Manuel de San Juan
Nepomuceno y Trigo, on March 24, 1750::

> I have learned that the recent petition of the Navajo
> Apaches of the mission of Encinal to found their pueblo
> at the place called Cubero, because of the greater
> abundance and convenience of the water, may produce some
> disagreements and ill-will with the mission of Ácoma in
> regard to the territory and appurtenances of each, which
> would occasion great injury to the conversion of the
> Navajos. Since it is necessary to watch over the
> latter and take care that the steps taken up to this
> time for their reduction to God and the king shall not
> be wasted, as well as to see that the old mission of
> Ácoma shall not be incommoded or offended, I have
> resolved that my lieutenant-general, Don Bernardo
> Antonio Bustamente y Tagle, shall go to these missions
> with my instructions for the purpose of preventing in
> the establishment of the Navajos quarrels and

31

---

[1] Thomas, Plains Indians, Instructions of Gov. Tomás
Veléz Cachupín to his Successor, Francisco María del Valle,
1754, p. 138.

[2] Jenkins Report, pp. 30-31.

disagreements with the Ácomas, so that both nations
shall remain satisfied, friendly, and content with
their possessions, territories, waters, and pastures.
Indeed, prudence requires such regulations [as will
assure] that these two missions mentioned, the one
because it is new and the other because it is old,
shall not suffer any harm, nor leave any motive for
the grievances, disturbances, and disagreements which
may alter the harmony of the affectionate intercourse
between the two pueblos, from which would follow, as a
consequence, pernicious results to the service of both
Majesties. 3

Before the investigation could be made, however, the Navajos
had driven the friars out.[4]

Most of the Navajo left the missions and moved
westward, but a few families remained temporarily in the
region and moved in and out for the next 125 years, raising
crops at times in the Cubero, Cebolleta, Juan Tafoya and
Cañada de Pedro Padilla areas, sometimes on friendly terms
with the Acomas and Lagunas, and often raiding them. Larger,
roving bands of Navajos returned periodically during the
same period to plague the pueblos.

32

When Bishop Tamarón of Durango came through the
region on his visitation of missions in 1760, along the road
from Zia to Laguna, thence to Ácoma, he noted seeing the huts
of a few Navajos who had remained near Cebolleta:

---

[4] Hackett, ed., Historical Documents Relating to
New Mexico, Nueva Vizcaya, and Approaches thereto, to 1773,
III, pp. 424-425.

[5] Hackett, Historical Documents, pp. 432-438.

On one side of this road, to the north, is the place
of the Cebolletas, where Father Menchero founded the
two pueblos already mentioned. The inhabitants are
Navahos and Apaches, and many of them live in those
cañadas. Some are heathens, and others apostates.
Some of their huts were seen. 5

Tamarón also reported that some of these Navajos came to
him at Laguna, asking for pueblo status, but that he could
not grant it:

. . . The Navahos were supplied with all they needed
at the expense of the royal treasury, and these Indians
lost it. The same ones came to me at the pueblo of
Laguna with the same petition for pueblos, saying that
they desired to become Christians. The Franciscan
Fathers informed me about the inconstancy of the Navahos and that they always said the same thing, but that
there was no way of subjecting them to catechism. I
observed that they did not come as they should. I
treated them kindly, I exhorted them, I left orders with
the missionaries to keep on trying to draw them in as
best they could. No other special fruit of that celebrated campaign was known. 6

As the church records of baptisms in the Ácoma-Laguna
area will show, his suspicions were well founded, for these
records fail to reveal Navajo conversions in the region,
except for a few captives, usually children, in spite of
later claims of the Navajos that they were Christian. Apparently, baptisms at the abortive missions of Encinal and
Cebolleta are not extant. No Navajo baptisms are recorded
at Ácoma, for which such records are relatively complete
since 1726, and at Laguna there were but three prior to
1770, reported by Fray Juan Pino, March 17, 1743.

5 Adams, Bishop Tamaron's Visitation, p. 67.
6 Adams, Bishop Tamaron's Visitation, p. 89.

Land Grants, 1753-1772

Land grants on the Rio Puerco, and to the west, made
to Spaniards from 1753-1772 mention but a few Navajos temporarily residing in a few places, although it is impossible
to determine whether they were Navajos or Apaches. A brief
description of each grant follows:

(1) Bernabé Montaño (Surveyor-General #49; Court of
Private Land Claims #7), granted 1753, re-granted, 1759.
The boundaries were the Zia road on the north; the cerrito
colorado on the south; the mesa prieta on the west; and the
brow of the Rio Puerco mountain on the east. No Navajos
were indicated as living on the land, and none were cited,
but the settlers were ordered to build the town as a fort-
ress with only one gate against attack. Raids forced the
abandonment of the settlement about 1785.

34

> They all left then, being compelled to do so on account
> of the hostilities of the Navajo Apache Indians, who
> were continuously massacring men, women and children at
> that place, the government sent a force of men to escort
> the settlers to another residence in the Rio Grande
> valley. (Testimony of Mateo Durán, 1870).

(2) Nuestra Señora de la Luz de las Lugunitas (Antonio
Baca) (Surveyor-General #101; Court of Private Land Claims #70),
1759, 1761. Given as boundaries were a white mesa on the
north; the mesa prieta on the southwest where the Zia road to
Laguna crosses the Puerco; the Agua Salada on the south (the
northern border of the Laguna claim); the "high

mountain where the Navajo Apaches cultivate" on the west.

No Navajos were indicated as occupying any part of the area,

and although cited, none appeared to contest the grant.

(3) Bernardo Miera y Pacheco and Pedro Padilla (Cañada
de los Alamos) (Surveyor-General #98) The boundaries were
stated as the Rio Puerco and the Zia road on the east and
northeast; the Cebolleta mountain on the west; the lands of
Salvador Jaramillo and Antonio Baca on the north; and on
the south "a cañada which at times some Apache Navajo
occupy." Alcalde Francisco Trebol y Navarre, in the writ
of possession of March 1, noted:

> I forthwith ordered the Laguna Indians, those of
> Cebolleta and the rest of the Navajo that they
> should appear before me.

In his communication to Trebol y Navarre of February 7,

Governor Mendinueta had stated that:

35

> Notice is hereby given that if the boundary line
> running towards the site of Cebolleta, that is to
> say, where a hamlet was commenced by the half-breed
> Apache-Navajo Indians should cut into the arable
> lands of the aforesaid hamlet, the boundary line
> shall cease at such a distance as not to cause pre-
> judice and injury to the aforesaid hamlet.

(4)Vertientes de Navajo or Sitio de Navajo, 1768, 1772

(Surveyor-General #195; Court of Private Land Claims #270).

This grant, made to Carlos José Peréz de Mirabal, in the most

confusing of all the land grants in the area, and by

description and later claim, overlapped the Agua Salada and

lay within the boundaries of the Cebolleta Grant later made

in 1800. It was bounded on the east by the lands of Salvador Jaramillo; on the west by the Cebolleta mountain; by the hill of Santa Rosa on the north; and on the south by a pass through which the Zia road ran towards Laguna, apparently about three miles southeast of Juan Tafoya (Marquez). Mirabal sold to Salvador Jaramillo in 1769. In the sale terms, he noted that "upon one side certain half-breed Apache-Navajo Indians have located." Since he did not specify upon which side, it is impossible to determine whether they lived on the north of south of the Agau Salada Creek. Mirabal stipulated that if Jaramillo were dispossessed "because of the liability of a turmoil among the Navajo Indians that dwell on it as they may desire to form a town thereon," he could not recover the price of the sale. Jaramillo sold part of the grant to Clemente Gutierrez in 1772 with the same stipulation, stating that some Apaches were in the center of the tract.

36

(5) The Baltasar Baca and Sons Grazing Permit, 1768 (Surveyor-General #104; Court of Private Land Claims #114). The boundaries were delimited as a Castillian league west from the Encinal; a mesa close to the Zuni road on the east; some white bluffs on the south; a mountain on the north. This land was clearly in the region used by the Acomas and Lagunas, as Governor Mendinueta specified that the Bacas

> Shall not injure the ranches and fields of the
> Indians of the pueblos of Acoma and Laguna in
> that vicinity and much less the un-Christianized
> Apaches of the Navajo province.

1769

(6) The Agua Salada (Luis Jaramillo)ₐ(Surveyor-General #103; Court of Private Land Claims #31). This grant was bounded on the north by the lands of Antonio Baca; on the east and south by the lands of Pedro Padilla and a high mesa: on the west by the lands of Salvador Jaramillo "On the slopes of the Navajo country." Luis Jaramillo stated that he had occupied the tract since 1753, when everyone else left because of the Navajo danger, and that he located in the worst part of the area "in order to prevent the entrance and guard the trail of the enemy." No Navajos were cited or mentioned, except raiders.

(7) Antonio Sedillo,(1769 (Surveyor-General #50; Court of Private Land Claims #15). The boundaries were the Rio Puerco on the west and north; a little red hill on the east; and the lands of Mateo Pino on the south. In placing Sedillo in possession, Alcalde Carlos José Peréz de Mirabal stated that eight Spaniards were present as well as "Navajo-Apaches who said that the petition was good and that they had nothing to interpose against the possession about to be given." It would appear that these Indians were possibly Apaches.

Period of Navajo Conflict, 1774-1784

Navajo attacks against Laguna and Acoma, as well as against the settlers, began in earnest in 1774. Governor Pedro Fermín de Mendinueta apparently began the policy,

37

continued by his successors, of making use of the Pueblo
Indians against the Navajo. In his report to Viceroy
Antonio de Bucareli y Usúa of September 1774, Mendinueta
reported:

> Against the Navajo tribe, which up until the present
> has continued making war, two expeditions have been
> made by the militia and Indians of the jurisdiction of
> Albuquerque, Laguna, and Queres. On these they killed
> twenty-one barbarians and seized forty-six individuals,
> men, women, and children, two of whom after being bap-
> tized died. Our people lost four killed and thirty-
> one wounded. In the different attacks which in this
> time they have committed, they have killed six Indians
> and wounded two and stolen and killed some cattle and
> horses. They have been pursued four times, and of these
> they were overtaken and deprived of the stolen property
> on three occasions. [7]

Raiders struck near Laguna again on October 5,
according to Mendinueta:

> On the fifth of the current month, a fairly large
> group of Navajos attacked some ranches near the pueblo
> of La Laguna and killed four of the dwellers there,
> took two captive, and killed a number of sheep. They
> were pursued by the alcalde mayor and some citizens and
> Indians. Although they overtook them and attacked, they
> were able to kill only two of the enemies, and, of our
> people, twenty-two emerged slightly wounded. [8]

Raids and pursuit continued during the next two
months, according to Mendinueta:

> The Navajo nation on the 15th of November attacked a
> party on a rancho of the Pueblo of Zia and killed a

---

[7] Quoted in Thomas, The Plains Indians and New Mexico,
1751-1778, p. 173.

[8] Mendinueta to Bucareli, October 20, 1774, A. G. N.,
Provincias Internas, Legajo 65, Part 13, expediente 10, folio
11.

sheepherder and captured another and returned with
them, taking at the same time a quantity of cattle and
sheep. On the following 17th, the same Indians captured a boy near the Pueblo of Laguna, and on December
26, two of the same nation took during the night from a
corral of the same pueblo, a bunch of sheep. During
the former and the latter, they were followed by the
Indians and only in the latter were they able to
retrieve the stolen property as the malefactors fled
into the mountains.[9]

Baptisms of Navajo captives at Laguna from 1770 to
1776 reflect this struggle. On June 13, 1770, <u>Antonio</u>,
"gentile of the Navajo nation," age 18, was baptized, his
godparents being Bernardo Pacheco and Estafania Domingo.
<u>José Antonio</u>, "adult Navajo," received the rite April 16,
1775, with Santiago Chaves, lieutenant alcalde of Acoma as
godparent. On June 19, 1775, 29 Navajo children were baptized, some with Laguna and some with Spanish godparents.
On February 16, 1776, <u>María Barbara</u>, "child of the Navajo
nation," was placed in the custody of Rámon Jaramillo and
Barbara Angel. On May 19, 1776, <u>Juan Manuel</u> "of the Navajo
nation bought by Juan Antonio, a Laguna Indian"was baptized.
The Navajo <u>Juan Antonio</u> was baptized and "placed under the
tutelage of Juan de Dios, a Laguna Indian," on July 24,
1776. A Navajo child, <u>Marta Antonia</u>, was baptized, December
20, 1776, and placed under Antonia Francisca Gabaldon.

María Mariana, "daughter of Lorenzo and María
Candelaria of the Navajo nation," was baptized June 27,

39

---

[9] Mendinueta to Bucareli, March 30, 1775, A. G. N.,
<u>Provincias Internas</u>, Legajo 65, Part 10, expediente 10,
folio 36.

1777. This last entry appears to be the only Navajo
baptism recorded which was not that of a captive. No other
Navajo entries appear in Laguna or Acoma records from 1777
to 1853.

Navajo attacks decreased for a few years following
1775. The Lagunas continued to plant their fields in the
region around Paquate, north of the pueblo, and from 1776-
1779 were back at the Cebolleta site.[10] Neither the map
of the Navajo country as seen by Fathers Dominguez and
Escalante in 1776,[11] nor the Miera y Pacheco map of 1779[12]
show the Navajos residing east of the Continental Divide.

By 1782, however, the Navajos had driven the Lagunas
out of Cebolleta.[13] As a result of raids and small-pox, the
Lagunas and Acomas drew closer to their home pueblos. This
was a familiar pattern for many years. As the Navajo men-
ace lessened, the pueblos would return to their former
planting and herding sites; in times of attack, they would
withdraw for protection.

40

_____

[10] Jenkins Report, pp. 31-38.

[11] This map is reproduced in Amsden, Navajo
Weaving, Plate 57a.

[12] This map is found in Thomas, Forgotten Frontiers, p. 90.

[13] Jenkins Report, p. 39.

Relative Peace, 1785 - 1800

During Governor Juan Bautista de Anza's campaign
against the Apaches, 1785-1788, some Navajos, largely under
the threat of the Comanches being used against them, were
persuaded by the Spanish to become incorporated with the
Acoma and Laguna militia to fight the Apaches, and relations
between the Navajos and pueblos were comparatively peaceful.

On August 17, 1785, Comandante General Rengel reported to
the viceroy, the Conde de Galvez, as follows concerning a
June campaign by these combined Indian forces:

He [de Anza] shows that to force the Navajo to comply
with his proposals he is prohibiting their crossing the
Rio de la Laguna which separates them from the Gilas,
by notice that whoever be met with on the other side by
a patrol of forty men whom he put there, will be treated
as declared enemies, seized and taken to the Villa of
Santa Fe to receive the punishment which may appro-
priately be imposed upon them; and he forbade all trade,
exchange and communication with the inhabitants of the
province, despatching orders that the latter should
abstain from relations with them under corresponding
penalties. As a result of this action, forty-six Navajos, among them seven of their chiefs, presented themselves on June 5 to the Alcalde Mayor of La Laguna,
indicating that they had determined to set out on the
12th on a campaign against the Gila. For this purpose
they asked him to aid them with eighty of our Indians.
Their request with our compliments acceded to, they set
out on the 16th, numbering one hundred and twenty horse,
thirty foot, and ninety-four Indians from the pueblo who
went to reenforce their detachment and witness their
operations. It was noted that among the first were
five chiefs of major popularity and those who had contributed most to the treason of their nation.
They continued in truth on their campaign for the
deliberate purpose of attacking the enemy where they
found them. Having reached the Sierra Azul, the heart
of their country, they attacked them spiritedly. They

41

killed more than forty and both parties having recognized
each other, burst forth into reciprocal threats to
destroy one another. The next night after this action,
the Gila party attacked the Navajo in a defile where the
latter suffered some wounded of whom two have died, and
lost ten horses. On their return on the 25th, the
governor ordered them rewarded opening to them as a
sign of appreciation, and as a stimulus to the continua-
tion of similar acts, commerce and communication with
the pueblos of the province which he had before closed
to them.
    After this they made two other campaigns with less
important results, with the virtue of having inspirited
the Navajos more with the desire for war which that
governor was trying to keep alive. . . [14]

A similar engagement of Navajos and Pueblos against
the Apaches took place in the fall.[15]

On January 18, 1786, Rengel directed Governor de Anza
to establish a strong command at Laguna as a threat to the
Navajo if they did not continue their campaign:

Provided that in order to bring them to this point,
your lordship may judge it a proper means to despatch
a sufficient number of arms and munitions to the pueblo
of La Laguna and the vicinity, as if to threaten them
with some hidden design against them if they do not
decide shortly, or to reassure them against the terror
they have of the vengeance of the Gilas. . . [16]

In March, 1786, de Anza met with a group of Navajo at
the Bado del Piedra, near Jemez, and drew up an agreement with
them that in return for royal protection they would set out

42

---

[14] Quoted in Thomas, Forgotten Frontiers, pp. 259-260.

[15] Quoted in Thomas, Forgotten Frontiers, p. 269.

[16] Thomas, Forgotten Frontiers, p. 272.

out on another campaign against the Apaches under one of the chiefs designated by the governor by the end of July; that thirty Navajos per month would serve as auxiliaries; and that they would accept an interpreter. Section 4 stated:

That from the moment the council was dissolved they should go down to occupy their old camps to plant their seeds, and that, concerning the security which the governor guaranteed them in conserving and sustaining them in that situation, they could proceed to build sod huts.[17]

On May 25, the interpreter reported "that the nation was in its old lands having finished sowing,"[18] and that they were preparing for the campaign. On June 8, "Don Carlos" and "Don Joseph Antonio," the chieftains named by de Anza, the interpreter and others arrived in Santa Fe reporting that they were ready. The interpreter listed their lands as follows:

43

The interpreter on his part informed the governor that the Navajo nation has seven hundred families more or less with four or five persons to each one in its five divisions of San Mateo, Zebolleta, or Cañon, Chusca, Hozo, Chelli . . .[19]

On October 5, 1786, Comandante General Ugarte in a letter to de Anza noting Navajo contributions in the

---

[17] Pedro Garrido y Durán, Chihuahua, December 21, 1786, extraction of official reports of Governor de Anza, quoted in Thomas, Forgotten Frontiers, p. 348.

[18] Ibid., p. 349.

[19] Ibid., p. 350.

in the summer campaign, detailed future conduct of Navajo
relations, instructing the governor to encourage them to
establish themselves in fixed settlements, and likewise to
encourage the pueblos to trade with them on friendly terms:

> One of the circumstances which can contribute more
> to guarantee the peace with the Navajos is that they
> organize themselves into formal settlements and devote
> themselves to cultivating the soil as it appears they
> have already done. This disposition your lordship
> will not neglect to encourage, facilitating it in case
> of need with some assistance to the poorest to settle
> them and induce them to abandon the wandering life, to
> which absolute scarcity of possession and means of sub-
> sistence elsewhere would invincibly induce them. . .
> For the better encouragement of commerce with the
> nation referred to, to animate their industry of which
> they have given some signs, and inspire them with
> affection for our trade, your lordship will allow the
> settlers and Pueblo Indians to engage in their own
> rancherías in times decided upon and under prearranged
> rules [set forth] in a separate order of this date.
> There attending to the fact that the affairs of the
> heathen are carried on by barter, and that in these
> agreements our people ordinarily commit many excesses,
> abusing the ignorance of the natives, it may be
> arranged among other things that your lordship draw up
> a tariff or regulation in which may be fixed the quan-
> tity, and species of effects which each one of the
> parties must deliver in exchange for those which he may
> receive. . .[20]

Matters continued relatively quiet during the 1790's,
with the Navajos still continuing to graze their stock on
the middle Rio Puerco, apparently near Guadalupe. In 1794,
Governor Fernando de la Concha wrote:

> This tribe [Navajo] lives in the southwest part of
> the province. Their settlements have a rather regular
> form, and most of them are very near to our Indian towns

44

---

[20] Thomas, Forgotten Frontiers, pp. 355-356.

located in this direction. They possess much cattle and
sheep, and a proportionate number of horses. In general
they occupy rough mesas of difficult access, and pasture
their livestock on the borders of the Rio Puerco and in
the Canyon de Chelly. They cultivate their lands with
careful attention. They always sow seasonally because
of the scarcity of water which occurs in their lands,
but despite this invoncenience they reap generally
abundant harvests, and enjoy some commodities which are
not known to the other barbarous Indians.[21]

On January 31, 1800, Governor Fernando Chacón issued
the Cebolleta grant to thirty Albuquerque residents, and the
new settlers were placed in possession by Alcalde José
Manuel Aragón on March 16, with boundaries of the San Mateo
mountains on the north and west, the Mesa del Gabilan on the
south, and the Zia road cañada and the cañada of Pedro Padilla
on the east. Although Laguna granted land lay very close
to the proposed settlement, and although the Lagunas had
used the land intermittently since 1748, whenever there was
less danger from raids, they were not cited by the alcalde.[22]
The Navajos were neither cited nor did they make any objection, although relations between the Navajos and Spanish
authorities were deteriorating seriously.

Within a few weeks, hostilities between the government and the Navajos had broken out anew. From 1800 to the

45

[21] Quoted by Donald E. Worcester, New Mexico Historical Review, XXIV (July, 1949), p. 254, "Advice on Governing
New Mexico, 1794."

[22] Jenkins Report, pp. 51-52.

incarceration of the Navajo by the United States government
at the Bosque Redondo reservation in 1863-64, relations
between the government of New Mexico and the Navajo tribe
were characterized by intermittent Navajo raids on the Spanish settlements and Indian pueblos, followed by punitive
expeditions and treaties of peace. Then, brief and uneasy
periods of comparative calm would follow, and a few Navajos
would attempt to return to some of their old temporary sites
in the Acoma-Laguna area, often on friendly terms with the
pueblos, but contrary to the treaty terms or agreements
which they had previously accepted. Other raids, other
expeditions, and other periods of relative quiet would
follow with regularity.

46

The remainder of this report to the end of the Spanish
administration in 1821 consists of a summary or translation
of pertinent documents relating to Navajo activities in the
Laguna-Ácoma area. Originals of the documents cited are
in the collections of the New Mexico State Records Center and
Archives (abbreviated NMSRCA), entitled Spanish Archives with
proper number, or in the Spanish collections in the General
Land Office, Santa Fe, New Mexico known as Twitchell Archives
(abbreviated GLO, Twitchell), Surveyor-General Records
(SG with appropriate number), or Court of Private Land
Claims (CPLC).

June 21, 1800, Fernando Chacón to Comandante General Pedro
de Nava, #1492, Spanish Archives, NMSRCA.

The governor, reporting on the pacification of the Navajos

and a reconnoissance of the Apaches, states:

> . . . I went out from the province on the 13th day of the
> said month [May] with 500 men from the troops of resi-
> dents and including two Indian officials, and advanced to
> the site of Tunicha, the center of the territory of the
> said nation, where I proposed to launch an attack on
> their haciendas which are nearby, but at a short dis-
> tance from the said site, twenty of the most important
> Navajos met me, asking peace, which I conceded to them
> on the 3rd day after they had surrendered twenty-eight
> cows, fifteen tilmas, forty-eight tanned skins and one
> Moquino Indian in restitution for the robbery they had
> committed, they afterwards promised, among other things,
> not to rebel further nor ask for gratuities as other
> gentile nations do, confirming their agreement with a
> general and sincere pledge between both nations. . .

March 26, 1804, Fernando Chacón to Nemesio Salcedo (Comandante
General), #1712, no. 76, Spanish Archives, NMSRCA.

The governor was notifying the comandante general of

a possible alliance of the Navajos with the Apaches of   47

Carrizal:

> After having prepared the information which I sent
> your Excellency relative to the new settlement of
> Cebolleta asked by the Navajos who came to this villa
> with the cordon, the justices of the jurisdictions of
> Jemes and Laguna informed me of the hostilities lately
> caused by them, as your Excellency will see by the two
> originals which I include. [copies not included.]

March 28, 1804, Fernando Chacón to Nemesio Salcedo, No. 75,
#1714, Spanish Archives, NMSRCA.

> . . . On February 26, six Navajos presented themselves in
> this capital, two of whom said they came to this villa
> where they would speak to you and asked that the site
> of Cebolleta be conceded to them, for which purpose you
> had given them a paper which they had lost in a fray
> occurring with the Apaches in the place of the Cañas.

Considering that in the account of these gentiles
of the communication which you sent them that you gave me
an order to be informed concerning their demand, I beg
leave to state that the said site of Cebolleta is situated almost in the center of the province and has never
belonged to the lands of the Navajo and although these
Indians have lived there temporarily, on this date it is
colonized by thirty residents for the reason that there
is not sufficient water for more, they have already built
a fortified plaza and planted the lands, having spent
much labor on the interior.

The aforesaid site of Cebolleta will not serve the
Navajos except as a lookout in order to observe our
movements, always abandoning it to carry off with great
repitition the horse herds and sheep which pasture in
the lands nearby, committing these outrages under frivo-
lous pretexts and without any motive, and this they
have succeeded in doing under previous governments and
twice in particular during my time until the year 1800
when they rebelled the last time, I determined immediately
that it should be occupied by the colonists who had
previously asked for it, and in the terms of surrender
which I made with all of the Navajo nation when I was
personally in the center of their lands and obliged them
to make peace, among other things, I informed them that
I had determined to cede the territory of Cebolleta in
consideration that it be made a domicile for Spaniards
to end the discords and pretexts for uprisings, to
which proposal they all agreed. I assigned to them
at once the limits from which they could go to pasture
their haciendas, many of which are the results of
pillages formerly committed, having been so successful that
there has not been a return to unrest.

As it has happened, now the above mentioned Indians
are repeating again their insistence, it has seemed
proper to me to convey to you every thing concerning the
new colony of Cebolleta and state for your consideration
that if the Navajos again occupy it, they will renew
their old and repeated vexations which this province
has suffered from that nation.

April 19, 1804, Nemesio Salcedo to Chacón, #1722, Spanish
   Archives, AGRCA.

48

The comandante general in answering letters from
the justices of Jemes and Laguna which had accompanied
Chacón's of March 28, authorized Chacón "to pursue and
castigate them [the Navajos] until they are again reduced to
peace."

<u>May 16, 1804</u>, <u>Chacón</u> <u>to</u> <u>Salcedo</u>, <u>#1730</u>, <u>Spanish</u> <u>Archives</u>,
<u>NMSRCA</u>.

In transmitting a diary of events since April 1
concerning Navajo hostilities, Chacon stated that the uprising
had resulted in the theft of thirty ewes, fifty-eight head
of cattle, twenty-four horses, and the death of nine sheep-
herders, and one boy taken captive. As a result, the campaign was being carried into Navajo territory. Extracts of
the diary follow:

On April 17, the alcalde mayor of Rio Abajo reported
that Navajos came into the Cañada de los Alamos in the
Rio Puerco, stealing two cows and eight heifers.
On the 9th, the alcalde mayor of Laguna reported that
the Navajo Segundo, one of the principal chiefs of the
nation, arrived at that pueblo with the stratagem of
saying that among themselves they had no news nor any
trouble; that those who had stolen the horse herd were
poor and hungry, but that they would recover all and
restore them, for they wanted peace with the Spanish. . .
Dated the 14th, the lieutenant of Jemes stated that
some Navajos had arrived at that place with the hoax
that the chiefs of the nation wanted to know the number
of stolen animals, but that when they left, they carried
off ten heifers and some animals from the horse herd. . .
Dated the 30th, the alcalde mayor of Laguna stated
that on the 14th during the night, more than 200 Navajos
broke into the plaza of Cebolleta and sacked three houses
which had outside doors, carrying off twelve cows and
fifty heifers which were pastured in the marsh. Without
doing more there, they went to the ranch of some sheep-
herders, killed three and seized a young boy, taking also
the sheep they were guarding; that on the following day
he went out to overtake them, and in the place of the
cañoncitos saw that they were dividing the spoils into
various portions, that he decided to follow the major
group, and overtook them in the middle of the night,
taking from the aggressors more than sixty sheep and
ten cows. . .

49

<u>June 8</u>, <u>1804</u>, <u>Salcedo</u> <u>to</u> <u>Chacón</u>, <u>#1735</u>, NMSRCA.

Salcedo approved the policy of not making peace with the
Navajos and authorized the continuing of the campaign into
all their lands.

July 16, 1804, Salcedo to Chacón, #1743, Spanish Archives, NMSRCA.

In asking for a report on the Navajo campaign, the comandante general emphasized that it was necessary to continue the campaign until the Navajos were completely subdued.

September 16, 1804, #1754, Salcedo to Chacón, Spanish Archives, NMSRCA.

In answer to Chacon's letter of August 28 concerning progress of campaign, and request of alcalde mayor of Laguna that Cebolleta be abandoned, the comandante general stated:

> At the same time you have informed me of the attack which was made by 900 to 1000 Navajos against the colony of Cebolleta in which the sergeant of the detachment was killed, one settler and an Indian, and four soldiers, ten colonists and one woman were wounded, and twenty-two gandules were killed and forty-four wounded in this action. By separate order of today, I tell you what must be done relating to the precise necessity of keeping this site of Cebolleta colonized for which purpose I approve of all the actions to which you refer and that you have taken to continue the castigation of this recalcitrant Navajo faction, preventing it from having any of its wishes considered until such a time as they will have been well punished and they ask for peace upon the just conditions which it will require.

50

September 26, 1804, Chacónoto José Manuel Aragón, alcalde mayor of Laguna, GLO, SG, #46, Town of Cebolleta

Chacón informed Aragón of Salcedo's decision that Cebolleta not be abandoned. See Exhibit 8, Pueblo of Laguna, and pp. 52-53, Jenkins Report.

October 5, 1804, Salcedo to Chacón, #1763, NMSRCA.

Don Nicolás Farín, with a detachment of thirty men is to be stationed at Cebolleta to safeguard the settlers.

October 5, Salcedo to Chacón, #1766, Spanish Archives, NMSRCA

Repeats the instructions that the campaign against the Navajo must continue.

November 20, 1804, Chacón to Nicolás Farín, Spanish
 Archives, #1774, NMSRCA.

Chacón instructs the lieutenant about the disposition
of auxiliary troops from Sonora. When they arrive at Laguna
or Ácoma, they are to be divided into two parts and sent
against the Navajos to operate on two fronts which have been
verbally agreed upon, without forgetting "That in no way shall
they give quarter to the enemy until he shall have been well
punished and given the greatest damage."

November 26, 1804, Lieutenant Colonel Antonio Narbona to
 Chacón, #1776, Spanish Archives, NMSRCA.

A detailed account of the Navajo campaign from his
headquarters in Zuni

December 10, 1804, Narbona to Chacón, Spanish Archives,
 #1778, NMSRCA.

In this account, written from Laguna, Narbona stated   51
that on December 3rd, he had attacked a Navajo ranchería
at the foot of the sierra of the Cañon de Chelly, but his
troops are exhausted. and the weather bitterly cold, and he
is awaiting further orders.

December 13, 1804, Chacón to Narbona, Spanish Archives, #1780,
 NMSRCA.

In answering Narbona's communications of November
26, and December 10, the governor emphasizes that the campaign must be continued.

January 11, 1805, Salcedo to Chacón, #1788, Spanish Archives,
 NMSRCA.

The comandante general was most critical of the conduct

of the war in the Canyon de Chelly region, and states that

he is sending fresh troops from Nueva Vizcaya, and that

Chacón is to order the colonists who have abandoned Cebolleta

to return. In a special note, he emphasizes that the war

is to be prosecuted from the sierras of the Rio Puerco to

the Cañon de Chelly.

January 24, 1805, Narbona to Chacón, #1792, Spanish Archives,
NMSRCA.

Narbona gives a detailed account of the battle of
January 17-18 at Cañon de Chelly, with the result that the
chieftain, Cristobál is asking for peace.

March 27, 1805, Chacón, #1801, Spanish Archives, NMSRCA.

Conditions Which Should be Met by the Navajo Nation
When Peace is Made.

52

(1) They shall have no right to the settlement of
Cebolleta, nor shall they use it as a pretext for a new
uprising;
(2) Neither shall the animals or herds be reclaimed
which are now among the Spaniards of this nation; . . .
(4) They shall not cross with their herds or haciendas
from the limits of the cañon de Juan Tafoya, the Rio
del Ojo; and the San Mateos seeking to betake themselves
with their goods to the Rio of San Juan;
(5) The slightest robbery or hostility which they shall
commit shall result in arms being taken up against them
unless they surrender the things stolen and the aggressor
. . .

May 15, 1805, Governor Joaquín Real Alencaster to Salcedo,
#1828, Spanish Archives, NMSRCA.

Consequent to your communication of April 26, and in
fulfillment of what you have arranged for me, I have
agreed upon peace with the principal chiefs of the Navajo
nation, Cristobál and Vicente in the name of and in
representation of them all, on the 12th day of this May
with the following conditions: (1) that at no time shall
they make any claim to the lands of the site called

Cebolleta; (2) that they shall restore to us the two
children that they have surrendered to me, and any other
captives which are found in their power; (3) that they
will make no alliance, treaty, nor communication with a
nation or faction hostile to us, and that on the
occasions which arise, they will also make war; (4) that
if any of their nation commit a robbery or other outrage
on those of this province, they will surrender him to
their chiefs that he may be punished; (5) that on our part
we will permit them commerce, stock-raising and planting
of fields and other enterprises which they may wish to
engage in, verifying it as I have done to the interpreter, Josef Antonio García.

September 1, 1805, Real Alencaster to Salcedo, #1881,
Spanish Archives, NMSRCA.

This is an answer to Salcedo's of June 1, 1805,

approving the Navajo peace and the appointment of García

as interpreter.

October 11, 1805, José Manuel Aragón, alcalde of Laguna to
Real Alencaster, #1902, Spanish Archives, NMSRCA.

The residents of Cebolleta have told me that the
Navajos are wreaking much damage, robbing them of the
corn from their fields; that forty or so families of
the said Navajos have come to live at the site of
Cebolleta itself, and during the day and in full view
are pulling up the corn from the fields to feed themselves. The said settlers tell me that they are sustaining many losses, and at the same time are suffering
and having to endure many things from these gentiles,
that it would be better to leave the site so that they
will not suffer all the years to come from losses
without being able to remedy them, and that it is
grievous to them to work all year so that the Navajos
may have provender. . .

53

December 15, 1805, José Manuel Aragón to Real Alencaster,
#1929, Spanish Archives, NMSRCA.

Vicente, the Navajo, has come to look for a horse that
was stolen by the Navajos and sold in the Pueblo of
Ácoma, and asks that it be returned to him. He also tells
me to write to you complaining that in the cañon de
Juan Tafoya and the Serro Chato, where he is living with
his people, he was beaten with sticks by some Spanish
sheep-herders because he went to ask them not to put

their flocks where he had his horses. He also wants me
to ask that you give an order to have the sheep-herders
restricted from trespassing in the future to avoid any
trouble. . .

November 20, 1807, Real Alencaster to Salcedo, #2089, Spanish
Archives, NMSRCA.

Real Alencaster reported the visit of the chieftain El
Segundo who returned an accused criminal from Jemes, and came
to show his loyalty to the peace treaty. Through the
interpreter, he assured the governor of his good intent and
hostility to the Gila and Mescalero Apaches.

May 23 - July 9, 1808, group of twenty-one documents concerning
decisions in a quarrel of group of Navajos under Segundo
and settlers in the cañon of Juan Tafoya, Rio Puerco,
and cañada de Pedro Padilla areas (incomplete), #2105,
Spanish Archives, NMSRCA.

The regions of the quarrel are not precisely established in these documents, but one of them clearly lay south
of the line marked out for the Navajos in the March 27, 1805
statement of Governor Chacón. The cañon de Juan Tafoya was
the southern limit of the line set; the lands in question on
the Rio Puerco were within the Bernabé Montaño grant; the
cañada de Pedro Padilla was stated as being "three long
leagues from Cebolleta" and lay south of the March 27, 1805
boundary. Since the Navajos were peaceful at this time, the
authorities were anxious to placate these small bands by
permitting them to harvest their small crops. Although
the disputes were resolved in favor of the Navajos, none
of the decisions made any pretense of establishing Navajo
rights to the lands.

On May 31, Lieutenant Bartolomé Baca, in compliance
with instructions given to him by the alcalde of Albuquerque,
Lorenzo Gutierrez, set forth with four men from Tomé to investigate complaints which the Navajo Segundo had made to Governor
Real Alencaster in the three regions. Excerpts from Baca's
diary follow:

. . . Having received the order, I began my march on the
last day of May at 1:00 a.m., and on the same day at 3:00
p.m. I arrived on the other bank of the Rio Puerco which
has a small spring of water where I found the captain
Segundo with others of the same nation. Notwithstanding
that I had come at the request of the said Navajos for
the complaint they lodged with my superior, I ignored their
presence for an hour as I was indisposed and had arrived
thoroughly fatigued; shortly after I got up, they began to
question me if I had come to investigate their complaint
and although I had explained it, I told them that in the
morning we would treat of their business. The chieftains
Segundo and Delgadito answered that I should attend them
and looking at these gentiles, I listened to the complaint
of the said chiefs with the rest of their people having me
see a small field that they had made on the Rio Puerco
which they had also planted last year, but where five
residents have now intruded, three from the Albuquerque
jurisdiction of Alcalde Don Lorenzo Gutierres and two from
the Corrales jurisdiction of the alcalde of Alameda, Don
Cleto Miera. Those from the first one are Juan Candelaria,
a half-breed of the said Candelaria, and José Gonzales.
Those from the second are Juan Miguel Santellanes and Juan
Antonio Torres, and finding the last ones there with
one from the alcaldia of Albuquerque, I ordered them to
speak, and having them see the complaint lodged by the
Navajos, I asked them what their reason was for intruding
into the field with the said Navajos, and they answered
me that they had come there having the consent of the
lieutenant. I asked them for the said license in writing;
they said they did not have it, for which reason I ordered
them to depart to their own lands at once, making them see
that lands could only be given by the Superior Government
and having placed before them that it had not come to my
attention that the lieutenant of an alcalde mayor had
such authority, I determined that they should lose that
which they had planted, but excused them from penalty
since by their innocence they had gone out from the limits
without a proper order and used the said field, that the
said field should be given to those of their nation
who needed it most, the chief making the division.

55

On the 1st of June I arrived at the Sierra of Navajo
in the cañon commonly called Juan Tafoya, where the said
nation is complaining of the pasturing of sheep in the said
cañon, and where because of the scantiness of the existing
water, they cannot raise their crops, for which reason I
ordered the majordomos of the said herds to meet and in
the presence of the Navajos I ordered them not to damage
or injure the Navajos with ill treatment under penalty of
a twelve peso fine and so many days in jail for the first
offense, and for the second the fine would be made by my
superiors and as they agreed, I pointed out to them the
point where the Serro Chato descends into the same cañon
for the pasturing of their flocks.

On the 2nd, the said Navajos placed before me the
complaint that the settlers of Cebolleta were interfering
in the cañada which is commonly as Pedro Padilla, telling
me that they understood that only Cebolleta and the region
immediately around it was conceded to the settlers by
the governor, whom they call "Captain," and not the areas
which are away from the said settlement of Cebolleta
and that when they explained their complaint to the "Captain," that it was because he had taken Cebolleta from
them, the "Captain" said that they could keep the other
lands which they had planted, and seeing that these lands
are in the said canada they have now been hindered by the
residents of Cebolleta for two years . . .   Since the
settlers are in the jurisdiction of the alcalde of Laguna,
I went with the Navajos and the four men who accompanied
me to the settlement of Cebolleta where I wrote to the
said alcalde, notifying him of the complaint which the
said Navajos have lodged against these settlers, dated
today, by which I have told him to come and bring the
grant which the said settlers hold, made by the said
alcalde and approved by the governor, in which he cites the
boundaries that the said settlers agree with the said grant
that the said cañada is within their boundaries notwithstanding that it is distant from the said settlement.
It is necessary for me to see the grant and that the
Navajos see it . . .   I then retired, returning by the
same route I had taken. . . .

While Baca settled the matter, temporarily at least,

in the cañon of Juan Tafoya, the issues over the Rio Puerco

lands and the cañada of Pedro Padilla remained unresolved for

over a month while additional investigations were made.   In

his letter transmitting the diary, on June 5, Baca noted:

it is a good thing for Cebolleta that the Navajos are
settled in the cañada to safeguard the entrance from the
Apaches, and also it is good for us all.

In his report to Governor Máynez. of Baca's mission, Alcalde Gutierrez, apparently unaware of the 1805 treaty, recommended that the Navajo be allowed to remain in the cañada of Pedro Padilla. Maynez sent Juan Rafael Ortiz, Alcalde of Santa Fe, to make an independent investigation of the rights of the various parties, and in a communication of July 2 to Gutierrez telling him of the mission, the governor noted that Ortiz

> could give a simple license so that the Navajos could plant on the said Rio [Puerco], but he cannot give them a right of property as royal possession.

Ortiz' report is as follows:

> . . . For the urgent business that I had at the Pueblo of Laguna, I passed by the Rio Puerco at the place which they call the dam, made by three residents of Alameda and Albuquerque together with the Navajo Indians, and having arrived at the dam with the residents who accompanied me, Francisco García, José García, Antonio Gonzales and Rafael Córdova, all residents of Corrales, six or eight Navajos and three women of the same nation approached me. They asked the said Francisco García who I was, and he answered them that I was the alcalde of the villa of Santa Fe; then the said Indians continued talking in their own idiom, and presently asked me by a note what was my motive towards the three poor residents who had come together with them to plant, to which I answered them that I was ignorant of all of it, as I was not of that jurisdiction, but nevertheless they continued to communicate with me that the three residents had made a little planting on the edge of this river and with their hands they made a little dam to hold back the last drops of water so that by this means they could provide for the dry season, which cost them three days and two nights of work, the same Indians telling me that at the same time, the residents did not sleep a wink, and that afterwards, when their fatigue was so great, and without having the slightest other complaint to make against the said residents, the chief of the nation, called Segundo, threatened it, and this was a bad thing for he had no more than a tiny piece of planting in the said place,

57

for his fields are further away, and for this reason the
said Segundo had not received any damage from the said
residents. Judgment should be given for the demand,
considering that by driving the residents from their
plantings, they would be given to him, so that he would
profit by them, as in fact they say happened, that the
lieutenant Bartolomé Baca came to the said Rio Puerco by
order of the alcalde, Don Lorenzo Gutierres, warning the
three residents, so that they immediately left, abandoning
their fields when they received the order, and the Navajos
said that these were the corn fields of the Spaniards and
they did not want to take them as they had cost them no
labor, and they were not the legal owners, and that they
were only caring for them so that the animals would not
eat them.

In respect to the cañada which is called Pedro Padilla,
I have not the slightest information that it can belong
to the Navajos although the Navajos claim it for their
own from the Governor, Don Joaquín del Real and the alcalde
of Laguna, but the governor himself told me it was neither
theirs nor was there any reason for them to be in the
said cañada within the boundaries of the province.
Following this, the alcalde of Laguna tells me that
neither in the time of Governor Real nor of Governor
Chacón did he have an order for possession in the name
of His Majesty for the said Navajos in the said cañada,
much less in any other place close to the Rio Puerco,
for these lands have always been considered as royal in
virtue of which those of the Rio Abajo can pasture and
shelter in them all their sheep flocks and part of the
cattle and horses, and if the said Indians were allowed
to make any plantings in the said cañada and on the Rio
Puerco, as has been verified for this year and the one
past, it is only an act of charity, for at no time can
they allege any right.

58

The matter was temporarily resolved by Governor
Maynez on July 9, 1808:

The expediente which is now in my hands which your
Excellency sent me dated the 7th of the present month
has the result that without having been convinced of the
reasonableness of the residents of Cebolleta, I order
your Excellency to turn over to the Navajos the cañada
of Pedro Padilla, but it follows that from such a decision
various appeals and much work results.
My order of June 23 is contrary to having me agree
promptly with your opinion in favor of the Navajo nation,
leaving aside the claims of those from Cebolleta, and
this is not to command that your Excellency place the
Navajo in the use or ownership of the said site and in
carrying out what follows, your Excellency must exercise

much patience in order to take from them the use which
has been given them.

The total result is that neither party has proof of
ownership of the said cañada and thus they are the boundaries of the two parties, and in this concept and to
get to the root of the struggle, it results that ulti-
mately it remains as a common boundary, so that the
herds of the settlers of Cebolleta and those of the
Navajo nation shall pasture in it freely, without
claiming it, both parties paying for damages done to
planting according to universal custom.

Concerning the point of the planting by the settlers
on the Rio [Puerco], seeing that your Excellency is
certain that the Navajo has the right of preference, I
repeat my first decision that they should not lose their
fields, I now declare that for the present they do not
pay fees, but that the taking of the water remains to the
benefit of the Indians as does the other work of breaking
the soil, and that in the future the residents shall not
plant there without having settled the matter with the
Navajos, at least that they justify a better right than
the Navajo, in which case I will determine as it seems
fair. I expect that you will carry out these propositions
with prudence, equity and justice in every way that it
may be possible.

It is clear that the apparent preference given to the

Navajos in these three sites was a matter of expediency, and

no rights to the land were conferred upon them. There is

no evidence in other documents throughout the remainder of

the Spanish period that these small bands continued to occupy

the Rio Puerco lands or the cañada of Pedro Padilla.

The next few years were peaceful, and a few Navajos

planted small fields in the Cubero region.

April 16, 1816, José Vicente Ortiz, alcalde of Laguna, to
Governor Pedro María de Allande, #668, GLO, Twitchell.

. . . Padre Peña, priest of this jurisdiction tells me
that some fifteen Navajos have arrived at his convent
saying that they are abandoning their habitations at
the places they call Encinal, San José and Cubero, where
they have their plantings and are going to join their
companions at Chelly for fear of the Comanche . . .

August 20, 1816, Josef Mariano de la Peña to Interim Governor Allande, Pajarito, #2668, Spanish Archives, NMSRCA.

This is a request for orders as alcalde Bartolomé Baca has recalled the troops because of a call for help from the alcalde of Laguna, due to an expected Navajo attack on Cebolleta.

June 25, 1818, Interim Governor Allande to the alcalde of Jemez, #2727, Spanish Archives, NMSRCA.

The governor stated that he had received two communications that the Navajos at the site of San Miguel had killed Juan Alire of Corrales on the 20th. and wounded four sheepherders, and he had sent a group of men to reconnoiter the camp of the culprits. He also stated that Don Mario Mestas of San Isidro had witnessed a great movement among the Navajos and that they were threatening a general uprising. The recent murder had been the work of the two sons of Vicente, and he had dispatched the interpreter, Antonio García, with some settlers and Indians to see the chiefs and find out their intentions, as well as to recover the stolen animals and the murderers.

July 7, 1818, José Vicente Ortiz, alcalde of Laguna, to Allande, #2732, Spanish Archives, NMSRCA.

Ortiz informed Governor Allande that he had completed the recently ordered reconnoissance of the San Mateo region as far west as San Miguel, and that he had seen much evidence of Navajo theft of stock. He also had furnished men to assist the lieutenant of justice of Zuñi who was badly in need of additional arms and munitions.

July 10, 1818, Interim Governor Pedro María de Allande to the alcalde of the Partido of Laguna, #2733, Spanish Archives, NMSRCA.

Being aware of what your Excellency has informed me in your communication of the 7th of this month, I warn your Excellency to be very careful for last night I had news from the alcalde of Jemez, dated the 8th, that when the interpreter, Antonio García, with eighteen men spoke with the principal men of the Navajo nation at my order concerning the present events, he found them near Tunicha with the chieftain Joaquín, who indicated a general uprising of his people against us, and also that this uprising would soon occur, this news having been verified.

In view of this, a group of sixteen men from the troops of this company of Santa Fe went out this morning for the jurisdiction [of Jemez] to wait in the site of Badito; meanwhile Captain Bartolomé Baca with his whole company is arriving to halt the depredations which the Navajo can commit, and your Excellency should must also take all your people quickly, in order to pursue and punish them if you can do so.

Your Excellency is to give an escort to the lieutenant of justice of the Pueblo of Zuñi so that he can return to the said pueblo, as the enclosed indicates, for it is not now convenient for me to go to the Navajos, and I say this to your Excellency by virtue of what you have said to me in the afore-mentioned communication.

61

July 10, 1818, Interim Governor Allande to the lieutenant of justice of the Pueblo of Zuñi, #2731, Spanish Archives, NMSRCA.

In answer to that which your Excellency tells me in your communication of the 9th of the present month, I say that I have not yet decided to go to the Navajo nation as matters stand, but I have sure information that they have risen up on all routes for an attack, by virtue of which it is now important that your Excellency go to Zuñi [the official was at Laguna] to assist the alcalde there, and that you both take great care, gathering together the flocks and horse herds and placing them under an escort so that the enemy does not take them, and that after you carry out this last, that you pursue and punish them. I am now telling the alcalde of Laguna to assist your Excellency in the escort.

July 21, 1818, Ignacio María Sánches Vergara, alcalde of Jemez, to Pedro María de Allande, #2736, Spanish Archives, NMSRCA.

Sánches Vergara stated that on July 20, the chieftain Joaquín arrived at the pueblo with his brother and two nephews to state that he was still loyal, and that he had come to relate the warlike preparations of the majority of the Navajo, as well as his efforts to dissuade them, and when he could not do so, he had separated his band from the rest of them. His account shows that the rebels could be destroyed by an attack from five or six different places. The alcalde ended his communication with the statement that, under the circumstances, he had extended to Joaquín the greatest courtesy.

January 31, 1819, Fr. Mariano Peña, Laguna, to Governor Facundo Melgares, #2790, Spanish Archives, NMSRCA.

62

On September 1, 1818, I gave ecclesiastical burial, by order of Captain Don Bartolomé Baca, to José Antonio Valverde of Tomé, Pablo Urrivali of Sabinal, to Justo Chaves of Belen and Juan Trujillo of La Joya, who died at the hands of the Navajo.

At this mission of San José de la Laguna on November 4, 1818, I, Fray Mariano Peña, Minister of this mission, gave ecclesiastical burial to Diego Antonio Sanchez, a soldier of the Company of Santa Fe, married to María Manuela Gallego, of a wound received from the Navajo enemy.

February 1, 1819, Facundo Melgares to the alcaldes of Alameda, Albuquerque, and Belen, #2791, Spanish Archives, NMSRCA.

In a circular to the alcaldes of the Margin, Governor Melgares warned them that they should be on guard against a large group of warlike Navajos reportedly on their way to the Rio Abajo, and that their militia should meet the threat with the most vigorous resistance.

March 8, 1821, Juan Antonio Cabesa de Baca, Jemez, to Governor Facundo Melgares, #2971, Spanish Archives, NMSRCA.

In dealing with the Navajo chief "General Joaquín's attempts to recover recently stolen stock, Cabesa de Baca reported:

> The said General also says for me to tell you that having examined the rancho which they call Pedro Padilla for sowing, he believes it will be incapable of raising a harvest. Because of the deep snow, the Rio Puerco is flooding their tillage as it is still rising; also that if this is the case, it would be well to give him help from Laguna and Cebolleta near the said site [Pedro Padilla], so that they could plow with a pair of oxen during this month of March the land which they are going to sow.

This would seem to indicate that a small band, back temporarily in the Pedro Padilla and Rio Puerco region after the disturbances of 1818-1819 were on friendly terms with Laguna. The situation changed, however, within a few months.

July 9, 1821, Captain Bartolomé Baca to Facundo Melgares, #2992, Spanish Archives, NMSRCA.

63

Baca was then stationed at Cebolleta, and suspicious of the motives of the Navajos and the sincerity of their alleged desires for peace, asked for sufficient reinforcements to punish the Navajos if it became necessary.

July 16, 1821, Facundo Melgares to the First Constitutional Alcalde of the Capital, #2995, Spanish Archives, NMSRCA.

In answer to Baca's request of July 9, Melgares orders a detail of forty armed men and additional munitions to be sent from the alcaldia of Santa Fe to march to Cebolleta and reinforce Captain Baca.

October 23, 1821, Juan Armijo to Facundo Melgares, #3060,
Spanish Archives, NMSRCA.

This document is a detailed account of a militia
expedition against the Navajos, October 3 - 23, from Cebolleta
to the Chusca Mountains and Ojo del Oso. Armijo's actions
were hampered throughout by insubordination and defection of
the white troops. On the 4th, shortly after leaving the San
Lucas site in the Cebolleta mountains, the first major
insurrection among the troops occurred, one large group
defected, and a smaller one was persuaded to stay with the
expedition.

> And seeing myself with only the Indians of Isleta,
> those of Laguna and Acoma, with their officials and
> those leaders who had surrendered to me, I continued
> my march, under these circumstances, to the place where
> I had determined to go if those who had surrendered
> confirmed their good intentions, and arrived at the
> site of Seven Springs [Seven Lakes?] to make camp with
> the people who remained with me.

64

Other defections occurred, and the only engagement of the
expedition was near Ojo del Oso, where the militia killed
seven Navajos. There were many later incidents when the
pueblo militia played an important role in actions against
the Navajos.

Summary

The first Navajo settlement in the Acoma-Laguna area
at Encinal and Cebolleta, 1748-1750, were the result of
pressure from the Utes against the Navajos and the promises
of Spanish authorities to give them subsistence and gifts in
return for their acceptance of the viceregal Indian policy of

fixed settlments and ministrations of the Franciscan friars
for more effective control. This policy quickly broke down,
however, because of Navajo refusal either to give up their
way of life or to adopt an alien religion, and, because of
the pressure of the more agricultural and pastoral Indians
of Ácoma and Laguna who would effectively utilize the land
which the Navajos spurned.

Throughout the Spanish period to 1821, however, small
bands of Navajos continued to move in and out of the region,
sometimes cultivating small plots in the Cebolleta, Cubero,
Pedro Padilla cañada, on the Rio Puerco, and in the cañon of
Juan Tafoya on the Agua Salada, northeast from Cebolleta.
There is no historical evidence that even small bands utilized
any area south of the San José River. In 1760, Bishop
Tamarón saw the habitations of a few near Cebolleta, probably
in the cañada of Pedro Padilla, but when the Navajos approached
him at Laguna to give them the right to missions in the area,
he refused. Spanish policy after that period did not grant
the Navajos any rights in the Ácoma-Laguna area, although
they were on occasion permitted to stay in some areas.

During the period of land grants to Spaniards west of
the Rio Puerco in the 1760's, grants which were encroachments
into territories used by the Lagunas for herding, and in
case of the Baca grant, used also by Ácoma, a few of these
small bands lived temporarily in widely scattered parts of

65

the grants, although it is difficult to determine whether
they were Navajos or Apaches. During this period, also the
pattern was established which was to continue until after the
return of the Navajos from Bosque Redondo in 1868. While
the Navajos were in temporary occupation, often they were on
friendly terms with the pueblos who did not object to their
presence, but as Navajo raids from outside the area and by
those living around Cebolleta, especially, increased, tension
became greater, for the herds of the pueblos were a powerful
temptation for Navajo raiders. During periods of raids, both
on the pueblos and on the Spanish settlements along the Rio
Grande, the pueblos would move their herds nearer the home
villages; in times of peace they would again return to former
herding and farming sites. The years 1775-1779 were relatively peaceful, and the Lagunas returned to Cebolleta; by
1782, they were again driven out. The Domingues-Escalante
map of 1776 and the Miera y Pacheco map of 1779 showed the
Navajos as west of the Continental Divide.

66

Church records reveal no baptisms of Navajos in the
area during the Spanish period, with the exception of a few
captives, usually children, during the years of raiding, 1770-
1775.

During the Navajo campaign of 1774, the Spanish authorities began the policy, continued by the Mexican and United
States governments, of using pueblo militia to augment their
forces against the Navajos.

Navajo affairs were comparatively quiet from 1785 to 1800. As a part of his policy of frontier Indian defense, Governor Juan Bautista de Anza succeeded in persuading the somewhat reluctant Navajos to break their former ties with the Apaches, and to join with the Spanish and pueblo militia against the latter, 1785-1788. The Navajos were in the meantime prohibited from crossing the San José River. In 1786, de Anza, at the urging of authorities in Mexico, attempted to reinstate the old policy of establishing the Navajos in fixed settlements for better control and administration. To this end, he permitted them to select one of their chiefs to speak for them in dealing with the authorities, to accept an interpreter. and, of much greater importance, encouraged trade and close relations between the Navajos and the Pueblo Indians.

67

This uneasy peace lasted until the late 1790's. From 1800 to 1821, however, relations of the Navajos with the Spanish and with the Pueblos Indians of Acoma and Laguna were characterized by periods of Navajo raids, followed by brief periods of peace, followed by more raids, and more campaigns. During this period, some small bands still continued to move in and out of the pueblo area. Raids and pursuit began in June, 1800, with Governor Chacón pursuing the Navajos to Tunicha where peace was made. Constant warfare occurred during 1804 and 1805. A Navajo request in February, 1804,

to reoccupy Cebolleta was denied because of the depredations
committed by the group who had temporarily occupied this
site and the nearby regions. Attacks on the Rio Puerco and
Jemez, a raid by 200 warriors on Cebolleta in April, and
another by 1,000 in August resulted in a full scale campaign.
The Cebolleta settlers fled to Laguna, but were ordered back
by Comandante General Nemesio Salcedo in September. Lieutenant
Colonel Antonio Narbona led the campaign into the Cañon de
Chelly heart of the Navajo country. Peace terms dictated by
Governor Chacón on March 27, 1805, forbade Navajo occupation
of the Cebolleta area, and established a cordon south of
which the Navajos were not to go, consisting of the cañon of
Juan Tafoya, the San Mateos, and the San José River. Peace
stipulations in May denied any Navajo claim to Cebolleta.

68

In October, the settlers of Cebolleta again complained
of the Navajos destroying their crops, but again were not permitted to abandon the grant.

As soon as calm returned, a small band under the chieftain Vicente, returned to the Juan Tafoya and Serro Chato and
came into conflict with Spanish sheepherders in 1806. A few
families under Segundo and Delgadito again planted small
fields in the Rio Puerco region and in the cañada of Pedro
Padilla, clearly forbidden in the peace terms of March 27,
1805. In 1808, a quarrel between the Navajos and settlers was
resolved by permitting the Navajos, since they were then

peaceful, to use the regions, but at no time were they given
a right to the land.

In April of 1816, a few Navajos who were using lands
in the Cubero region abandoned them and moved to Cañon de
Chelly because of fear from the Comanches.

Trouble again arose over Cebolleta in August, 1816, and
additional troops were sent to ward off an attack. In June,
1818, a Navajo raid in the San Miguel district west of the
Cebolleta mountains, and also along the Rio Grande, led to
another campaign, and the alcalde of Laguna was ordered to
use his forces, including the pueblo militia, to provide military escort and assistance to officials at Zuni, as well as
to patrol his own area. No evidence of Navajo occupation in
the Acoma-Laguna area was indicated during this conflict, but
in the spring of 1821, the chieftain Joaquín was requesting
assistance for small groups of Navajos were were attempting to
farm in the Rio Puerco and cañada of Pedro Padilla sites.

69

By July, 1821, however, raiding had begun anew, and
additional troops from Santa Fe were ordered to Cebolleta.
Juan Armijo led a detachment of Spanish and pueblo soldiers
into the Chusca and Ojo del Oso country in October in a man-
euver hampered by defection of the white troops, so that the
small success which he had was due largely to the lpyalty of
the Indians of Isleta, Laguna, and Acoma.

BIBLIOGRAPHY

I. PRINTED SOURCES

Adams, Eleanor B., Bishop Tamaron's Visitation of New Mexico, 1760. Albuquerque: Historical Society of New Mexico, Publications in History, XV, February, 1954.

Amsden, Charles Avery, Navaho Weaving; its Technic and History. Santa Ana, Calif.: The Fine Arts Press in Cooperation with the Southwest Museum, 1934.

Hackett, Charles Wilson, ed., Historical Documents Relating to New Mexico, Nueva Vizcaya, and Approaches Thereto, to 1773. Adolph F. A. Bandelier and Fanny R. Bandelier, collectors. Washington: Carnegie Institution, 1937, Vol. III.

Thomas, Alfred Barnaby, Forgotten Frontiers . . . . Norman: University of Oklahoma Press. 1932.

Thomas, Alfred Barnaby, The Plains Indians and New Mexico, 1751-1778. Albuquerque: The University of New Mexico Press; Cuatro Centennial Publications, Vol. XI, 1940.

Worcester, Donald E., "Advice on Governing New Mexico, 1794," New Mexico Historical Review, XXIV (July, 1949).

II. DOCUMENTARY COLLECTIONS

Archivo General de la Nación

Provincias Internas, Legajo 65, Part 3, expediente 10, folio 11.

Provincias Internas, Legajo 65, Part 10, expediente 10, folio 36.

Surveyor-General and Court of Private Land Claims

Bernabe Montaño, SG #49; CPLC #7.

Nuestra Señora de la Luz de las Lagunitas (Antonio Baca), SG #101; CPLC #70.

Bernardo Miera y Pacheco and Pedro Padilla (Cañada de Los Alamos), SG #98.

Vertientes (Sitio) de Navajo, SG #195; CPLC #270.

Town of Cebolleta, SG #46.

Baltasar Baca and Sons, SG #104; CPLC #114.

Agua Salada (Luis Jaramillo), SG #103; CPLC #31.

Antonio Sedillo, SG 50; CPLC #15.

Twitchell Archives (Federal Land Office)

#668, José Vicente Ortiz to Pedro María de Allande,
April 16, 1816.

Spanish Archives (New Mexico State Records Center and
Archives)

#1492, Fernando Chacón to Pedro de Nava, June 21, 1800.

#1712, Fernando Chacón to Nemesio Salcedo, March 26,
1804.

#1714, Chacón to Salcedo, March 28, 1804.

#1722, Salcedo to Chacón, April 19, 1804.

#1730, Chacón to Salcedo, May 16, 1804.

#1735, Salcedo to Chacón, June 8, 1804.

#1743, Salcedo to Chacón, July 16, 1804.

#1754, Salcedo to Chacón, September 16, 1804.

#1763, Salcedo to Chacón, October 5, 1804.

#1766, Salcedo to Chacon, October 5, 1804

#1774, Chacón to Nicolás Farín, November 20, 1804.

#1776, Antonio Narbona to Chacón, November 26, 1804.

#1778, Narbona to Chacón, December 10, 1804.

#1780, Chacón to Narbona, December 13, 1804.

#1788, Salcedo to Chacón, January 11, 1805.

#1792, Narbona to Chacón, January 24, 1805.

#1801, Chacón, "Conditions for Peace" March 27, 1805.

71

Spanish Archives (continued)

#1828, Joaquín del Real Alencaster to Salcedo, May 15, 1805.

#1881, Real Alencaster to Salcedo, September 1, 1805.

#1902, José Manuel Aragón to Real Alencaster, October 11, 1805.

#1929, Aragón to Real Alencaster, December 15, 1805.

#2089, Real Alencaster to Salcedo, November 20, 1807.

#2105, Documents relating to quarrel of settlers with Navajos, May 23 - July 9, 1808.

#2727, Allande to Alcalde of Jemez, June 25, 1818.

#2732, José Vicente Ortiz to Allande, July 7, 1818.

#2733, Allande to Alcalde of Laguna (Ortiz), July 10, 1818.

#2731, Allande to Lieutenant of Justice, Zuñi, July 10, 1818.

72

#2736, Ignacio María Sánches Vergara to Allande, July 21, 1818.

#2790, Fr. Mariano Peña to Facundo Melgares, January 31, 1819.

#2791, Facundo Melgares to Alcaldes of Alameda, Albuquerque, and Belen, February 1, 1819.

#2971, Juan Antonio Cabesa de Baca to Melgares, March 8, 1821.

#2992, Bartolomé Baca to Melgares, July 9, 1821.

#2995, Melgares to First Constitutional Alcalde of Santa Fe, July 16, 1821.

#3060, Juan Armijo to Melgares, October 23, 1821.

RECORD OF NAVAJO ACTIVITIES AFFECTING THE ACOMA-LAGUNA AREA

DURING THE MEXICAN PERIOD, 1822-1846

by

Ward Alan Minge

Myra Ellen Jenkins

74

This report contains pertinent documents extant for the Mexican Period, 1822-1846. They are translated in part or in full, whatever the contents seem to warrant. Unfortunately, the collections for this period are fragmentary and the data not easily drawn into smooth narration. Where not specifically relating to the Pueblos of Acoma or Laguna, the documents are based on references to the <u>Alcaldia de Laguna</u> of which these two Pueblos are members and the Jurisdiction of Jemez within which they find their boundaries and under whose commanders they are often enlisted to withstand invaders. Towards the end of the Mexican Period, from 1844 on, they are part of the Third District, or <u>Rio Abajo</u>. While some of these documents may be found in secondary sources, the authors choose to utilize the originals whenever possible. These are located in the Federal Land Office collections in Santa Fe, New Mexico, or the Mexican Collections of the New Mexico Records Center and Archives, Santa Fe, unless otherwise indicated. Summary remarks follow at the end of the report.

75

*   *   *   *   *   *

April 24, 1822. Governor Facundo Melgares to the First Alcalde of the Capital of Santa Fe, New Mexico.

The Governor orders preparation for Navajo hostilities and warns that the "Navajos may attempt a bloody vengeance on the inhabitants of the Province." The Alcalde should assemble 50 armed men as soon as possible, and the people of the Province should prepare themselves for such an attack.

1

April 26, 1822. Records of the New Mexico Junta Provincial, Santa Fe.

Classification of inhabitants of New Mexico for a levy to conduct a campaign against the Navajos. [Neither Acoma nor Laguna are mentioned in this levy. That they contributed men and equipment for militia and guard work from time to time is submitted in subsequent citations and in exhibits.]

May 6, 1822. Governor Facundo Melgares to all Alcaldes.

The Governor orders a rendezvous of all the troops at Cebolleta for Navajo campaign.

June 15, 1822. Alejo Garcia Conde, Durango, Mexico, to Governor Facundo
                 Melgares, Santa Fe, New Mexico.

Conde refers to 13 Navajos killed at Jemez, New Mexico, and the hostilities which follow. He asserts that the "Navajos have been untrustworthy of the faith and confidence of the Mexican government," and discusses a plan for concerted moves from Chihuahua and Sonora, Mexico, and New Mexico against the Navajos.

June 30, 1822. Manuel Armijo, Albuquerque, New Mexico, to Governor Facundo
                 Melgares, Santa Fe.

Armijo describes an attack on the settlement of Atrisco, New Mexico, by Navajos during which they "killed a child and others and wounded a woman." He gave pursuit "as far as the Puerco River."

September 12, 1822. Governor Facundo Melgares to Alcaldes.

The Governor advises Alcaldes that peace negotiations are to be held with the Navajos.

September 21, 1822. Antonio Chavez, Belen, New Mexico, to Governor Facundo
                  Melgares, Santa Fe, New Mexico.

2

Mr. Chavez reports of depredations south of Albuquerque saying that the Navajos were followed "to the Puerto de los Ojos de Toribio, where he and his men gave up the chase."

<u>February 5, 1823.</u> Copy of peace treaty with Navajos and the terms thereof as recommended by Governor Jose Antonio Vizcarra, New Mexico.

Points of interest which the Political and Military Leader of the Province recommends to the individuals who compose this meeting in the name of the Province with the object of celebrating a better peace with the Navajo Tribe.

1. That all the captives which they may have made of our people be returned without hiding any and the same with the fugitives if there are any.

2. That there be returned to them those who fled to us; whenever they may wish to go back; but if they should wish to receive the saving waters of Baptism it does not appear the desire of Catholics to deny them, before favoring them on the contrary, and exhorting them to the end that the number of faithful adoring the True God of the Christians is multiplied.

3. That it be demanded of them to the last that they return what they have stolen in the Province from the last peace celebrated with them; returning to the injured what was robbed, in its entirety.

4. And lastly, that it be energetically proposed to them to be converted   77 to the Catholic religion, reducing themselves to Pueblos, that they will be settled in the places which may be convenient, in order to pursue these results in the propagation of the faith in Jesus Christ, and that we fulfill with perfection attributes of Christians reducing an infidel nation to society of the Catholics.

Pueblo of Laguna

<u>February 12, 1823.</u> Record of the meeting held between Governor Jose Antonio Vizcarra and the Navajo Tribe, Camp at Paguate, New Mexico.

The meeting held to consider the terms of the treaty between the Navajos and the Governor of the Province proceeded as follows:

In fulfilling the first article, they returned the captives that were found among them.
Concerning the second, they reclaimed those of their Nation that existed among us but with the agreement that they would be returned them when they had met all my proposals and would give proof of proceeding as promised.
As to the third article, they said that they were starving and for that reason they did not have the wherewithall to pay for the robberies, but that

3

they promised not to rob again and that if they did not comply they should
be punished.

In fulfillment of the fourth and last, they pledged to answer within the
span of four months counted from the first of March; respecting which they had
to speak with the entire Nation, by virtue of which and for the due permanency
were signed in the name of the General Juanico, and those of his Tribe this
[agreement] the Captain Don Bartolome Baca and Don Antonio Sandoval.

February 12, 1823.   Copy of a plan for war in case the Navajo did not live up
to the agreements of the Treaty. [This copy is not signed
but from the internal information was agreed to by all the
Alcaldes, leading citizens and officers, including the
regidores.]

This plan, as agreed to by the above cited officials, included division

of booty. One thousand men would enter the province of the Navaje with the

object of making war and raiding. Two hundred men would be left in the interior

of New Mexico for ordinary precautions but the remainder would proceed with arm

and the booty taken from the Navajos would be divided by the men actually takin

part in the war. Further, if after celebrating the peace there would be

78 encountered any thief, "he would be killed in the act or imprisoned if he

surrendered or offered no resistance."

June 17, 1823.   Governor Jose Antonio Viscarra to the Illustrious Municipal
Government of this Capital.

Governor Viscarra announces plan to attack the Navajos in their own

country, which campaign is to last for 4 or 5 months and will include 1,500

troops. He announces that he will depart on the next day, June 18, and leaves

in his place of government and second in command, D. Francisco Xavier Chavez.

[There is a diary of this campaign but the dates are not useful and nothing

is revealed specifically relating to landmarks or boundaries, excepting that

the troops spent much of the time around the Canyon de Chelly.]

4

June, July, August, 1823. Military personnel records of the men who participated in this campaign. For example, the personnel records for Captain Donaciano Vigil, Santa Fe, December 31, 1842.

Captain Donaciano Vigil /in December 1842 he was 39 years of age7 took part in the war against the rebellious Navajos during June, July, August, 1823, during which the Mexican troops killed 50 Navajo warriors and imprisoned 36 of both sexes.

January 16, 1824. Governor Jose Antonio Viscarra to Committee.

The Governor discusses the possibilities of another peace treaty with the Navajos in an attempt to "create harmony in this unhappy Province."

February 9, 1824. Official record of Jose Antonio Chaves /no addressee7.

Reports of a chase against some Navajo horse thieves and that Laguna Pueblo "lent some people on foot." They had no success but the Navajo Chino told them there was a party of bad Navajos at the Rito Quemado.

February 27, 1824. Juan Crus Baca /Jues de Paz7, Belen, New Mexico, to Governor Bartolome Baca, Santa Fe.

Mr. Baca describes how Mr. Toribio Trujillo appeared before him with three Navajos which he had captured menacing his ranch at Lomita del Berrendo.

April 6, 1824. Gaspar de Ochoa, Durango, Mexico, to Comandante General of New Mexico.

He states that he cannot send approval of treaty with the Navajos until he knows the terms. /Such treaties always required the approval of higher authorities in the Supreme Government of Mexico causing unfortunate delays.7

October 30, 1824. Gobierno, Santa Fe, to Alcalde of Laguna.

Acknowledgement of information that Navajos have stolen horses of Mr. Luis Baca.

<u>December 13, 1824</u>. Jose Antonio Valverde, Jemez, New Mexico, to the
Governor in charge of same.

He sends notice from Jemez that the Navajos have been raiding and causing
much damage, taking six sheep from the Pueblo of Santa Ana and destroying
houses.

<u>March 24, 1825</u>. Pablo Baca, Belen, New Mexico, to the Governor of this
Province, Antonio Narbona.

Baca describes raid committed by Navajos near Belen. Some animals were
stolen from Antonio Chaves and Mr. Baca requests the aid and support of 150
troops for 15 days to go in pursuit.

<u>May 28, 1827</u>. Manuel Armijo to the Comandante General, Colonel Antonio Narbona
Armijo sends notice that Navajos have stolen 40 animals in the vicinity
of Rio del Oso at San Juan de los Caballeros.

80 <u>May 29, 1827</u>. Comandancia General of the Territory of New Mexico to the
Comandante General, Simon Elias.

Colonel Narbona complains that the repeated attacks and depredations of
the Navajos have continued and will continue "in spite of the peace celebrated
with that Tribe" because of the lack of military protection and supplies.

<u>June 13, 1827</u>. Mariano Martin, Abiquiu, New Mexico, to the Governor of the
Territory of New Mexico, Manuel Armijo.

Sends notice that Navajos enter the vicinities of Abiquiu and Canada
and steal animals, unharmed.

<u>June 18, 1827</u>. Notice of the Comandancia General [no addressee].

Navajos have taken animals from the neighborhood of the Pueblo of Isleta
and are being chased.

6

<u>June 27, 1827.</u> Manuel Armijo, Santa Fe, to the Comandante General, Colonel
        Antonio Narbona.

Mr. Armijo relays information he has received from Jemez that Navajos
have stolen animals at el Valle, and that a party of troops will leave
Santa Fe on June 29 to help retrieve them.

<u>July 11, 1827.</u> Mariano Martin, to the Governor of the Territory of New Mexico,
        Don Manuel Armijo.

The Navajos commit raids in the vicinity of Abiquiu, New Mexico, almost
every day. Martin describes further how they are trying to stop these raids
with 36 men under the retired Sergeant Pablo Trujillo.

<u>August 4, 1828.</u> Juan Jose Arocha, Comandancia Militar de Nuevo Mejico, to
        The Governor of this Territory.

The Navajos have stolen 29 sheep from Joaquin Padilla near Belen.

<u>August 4, 1828.</u> Acoma Exhibit # ___, and Laguna Exhibit # ___. Militia lists,
        signed by Manuel Jaramillo, Laguna, New Mexico.

"List comprising the number of residents for the militia there are at
this Pueblo of the Lord San Jose de la Laguna between the ages of 28 to 50
years," and includes ___ Acomas and ___ Lagunas.

81

<u>November 12, 1828.</u> Jose Antonio Sandoval, Jemez, to the Governor.

Notification from Sandoval relating of thefts and murders committed by
the Navajos in the Jurisdiction of Jemez. This document lists the goods,
animals, and deaths committed against the persons of Jesus Gallego, the
Alcalde Tomas Sandoval, and Antonio Montoya, who lost a child; men and arms
are requested from the Jurisdictions of Alameda, Cochiti, and Jemez, the
latter Jurisdiction included Laguna and Acoma.

<u>February 21, 1829</u>. Jose Antonio Sandoval, Jemez, to Governor Manuel Armijo.

Mr. Sandoval sends notice of robberies committed by Navajos against the persons of Jose Antonio Sandoval, Jose Maria Garcia, and Fernando Montoya, in the Jurisdiction of Jemez.

<u>March 7, 1829</u>. Miguel Garcia, Jemez, New Mexico, to the Principal Comandante, Don Juan Jose Arocha.

The Navajos rob 130 sheep from Francisco Sandoval, Jurisdiction of Jemez, and they are pursued to the "Mesa Azul, and to where they have their rancheria at San Lucas and Rincon del Visente, and the sheep were taken to el Carrizo."

<u>March 8, 1829</u>. Jose Antonio Sandoval, Jemez, to the Governor of the Territory, Don Manuel Armijo.

The Navajos steal 130 sheep from Francisco Sandoval, Jurisdiction of Jemez, and flee to their own hills. Jose Sandoval complains of the continuous depradations and insults, misery and pain, caused by the Navajos and asks for help of the troops.

82

<u>March 10, 1829</u>. Instructions for the troops leaving for the Pueblo of Jemez.
[Probably composed by Manuel Armijo]

Fifteen men with arms and ammunition are ordered to leave for Jemez where they are to be stationed and to patrol the frontier for the peace and harmony of the inhabitants.

<u>April 14, 1829</u>. Military personnel records of the men who participated in this campaign. They all agree in the fundamental data presented below in the personnel records for Sergeant Jose Bustamante, December 31, 1842, when at that time he was stationed with the Permanent Company at San Miguel del Vado on the Pecos River.

"Sargento Jose Bustamante, . . . participated in an expedition against the

8

rebellious Navajos, returning on the 14th of April 1829, under orders of

Captain Don Jose Antonio Vizcarra." They had a battle during which 11

warriors and 3 women were killed, and they made prisoner of 22 of both sexes.

/There is very little known of this campaign. Where were the battles? Who

participated? Obviously, it was successful and led to the treaty below./

<u>July 15, 1829.</u> Treaty of Peace and Friendship Celebrated with the Navajo
Nation by His Excellency, Governor of the Department of New
Mexico.

Having repeatedly petitioned the said Tribe through their envoys, and
finally the Chieftain Cayetano, being one of the most important of the said
Nation, coming with six of the principal leaders and having spoken to me in the
name of the entire Nation that they desire to be given the terms which the
Governor of New Mexico may wish, and in view of their humiliation and what
appears to be good faith, he /Cayetano/ has agreed to present them to me with
the chieftains and other notables of the Nation, concerning this very interesting
affair, and after some difference we have agreed to the following articles:

1. There will be peace and commerce to carry out what those of the
   Navajo Tribe have promised with the citizens of the Department of
   New Mexico; with those of the Department of Chihuahua; and with
   those of Sonora as well as with all the citizens belonging to the
   Mexican Republic as well as with all the other citizens of the
   potential friends of the Mexican Republic.

2. In fulfillment of this agreement and in order to carry out the good
   faith which animates the agreeing parties the Navajo chieftains
   have agreed to surrender our captives which are in their Nation who
   were seized from the fields in which they were caring for their flocks
   without protection and have agreed also those of their own remain
   among us as a just reprisal, acquired through an honorable war,
   without betrayal.

3. As the principal bases for these agreements is to end the horrors
   of war and return to the sweet name of a stable and lasting peace,
   the aforesaid chiefs and principals of the said Tribe have agreed
   to make what safeguards as may be possible that their people in no
   way again disturb the order with the citizens of the Department of
   New Mexico.

4. It is understood that trade will remain on the same terms in the
   Department of New Mexico as it was before the present war.

5. As the purpose of this treaty is to remove every resentment, it is
   suggested to the Navajo chieftains that in case their people cause
   any death to the Mexican sheepherders, that they will give up the

83

murderer to the government so that he can be punished, the
government suggesting at the same time that in case the sheep-
herders cause any death that 30 sheep be paid for the dead man,
and the malefactor be punished according to law.

6. In case any Navajo Indian woman succeeds in escaping by fleeing from
the house of her master, on arrival of the said woman in her own
land, when it is verified, that she remain free and without any
obligation of the nation to give anything for her ransom.

7. In any case whatsoever, that the enemies of both nations attempt to
invade, it shall be the obligation of the contracting parties to
stop the aggression and give immediate notice so that they may free
themselves from the insult which is being prepared for them, the
Navajes being allowed, for if they agree, to have one of, or two of,
their Tribe live on the frontiers of Cebolleta and Jemez in order to
anticipate such information, if there are Sahuanos, Comanches, or
other barbarous tribes, that they be prepared to defeat them or in
any case to impede their passage, and that they give the same
obligation to the Navajos if the Gila Apaches or other nations prepar
to invade the Department.

And in order to carry out all and each one of these articles which make
up this Treaty, His Excellency, the Governor, will be authorized on the part
of the Republic of Mexico and at the invitation of the Prefects, who also were
present, and for the Navajo Chieftains, above listed, placing as a sign, each
one, a cross for the due certification of the Treaty celebrated at San Diego
84 de Jemez, at Jemez, New Mexico, July 15, 1829.

August 3, 1829. Jose Antonio Sandoval, Jusgado de Xemes, to the Governor of
the Territory.

The Justice Sandoval asks for help. The Navajos have raided the Pueblo

of Santa Ana, stealing 4 horses after which they were chased, unsuccessfully,

"to the Cerro Cabezon."

August 15, 1829. Jose Antonio Sandoval, Jusgado de Xemes, to the Governor
of the Territory, Don Jose Antonio Chavez.

Sandoval reports that the Navajos have stolen 30 animals at Abiquiu, New

Mexico.

<u>September 11, 1829.</u> Jose Antonio Sandoval, Jusgado de Xemes, to the
                       Governor of this Territory, Don Jose Antonio Chaves.

   Justice Sandoval reports the Navajos sacked and robbed the vicinity of

the Pueblo of Jemez, "taking goods and animals from the Mayordomo, also from

Juan Casados, and killing one of the animals belonging to a Pueblo of Jemez

Indian and three more."

<u>September 26, 1829.</u> Jose Antonio Sandoval, Jusgado de Xemes, to the Governor
                       of this Territory, Don Jose Antonio Chaves.

   Navajos robbed the citizen Juan Montoya, Jurisdiction of Jemez, of six

horses and one mule. Sandoval complains of the despotism of the Navajos.

<u>January 31, 1830.</u> Miguel Garcia, Canon, to Alcalde Don Jose Antonio Vizcarra.

   Navajos steal 11 animals from Jose Segundo Garcia, Jurisdiction of Jemez,

and Cebolleta.

<u>July 30, 1830.</u> Jose Antonio Chaves, Governor of New Mexico, to the Appointed   85
               First Constitutional Alcalde of Santa Fe.

   Navajos plan and promise to meet on August 11 to satisfy the claims of

damages and robberies committed against the Mexican Nation. They will meet

with representatives from New Mexico on the Puerco River at <u>Ojo del Chico.</u>

          In a letter dated 27 July, the Alcalde of Jemez tells me, among
     other things, the following:
          The Chieftains of the Navajo Nation have discussed and are in
     accord with the Interpreter /the Mexican interpreter Garcia7 that on the
     11th of August next there is proposed a reunion for the Nation in order
     to satisfy the damages and robberies that have been made by the malevolents
     of their Nation with these interests which the Chieftains have solicited
     and are gathering together among the Nation with which consideration Your
     Highness will be able to believe that they wish peace, this reunion which
     they cite for Your Highness, they say will be in the vicinity of the
     Puerco River, at a place called Ojo del Chico, which is up to where the
     Interpreter has been able to follow what may be the place, that they wish
     to come for two ends to satisfy the robberies and to treat with our
     representatives, and for this purpose there will unite up to 700 Indians
     more or less, at the said place and await there three days for your answer

/The Governor circulated this information in order that as many people who
may have had claims could meet with the Navajos. Unfortunately, there does
not appear to be any follow on correspondence./

September 28, 1831. Jose Antonio Vizcarra, Comandancia General del Nuevo
  Majico al Sor. Gefe Politico de Este Territorio.

Vizcarra discusses in very general terms the excesses caused by the
Navajos in the Jurisdiction of Jemes.

Summer, 1832. Lansing Bartlett Bloom, "New Mexico Under Mexican Administration,
  1821-1846," Old Santa Fe, Vol. I, No. 4, April, 1914, p. 355.

   This summer, the Apaches were still harassing both Chihuahua and New
Mexico. Writing in September, Escudero stated that commerce had pro-
gressed more since 1824 than in three hundred years before the Independence
but that the frontiers were so little respected by the barbarous Indians
that they were desolating the internal States, regardless of troops and
of the national power.
   New Mexico was beset by the Navajos also, and an expedition against
them was occasioned by troubles in the jurisdictions of Jemes and Laguna
during 1832-1833. In August, 1833, Apache hostilities were reported
86   from the same region.

October 15, 1832. Record Book of the Comandancia General, Santa Fe, copy
  of report to the Comandante General Inspector.

The detachment at Socorro was robbed by the Navajos "who have taken the
mounts of the troops at Socorro." This occurred on 1 October and another
robbery on 7 October. The troops were unable to give chase because they had
no horses.

October 31, 1832. Record Book of the Comandancia General, Santa Fe, copy
  of report to the Comandante General Inspector.

   On the 12th of October there were present in this city, 25 warriors
of the Navajo Nation with the Chieftains Narbona, Francisco Baca, and
others, and having been bitterly upbraided by the Governor and by me over
the robbery of horses that occurred against the troops at Socorro, they
answered that they knew nothing of the robberies and that they were made
in the vicinities of other gentiles, . . . Chieftain Jose Caballero
presented himself to me on the 28th of October, giving notice of having
gone to Tunicha and taking the said mounts belonging to the troops along
with other animals with the exception of six belonging to the Company
which had been lost and three which were dead, without the cited Navajo
Nation offering any resistance with arms, . . .

March 15, 1833. Record Book of the Comandancia General, Santa Fe, copy of
report to the Comandante General Inspector.

The Governor of the Territory having ordered in accordance with the
Excellent Diputation which accuses the Navajo Nation of robberies and
excesses which they are experiencing with some frequency against the
cattle and sheep herders, the inhabitants of the country have met together
finally to march on a campaign the 20th of the current month, to the camp
of the Siete Lagunas taking along all the existing troops of the permanent
company of Santa Fe, and there will join at Jemez on the 24th 500 residents
by order of the same Governor; . . .

November 24, 1833. Jose de Madariaga, Tome, New Mexico, to the Governor of
this Territory, Don Francisco Sarracino.

Reports that 30 of the best troops, armed and equipped, are sent to the
Rito de Laguna with provisions for replacements to help stand off the Navajos.

November 24, 1833. Gobierno to the Citizen Alcalde of Jemez.

The cattle stolen by the Navajos have been taken from the thieves by the
allied Chieftains Baca, Narbona, and Sebolla. The Governor requests more
information regarding this rumor.

87

February 6, 1834. Blas Antonio Chaves, Alcalde of Jemez, to Governor Don
Francisco Sarracino, Santa Fe.

In answer to the Governor's request for men and horses to conduct a
campaign, Mr. Chaves is only able to raise a few men and few horses of good
quality. He describes the Pueblos of Santa Ana, Zia, and Jemez, and the
entire jurisdiction as being very poor and demoralized because of the Navajo
depradations.

February 23, 1834. Miguel Garcia, Jemez, to Commander of Arms, Blas Hinojos,
Santa Fe, New Mexico.

Mr. Garcia describes a Navajo attack on the Ranchos de Tres Ganados in
the vicinity of the Canada de las Milpas of the Pueblo of Zia. The attack

occurred during the night of February 21. They killed one man named Marcos Gallegos, "took captive two children, a burro, and other equipment from the ranches." Thirty-six men gave the Navajos chase to the Mesa Prieta when they became bogged in mud and after reaching the top decided to return.

July 11, 1834. Rafael Garcia de Noriega, Jemez, to the Political Leader of the Territory.

Garcia de Noriega describes a raid in the Canyon at Jemez in which the Navajos, on the same day, have taken a mule and three horses which were near the settlements. He further sets forth a plea for raising 300 men to fight the Navajos who are planning to conquer the territory, he believes.
Note in Margin: /Probably in answer but unsigned/ attempts to discourage such an enterprise but recommends the thefts must be stopped, that if the guilty be captured they should be brought to Santa Fe for punishment.

88

August 14, 1834. Ambrosio Culaque, Jemez, to Governor Don Francisco Sarracin
Extends notice that the Navajo Francisco Baca has taken his family away from Cebolleta to parts unknown but far away.

September, 1834. Manuel Sanchez, San Miguel de la Bajada, to the Governor of the Territory, Don Francisco Sarracino, (September 24, 1834).

The above cited is in response to personal requests by the Governor to join in a campaign he is organizing against the Navajo Nation.
/See also annotated list from the jurisdiction of San Juan, New Mexico, which includes all the individuals named to participate in the campaign against the Navajos. List includes 7 Indians from the Pueblo of San Juan and in all 60 men. Unfortunately, the majority of militia lists for this campaign are still missing. From other correspondence, however, there is positive evidence that the Pueblos of Sandia, Jemez, and Cochiti contributed men./

14

October 13 - November 17, 1834.   Military personnel records of the men who
                                  participated in this campaign, for example,
                                  the personnel records for Captain Donaciano
                                  Vigil, Santa Fe, December 31, 1842.

Captain Vigil's records show that he participated in a war against the
Navajos which lasted from October 13 to November 17, 1834, during which time
he was under orders of Captain Blas de Hinojos, and during which time there
were 16 Navajos killed, 3 taken prisoner, and the capture of goods and grain.

January 12, 1835.   Miguel Garcia, Jemez, to Blas de Hinojos, Comandante General
                    of this Territory.

Interpreter Garcia reports to Captain Hinojos that two Ute Indians have
arrived at Jemez for trading. These same Indians tell of the close relations
some of the Utes are having with the Navajos; the "rich Navajos have settled
their rancherias in the Silver and Datil Mountains for that year." As a
postscript, he adds that on January 13, a large party of Navajos approached
Jemez and on the 14th they took 50 animals of which 18 were retrieved by the
Alcalde of Jemez and one Navajo was killed.   89

March 1835.   Rev. Lansing Bartlett Bloom, "New Mexico Under Mexican Adminis-
              tration, 1821-1846," Old Santa Fe, Vol. I, No. 4, April 1914,
              p. 366.

In discussing the Navajo problem, Bloom cites that there was a diputation
convened in this month because of the "grievous state in which the war with
the barbarous Indians holds the Territory, and the need to check on proper
measures."

March 13, 1835.   Military personnel records of the men who participated in
                  this campaign. For example, the records for Lieutenant
                  Colonel Jose Silva, Santa Fe, December 31, 1842, indicate
                  that the troops returned from this campaign on March 13, 1835.

Jose Silva was a Second Lieutenant during this campaign under the orders of Captain Blas de Hinojos, during which campaign the New Mexicans killed 35 warriors, captured 4 persons of both sexes, 14 horses, 6,604 sheep, 109 cattle, and returned from the expedition on March 13, 1835.

__March 3, 1835.__ Juan Rafael Ortiz, Gobierno Politico of New Mexico, to the First Alcalde of this City /Santa Fe7.

Ortiz orders a detachment, consisting of 15 men and supplies, to be stationed at Canon de Santa Clara in order to hold off Navajo invasions. They are to be stationed there for 15-day intervals.

__March 10, 1835.__ Julian Tenorio, Jusgado Primero de Alburquerque, to the Governor of this Territory.

Justice Tenorio praises the actions and valor of Manuel Armijo for chasing Navajos who had stolen cattle from the Jurisdiction of Alburquerque, and retrieving same. /Note in the margin of document thanks Armijo for the Governor. In the entire correspondence there are no places or sites of the Navajos./

90

__June 7, 1835.__ J. F. Baca, Jurisdiction of Socorro, New Mexico, to the Politi and Military Leader of the Territory of New Mexico, Albino Per Santa Fe.

Mr. Baca describes how on the day before yesterday "a large number of Navajos fell on the new settlement of Lemitar, taking 2,000 sheep and a sheep herder, and following behind them one man was killed and wounded two mor He continues that on this same day at 6 o'clock in the morning "around 200 Navajos attacked the vicinity and plaza of Socorro, taking with them horses, cattle, goats and sheep." They were chased to the Ojo de la Culebra but were not overtaken. He pleas for aid to deal with Navajo depradations.

<u>July 5, 1835</u>. Santiago Martin, Abiquiu, New Mexico, to Governor Albino Perez.

Word that the Navajo Narbona solicits peace with the Republic.

<u>August 11, 1835</u>. Copy of a letter sent by Governor Perez to each of the
Alcaldes listed in the margins: Santa Fe, Abiquiu, Cochiti,
Jemes, Laguna, Sandia, Alburquerque, Ysleta, Valencia, Tome,
Belen, Sabinal, San Ildefonso, Canada, Santa Clara, and San
Juan.

The Governor explains that the Navajos are soliciting peace and the

exchange of captives to show their good intentions. The Governor has asked

that the leaders of the Navajos meet with representatives of the Republic at

San Miguel de Jemez for negotiations. As listed the various Alcaldes would

send 605 men on horseback in all; Acoma and Laguna were to furnish 30.

<u>August 21, 1835</u>. Military records of the troops who participated show that
peace attempts were tried with the "rebellious Navajos"
by Governor Don Albino Perez, the Mexican Nation, and the
Navajo Tribe.

<u>July 21, 1836</u>. Copy of instructions for Jose Francisco Vigil who will march
in a campaign against the Navajo with the number of volunteers
offered him by the Alcaldias of San Juan, Taos, Ojo Caliente,
and Abiquiu, made in Santa Fe, July 21, 1836.

/Only the first order is revealing here while the rest deal solely with

carrying out the march, reporting methods, and so on./

Instruction 1. In the Navajo Nation there are at peace and trust the
people or <u>rancherias</u> of Narbona, Sandoval, Jose Tapia,
Caballada Mucha, and el Negrito, who have been at Zuni
offering the Governor their cooperation in order to
punish the dissidents of their Nation. For that reason
it is important to guard them and to respect their interests
which they deserve for this trust.

. . .

<u>September 16, 1836.</u> Copy letter #60 from the Record Book of letters sent
to the Comandante General, /Chihuahua/ by the Governor
of New Mexico.

"According to Your Excellency's orders of June 1, a campaign was
prepared against the Navajos which started on September 14, composed of
2,000 men in three divisions under the direct command of the Lieutenants
Jose Caballero, Francisco Garcia, and Jose Silva."

<u>November 1, 1836.</u> Copy letter #64 from the Record Book of letters sent
to the Comandante General, /Chihuahua/ by the Governor
of New Mexico.

A general report of the valor of certain individuals who participated in
the campaign. The only indication of where the three divisions may have
been comes from the notification of the death of one of the Lieutenants who
led a division, Francisco Garcia, near the Pueblo of Zuni and in which church
they interred the body. Further on the report cites:

In the different actions which they had against the Navajos, our
camp and theirs remained completely dispersed, resulting after a number
of days in the death of 19 warriors, one woman taken from them, and a
captive. Also, there was taken 108 cows and 1,537 sheep, and their
spoils which they left behind in their hasty flight when we gave them
attack.

<u>February 16, 1837.</u> Entry #67 from the Record Book of letters sent to the
Comandante General, /Chihuahua/ by the Governor of New
Mexico, being a report of the Navajo campaign.

As I said to Your Excellency in my official communication number
65 on 8 December last year, that I personally marched at the head of a
division of 2,000 men to open the campaign against the Navajo Tribe, but
as verified, not with the indicated number but with 750 auxiliaries and
60 soldiers of the permanent troops, the only force I could muster in
spite of my ordered arrangements not only taking every pecuniary recourse
with the troops but also respecting the troubled residents for the constant fatigue in the fearful campaign of such cruelty at this season
always rigorous in this country and in the current year more so than ever

92

So that of the 2,000 men that I ordered there could only be collected
the above cited 750 and these for the most part of those unhappy
wretches that in the Pueblos are those that regularly report fatigue
because those of better health hunt Indians but will not expose themselves personally to extreme adversities and I assure your Excellency
that only in strength of the compliment in my power, for the honor that
I feel I resolved to advance my fortunes, beginning the campaign about
which I am going to make an exact report to Your Excellency.

On the 9th of December I began my march from this Capital, sur-
mounting the obstacles whose import Your Excellency will be able to
imagine and nothing ponderous would be enough to show what they were.
I proceeded to Cubero and for the purpose of advancing from this frontier
against the Navajo, I indicated this place for the reunion of the people
I asked of the Alcaldes for the said campaign. At that place the forces
gathered consisting of all of five companies with their corresponding
leaders and officials, from among the countrymen recommended for the first
the citizen Julian Tenorio, resident of the Villa de Alburquerque, for the
second company, Fernandes Aragon, resident of Sandia, the third company to
the citizen Jose Martinez from Bernalillo, the fourth to the citizen Jose
Francisco Vigil of San Juan, and the fifth to the citizen Jose Gonzales
of Taos. This was on the 16th of December and I began my march for the
mountains where the Navajo live, according to my plan but receiving communications from various sources that the Pueblo of Zuni (the largest of
the Pueblos in the Territory and the most distant from its inhabitants)
was united with the Navajos I immediately directed myself toward it.
Before arriving at said Pueblo at a distance of 10 leagues, at 12 in the
night of 24 December with 300 horses in order that the dawn of the 25th
would find me taking all roads to the said Pueblo in order to take charge
of those indigenees in league with the enemy and to punish those in case
they may have been delinquent. What the intent of my arrangements and
having made numerous checks concerning the matter, from the proofs and
satisfactions they delivered up to me, I became convinced that they were
free of all charges, such that on the 26th they returned to me two
Navajos that they took and who were shot, having lost on this expedition
the citizen Francisco Garcia who froze to death on the same night of the
24th and, having frozen by the same coldness, 14 men but who lost none of
their extremities because of the promptness with which they were helped.

Notwithstanding the movement of the operations against Zuni, I
believed necessary, I ordered the commander of the second company, Fernando
Aragon, to separate from the Division with 200 men for the place of Ojo
del Gallo in order to direct himself to the points of Chusca and the Oso
where the Navajos regularly live for permanent water, so that in case
they were found there to give them battle and then to meet later at the
Quelites. This citizen, carrying out my orders exactly, arrived at the
destination and met with four rancherias which were found there /Chusca
and Oso/ and fought bravely, killing 20 braves and taking prisoner and
Indian woman and 14 children of both sexes, taking 5,300 sheep, 80 mules
and horses without further misfortune on our part than two citizens
wounded by arrows from which Jose Sebastian died, and 54 frozen somewhat
except the active soldier Juan Lucero who lost two fingers from the left
hand.

I believe it proper to observe what was called to my attention in that Pueblo, and that is the increasing desire for some years to have a priest as expressed by the principal leaders in order to know the numbers of creatures existing without the Sacrament of Baptism, appearing for this, opportunely, 63 innocent children of various ages for the Sacrament of Baptism, 31 marriages which lack the blessings of the Roman Ritual.

As the cold is extreme in this country and particularly during the time of this campaign, I can assure Your Excellency as is manifest that leaving this Capital, the entire march was made through snow, but particularly and with most rigor from the camp at Cubero when the horses broke the trail in order that the infantry and supplies might follow. But in spite of these obstacles I resolved to go to the Sierra de Tunicha, center of the Navajo country where they have their most secure refuge distant from this city a little more that 200 leagues, but that Nation being notified already of the defeats received against their lives and properties, they had dispersed in many directions as evidenced by the different tracks that were made during their dispersion and flight and which were recognized as having been recently made. From that point I ordered a party of 300 men under the command of the Ensign Diego Saenz to march in pursuit of the tracks of the Indians and animals which appeared most abundant, advancing as far as the mountains and naming as a meeting place the Ojo del Carrizo, near the Canyon de Chelley, to where I started with the remainder of the forces. After seven days and at the stopping place cited, the Ensign Saenz presented himself to me with an account of having fought with three rancherias which he was able to overwhelm and he killed 8 warriors, captured 2 large Indian women and two children, taking 2,000 sheep, and 18 mules and horses, without having suffered any misfortune save having withstood the extreme cold which froze the hands and feet of 140 men and of those one lost an ear and another three toes.

94

The report continues to relate of the diversities suffered from the extreme cold and that while still in the Tunicha Mountains there came a blizzard lasting all day and night of the 12th of January and which threatened to cut the expedition short. They were approached by four warriors who sued for peace. Governor Perez then relates that the campaign was successful in contributing toward the peace and security of the country and toward concluding the "desolating war." He then cites for bravery and good conduct the various units and individuals who took part in the expedition, including Sergeant Donaciano Vigil, the Governor's personal aide, the Lieutenant Colonel of the

cavalry, Pedro Madrigal, and the two aides de camp Jose Maria Gutierrez
and Clemente Sarracino._/

April 13, 1837. Govierno Secretaria, to the Alcalde at Cochiti.

Concerns the Alcalde's report of robbery of wood and a burro made at
San Felipe Pueblo by the Navajos on April 11. The Cochiti and Santo Domingo
Indians gave chase and killed three Navajos.

May 20, 1837. Vicente S. Vergara, Corrales, New Mexico, to the Governor of
This Department.

Mr. Vergara writes that the Justice of the Pueblo of Zuni, Salvador
Venado, has reported an attack of Navajos against some of the Indians of
the Pueblo of Zuni.

August 31, 1837. /Governor_/ to the Alcalde Don Julian Tenorio /at Albuquerque_/.

Letter gives Julian Tenorio charge of volunteer troops from Cochiti
to Valencia /area covered several Alcaldias_/ who will gather at the Pueblo of
Laguna or at Cebolleta for the purpose of withstanding the Navajos "who
threaten that frontier and to avoid a surprise attack."

95

September 3, 1837. Julian Tenorio, Jusgado de Alburquerque, to His Excellency
the Governor of This Territory.

/The Spanish is primitive in this one_/

At this same hour I am departing for Sebolleta. I do not know the
number of people that I will take but I believe there will be very few
because these people hide themselves so that almost half or more of
those of my command may be hidden; and I believe it will be the same
with the others but I will do nothing but comply with your orders, as
you will see:
Sir, at this same moment there arrived by mail from Cebolleta the
information that the Alcalde of that frontier is fighting in Acoma, he
went for the Indians and these together with the Navajos approached in
the Pueblo and they killed two residents. Also he says that the Indians

of Laguna have not wanted to help the said Alcalde and it is believed
that these Pueblos are in collusion "coludidos" with the Navajos, at
least Your Excellency well knows that with Acoma and Zuni there is no
doubt; in consideration Your Excellency will take whatever means con-
ducive to correcting these evils which threaten our Territory.

. . .

October 28, 1837. Manuel Martinez, Alcalde Interino, Ojo Caliente, New
Mexico, to Governor Manuel Armijo.

Manuel Martinez describes having taken part in fighting off a Navajo

raid on Ojo Caliente during which the Navajos "killed one man and took four

sheep herders and four saddle horses."

November 25, 1837. Secretariat to the Alcaldes of Sandia, Alburquerque,
Padillas, Isleta, Valencia, Tome, Belen, Sabinal, Socorro,
Sebelleta, Laguna, Jemez, and Cochiti.

The Governor empowers the Inspector de Milicias, Lieutenant Colonel

Mariano Chaves, with all matters of arms that occur in the entire district

96 of Rio Abajo. All such problems will be taken to him, especially those

respecting the Navajo invasions.

February 5, 1838. Comandante General, Santa Fe, to the Minister of War
and Navy, Mexico.

The Comandante complains of the terrible and frequent raids of the

Navajos which "have become each day more terrible with their frequent

incursions," for the past five years. He describes that many villages have

been left destitute.

September and October, 1838, Military Records of those men who participated
in the expedition against the Navajos during
these two months, for example, Captain Francisco
Martinez, personnel records for December 31, 1842.

22

As part of his service record, Captain Francisco Martinez took part in
a war against the Navajos in September and October 1838, under the command
of Manuel Armijo, during which the Mexican troops killed 18 warriors, 76 of
both sexes were taken prisoner, they captured 226 horses, 2,060 sheep, 160
hides, 6 serapes, and more than 1,200 costales of grain.

December 25, 1838. Copy of letter from the Record Book of the Comandancia
General, Santa Fe, New Mexico, with no addressee.

Describes how the campaign plan was to enter the heart of the Navajo
country and to map their pastures and fields. Jemez was to be the center
of operations for supplies and ammunition. The troops first moved from
Jemez marching four days into the vicinity of the Tunicha Mountains. Then
he moved the troops to a more habitable place called Tres Lagunas. A battle
ensued [location not given] during which 78 warriors were killed, 56 persons
of both sexes were imprisoned, they took 226 horses, 2,060 sheep, 5 serapes,
and other booty.

97

January 3, 1839. Simon Elias, Chihuahua, Mexico, to the Esteemed Governor
and Comandante General of New Mexico.

In response to requests of last November, two expeditions of 300 men
each are ready to leave Chihuahua to proceed against the Navajos on January 5.

January 4, 1839. Simon Elias, Chihuahua, Mexico, to the Esteemed Governor
of New Mexico.

Reports the return of 1,100 troops who had left Chihuahua for New Mexico
on 13 September last.

January 4, 1839. Simon Elias, Chihuahua, Mexico, to the Esteemed Governor
of New Mexico.

President of Mexico relayed message of satisfaction of the considerable success against the Navajos in New Mexico to the Minister of War and Navy.

February 11, 1839. Militia surveys of Acoma and Laguna /see Acoma Exhibit #_____, and Laguna Exhibit #_____/.

Militia surveys were conducted in answer to the Governor's Circular, dated February 11, 1839. Most of the surveys were submitted during the first week in March. These lists not only included the volunteers but also the horses, guns, and arrows contributed.

April 19, 1839. Circular to the Prefects of the First and Second Districts, copied from the Governor's Letter Book for 1839.

The Governor gives notice that he has gone to treat with the Navajos for a peace which they are soliciting after having killed a Laguna shepherd and committed other depradations.

April 26, 1839. Governor of New Mexico to the Prefect, Don Antonio Sandoval.

There appeared in Santa Fe on this day two Navajo Indians who solicited of the Governor that he order the Pueblos not to kill Navajos who might be ambassadors for peace. The point of contact for these ambassadors will be Jemez.

April 30, 1839. Circular to the Prefects of the First and Second Districts.

The Governor announces that the Navajos have been suing for peace many times, even through Ute ambassadors. However, they cannot be trusted and the Governor warns the Prefects that the Navajos be not allowed to enter the Pueblos because of their treacherous ways. They especially enter a Pueblo under the guise of peace and then turn on the people. There is only one point of contact to which they will be allowed to send ambassadors for peace and that is Jemez.

May 29, 1839. Governor to the Prefect, Don Antonio Sandoval.

The Governor acknowledges his note describing the incident at Cebolleta. where a party of Indians went to rob some Navajos on the outskirts of Cebolleta and another party was sent to bring them back in order to avoid trouble.

June 19, 1839. Governor to the Prefect of the Second District, Don Antonio Sandoval.

Governor orders the Captain Jose Francisco Chaves y Baca to "reorganize a company composed of the useful men of the Pueblos of Isleta, Laguna, and Acoma. These troop s will be used to open vacant plazas and to reoccupy any useless lands there might be."

June 28, 1839. Governor to the Prefect, Don Antonio Sandoval.

Governor has received notice of clandestine trade with the Navajos being carried on from that district. There has been one death already from this contraband traffic. There is also notice of a Mr. Saavedra who has been participating in this illegal traffic. The others are unknown. Governor orders that this business must come to a halt.

99

June 28, 1839. Governor to the Prefect, Don Juan Andres Archuleta.

The Navajos have agreed to celebrate a peace treaty on the 14th and 15th of July. The Governor advises that the Captain Don Pedro Leon Lujan and 50 men appear at Jemez for the occasion.

June 28, 1839. Governor to the Prefect, Don Antonio Sandoval.

Advises the Prefect to assemble the most respectable citizens for the

peace treaty, around 30 in number and counting among them the Sres.
Chaves, Oteros, and Pereas.

July 15, 1839. Peace Treaty made in the Pueblo of Jemez between the Republic
of Mexico and the Navajo Nation.

Celebrated on this day a treaty of peace with the Navajos. The treaty
is brief and in general terms Governor Armijo appointed Antonio Sandoval to
govern the Navajo Tribe and at the same time they are made subjects of the
Republic of Mexico and shall respect and obey the orders of the Mexican
government. The Navajos were given a copy of the treaty, signed by Manuel
Armijo and Antonio Sandoval.

July 1839. Francisco Sandoval, Commander of the Rurales and Justice of the
Frontier of Jemez to the inhabitants of New Mexico.

Since the treaty, the Navajos have frequently asked for their captives.
The Governor has refused because of the conduct of the Navajos which since
the treaty has not been good. However, the Navajos want the return of eight
of their people. They in turn will exchange all of the Mexican captives but
they will have to be paid for and he asks all the inhabitants of New Mexico
to contribute according to their consciences. All excess money left over from
the negotiations will be returned to the people proportionately. It is expec
that those parents who have captives among the Navajos will contribute more.
With this money he will attempt to deal with the Navajos.

September 7, 1839. Circular, Santa Fe.

Refers to Article 7 of the recent treaty with the Navajos. When either
party receives a notice of the threatened hostility of the other, the justice
should issue a speedy notice, being the places most likely for such: Abiquiu

Jemez, and Cebolleta. The warnings should be as secret as possible.

September 24, 1839. Governor to the Prefect, Don Antonio Sandoval.

Received notice that the Navajos have started hostilities. They have
"killed a man in the vicinity of Cebolleta, have robbed animals, . . ." They
are rumored to be ready and immediately will commence a war. The authorities
are notified to be on the alert, and to send warnings of any such activity as
soon as possible.

October 13 to December 13, 1839. Military personnel records of Lieutenant
Colonel Jose Silva, December 31, 1842.

Colonel Silva's records show that as a Lieutenant under orders of the
Colonel of the Rural Militia, Don Mariano Chaves, he participated in a war
against the rebellious Navajos which resulted in the death of 9 warriors, one
prisoner, the taking of 113 horses, and 10,000 or so sheep.

101

October 13 to December 13, 1839. Military personnel records of Captain
Francisco Martinez, December 31, 1842.

Captain Martinez' service records reveal that as part of his services
under the orders of the Lieutenant Colonel of the Rural Militia, Don Juan
Andres Archuleta, he participated in a war against the rebellious Navajos
in which 7 warriors were killed, they took a prisoner of both sexes, captured
32 horses, and also took 142 sheep.

October - December, 1839. Excerpts from a diary of the campaign against
the Navajos /probably from the records of Governor
Manuel Armijo/.

On October 27 received orders that the war with the Navajos had
commenced.

November 9 - 300 men under Captain Francisco Sandoval proceeded
to the punto de Chelly.

November 13-14 - Colonel Juan Andres Archuleta went by el Carriso,
exploring beforehand the mesa to the north of Chelly, the places of the
Calabasa Mesa and others in order to give the enemy chase.

November 15-16 - An expedition of 125 men under the command of the
Ensign Bentura Lovato explored the mesas of Chelly looking for Navajos.

November 17-18 - Two parties of 60 men each departed for Chelly, one
for the mesas and the other for el Carriso, intending to meet from these
places.

November 25-26 - Sent a party of 200 men, 100 cavalry and 100
infantry, to a place where the Canyon de Chelly meets the San Juan River.
They are under command of Captain Juan Cristobal Garcia.

First week in December the troops returned to Abiquiu after two months campaign.

November 4, 1839. Circular, published by the Governor.

In spite of the recent treaty of peace with the Navajo, these people
have newly declared war. The Pueblos are warned that they will descend upon
them to rob and kill. All demarcations are alerted to be prepared for action.

November 23, 1839. Circular, published by the Governor.

102

The inhabitants of the Department will be called upon to support the war
against the numerous tribe of the Navajo. . . . Only the strangers and
Mexicans from other departments will continue to care for their shops, . . .
and will be imposed upon by the municipal bodies, and taxed in accordance with
the laws.

July 2, 1840. Guadalupe Miranda, Secretary to the Governor of the Department
to the Treasurer and Administrator of the Public Treasury,
Don Jose Dolores Madrid.

There has been notice of an approaching caravan of New Mexican traders
from the United States. The Governor wishes to use the money from their
imports for another campaign against the Navajos. A listing of the cargo
and appraisals is to be made.

28

July <u>19</u>, 1840. Pedro Leon Lujan, Abiquiu, New Mexico, to the Subinspector
of the Rurales, Don Juan Andres Archuleta.

This night there arrived at his house two Navajos, sent by the Chieftain
Cayetanito, and they say that the entire Navajo Nation is gathered at the
Puerco River and anxious for peace and they wish to consult. Lujan plans to
leave one Indian behind and take the second with him to maker further arrangements.

<u>August 24</u>, 1840. Francisco Baca, Commander at Socorro, to the Inspector,
Colonel Don Mariano Chaves.

On August 22, the Navajos raided Sabinal taking 90 animals, killing
two men and a woman and wounding two more men. They were chased by Colonel
Francisco Chaves until the <u>Ojo</u> <u>de</u> <u>la</u> <u>Jara</u>, where they had to give up because
of the distance and they were exhausted, declaring further pursuit to be
useless.

<u>August 29</u>, 1840. Comandancia General to the Inspector of Militia, Colonel   103
Don Mariano Chaves.

Having received notice of the Navajo raid at Sabinal and the Pueblo of
Jemes, the Governor advises that another war against the Navajos should be
made and that the district of the south raise 500 men and 500 more will come
from the northern districts. The date for the campaign is set for September
15, 1840. Please advise. /A note added that they were in accord but that the
people had fought during the previous campaign./

October <u>1</u>, 1840. Governor to the Minister of War and Navy,,Mexico. From
the Letter Book of the Governor of New Mexico, 1840.

The Governor advises that because of the cruel war with the Navajos and
to free the Department of it he has ordered two companies of 500 men each to
march in an expedition.

<u>October 3, 1840</u>. Governor Armijo to the Minister of War and Navy, Mexico.
From the Governor's Letter Book, 1840.

After 18th of September when the Governor wrote of the campaigns
against the Navajos, a valiant man, Don Juan Ramirez of Sebolleta,
marched against the Navajo. He headed up 60 residents. Within a few
days he had the satisfaction of giving them battle at <u>Laguna Colorado</u>
on the <u>rancheria</u> of the Chieftain Cebolla, very astute, and who is
largely responsible for there not having been established a peace.
Ramirez put them to flight, captured members of both sexes, 26 horses,
one mule, took all their goods, and rescued one of the Mexican captives.
He accomplished all this without the loss of one man. . . .

n. d. First week in October, 1840. Governor Armijo to the Minister of War and
Navy. From the Governor's Letter Book, 1840.

Governor Armijo reports of the successes of the two Captains Don Jose
Salazar and Don Jose Francisco Vigil, each heading a company of 500 auxiliaries
and <u>rurales</u> in the latest Navajo campaign. Captain Salazar and his company
killed 13 braves, captured 8 Indians of both sexes, took 8 horses, and the
goods from one <u>rancheria</u>, and also captured the Chieftain Jose Largo, who as
a hostage asked a cessation of the war in order to make peace. Captain Vigil
and his company killed 20 warriors, captured 6 Indians of both sexes, 31 horses
and more than 200 <u>fanegas</u> of corn, which served his company for food, the
surplus they burned, and they also took such a quantity of blankets made by
the Navajos, which according to the prevailing prices amounted to more than a
thousand pesos. The latter officer and his men took the Indians by surprise
and gained the insurmountable mesa on which the Indians hide with their families
during times of war. It was estimated to be more than 600 varas in height and
could not be climbed by any animal, and the men scaled it one-by-one with
much work. It is fortified on top with wooden parapets and guarded day and
night. The Captain hid the company at a place four or five leagues away in

104

order not to be detected and on the night of 19 October at 11 o'clock, they
marched on foot over the land and to the top of the mesa, so quietly that
18 of the soldiers were on top before they were detected and whose operations
the Indians were now unable to stop and those who were not killed in the
action and did not want to be taken prisoner flung themselves off the cliff.
At this same mesa, in 1818, "the Governor Don Facundo Melgares spent 40 and
some days during a siege in which he did not succeed in conquering the Indians."
Captain Vigil reported that the mesa contained permanent water on the top and
the caves could store enough grain to sustain the Indians for a long time.

. . .

December 14, 1840. Jose Andres Sandoval, Rural Command of Jemez, to the
Governor and Comandante General of this Department.
By Extraordinary Speed.

Last night a Navajo appeared soliciting peace in the name of his
Nation, his name was Anceluno. He is living in Pena Blanca where there
arrived at his house Yerro de Narbona and other Navajo chieftains saying
that 20 ambassadors were consulting with the Navajo Nation, the major
part of the Nation being in some valleys on that side of de Chelly. Also
that the Navajos hoped to meet and settle a treaty sometime in January.
Also, that the family of Jose Largo /Navajo chieftain/ and all its
belongings had just moved into Encinal de Sebolleta.

105

/Response on same letter, probably dictated by the Governor/

How come can the Navajos succeed in approaching any other point than
Jemez?

They should check into the motives of Juan Largo.

December 30, 1840. Francisco Sandoval, Inspector of Militia, Jemez, to Don
Mariano Chavez.

Describes raid made on the Pueblo of Jemez by five Navajos on December
22 and that they took 11 animals and that they were chased.

<u>January 15, 1841.</u> Antonio Sandoval, Prefecture of the Second District, to the Secretary of State, Don Guadalupe Miranda.

A Navajo Indian appeared at Jemez on the 5th and wanted to know if it were true that Governor Armijo was disposed to discuss peace matters. He also stated that the Chieftain Narbona, commanding more than 30 Navajos and some women, was on the <u>Mesita Azul</u>. That on the 8th he would come to Jemez and proceed from there to the Capital in order to confer with the Governor.

<u>January 27, 1841.</u> Governor Armijo to the Minister of War and Navy, Mexico. From the Governor's Letter Book, 1840.

The Governor writes that he has been approached by many embassies from the Navajos who want peace. Finally, one of their leading chieftains with nine warriers appeared and through an interpreter assured the Governor that the entire Navajo Nation desired peace in good faith. The Governor asked at this time that all the Mexican captives be returned and that the Indians conduct themselves peacefully, not harming the Department or those who travel to <u>el Paso</u> or on any road. The Indians gave their promise to the Governor and that they would return in 25 days from the 25th of the current month to agree to a peace treaty to be held at the Pueblo of Santo Domingo on the bank opposite the River.

<u>March 8, 1841.</u> Francisco Sandoval, Rural Commander at Jemez, to /Governor Armijo/.

The Navajo chieftains with 100 braves appeared at his house to make further arrangements for peace. They were departing from Jemez to go to Santo Domingo because of problems over horses. They left Jemez on the 10th and would arrive on the 11th. The Navajo chieftains were listed as: Narbona, Jose Tapia, Sebolla Sandoval, Tarque Tuna, son of Calletano.

March 10, 1841. Copy of Peace Treaty celebrated at Santo Domingo between the Mexican Government and the Navajo Nation.

1. That peace and commerce will be opened with the entire Tribe of the Navajo with the citizens of this Department and Chihuahua, in celebration of the peace.

2. Entire Navajo Tribe of all parts of the Republic is obliged to turn over all captives. They must remember that they are citizens of the Republic.

3. The principal aim of this treaty is to end the horrible wars and instigate stable and lasting peace and the said Chieftains pledge themselves to guard the preceding articles, both as individuals and in the name of their tribes and in no manner to cause hostilities or injuries to individuals of the Republic.

4. The commerce will be reinstated as it was before the present war.

5. The treaty is to alleviate any resentment the Navajo Chieftains may have had against the Mexicans and to stop the killings of Mexican citizens. All murderers will be punished according to Spanish laws. Neither nation will be allowed to take slaves or captives.

6. Any captives of the Navajos who are among the Mexican citizens and who succeed in escaping their masters, the Government will not take action to reclaim them.

107

7. When the peace treaty takes effect, it is hoped that four chieftains will be named among the Navajos, under whom the Nation will deal with the outside world. These will be paid a small gratification by the Department to show the Mexicans' good faith. These will be elected by popular support of the Tribe.

8. In order to corroborate this good faith, both parties will be allowed to pasture their herds and animals with full confidence that they will not be harmed.

9. In order not to break the peace and in accordance with article seven, the Navajo Chieftains, in case their are thieves or murderers, either among the Navajos or the Department of New Mexico, will be made to surrender the killer or killers in order that they may be punished, to return what is stolen, and for the Mexican thieves, the Governor promises to return the goods stolen, and if there be a death committed by a Mexican, and it is verified, the Governor promises to pay 500 sheep.

March 12, 1841. Juan Andres Archuleta, Inspector of the Rurales of the
First District, to the Governor and Comandante General of
the Department.

Informs Governor Armijo that he has had the honor to participate and
conclude the peace treaties and that the Navajos have now returned to their
lands. Four captives were returned by the Navajos. He did not formulate
the articles of the treaty because "the Navajos concurred in all things and
for this reason he ommitted the treaty so that the Governor could arrange and
sign things when he was well, if it was his wish to do so."

March 14, 1841. Francisco Sandoval, Commander of the Rurales of Jemez, to
the Governor.

Sandoval gives his version of the negotiations for peace and they are
somewhat different than as presented in the version above. He says the
Navajos went away dissatisfied with the offers of the treaty for the
following reasons:

108

    1. They are not satisfied if settlement is not made of the spoils
taken from their nation from the times of the campaign of the Captain Don
Jose Salazar.

    2. That more than ten times they had relinquished captives and that
at no time had the Mexicans returned theirs.

    3. That if they plan to return the captives this may be accomplished
at the points of Chacoli or Jemez.

    4. While waiting decision for what they ask, they request that herds
be allowed on the road that goes from Jemez to Laguna, and that they be
allowed to watch and guard them from any harm.

    5. He has done what he can to dissuade them of their discontent.

    6. And for a last resort, that we should offer if the captives are
the cause of the discontent, to take pains to approach the Governor about
those which have not been returned, but in vain was this proposal when
they manifest such interests as theirs.

In conclusion, the Navajos are awaiting an emissary from the Governor as to his decisions, within twelve days from this to bring them the results on which cannot be agreed.

__March 26, 1841.__ Armijo to the Commander of the Frontier at Jemez.

Received his note. Is pleased with the comportment of Cebolla Sandoval, Navajo Chieftain, and the good work he is accomplishing in his Nation in order not to break the peace established; tell him that the Governor is very pleased with this work and that if it is effective he will offer him equal recognition as the Navajo Francisco Baca and will treat him with equal confidence; explain to him the sentiment of this letter and that the Governor will not go back on his word; tell him also to continue to exort the Navajos to continue negotiating the peace and that he should tell them the reasons the Governor has not returned their captives and that he will do so if they wish to make peace. They should be assured the Governor has no fear of them and that he tells them no lies, and if they wish to continue the peace nothing remains except to arrange the treaties.

__April 6, 1841.__ Francisco Sandoval, Commander of the Rurales at Jemez, to the Governor and Comandante General Don Manuel Armijo.

Two Navajos have appeared, invited by Armijo and Narbona, who wanted to know ex our peace plans. He answered that the Navajo Nation should place its trust with the Captain Navajo Armijo, who had gone to all their rancherias exhorting them to the acceptable terms offered by the Governor. They had heard all the bad rumors and that the Rancheria of Jose Largo, which is separated and in the land of the Apaches, was inclined to go along with peace. They were desirous of extending their habitations and planting but they could not make peace because they were committed to the Utes.

109

__May 8, 1841.__ From the Governor's Letter Book of the Communications sent by This Government to the Ministry of War and Navy, 1841.

After the treaty, the Navajos seem to have settled down. They have not stolen or molested the sheep herders in fact have dedicated themselves to planting along the margins of the Puerco River, very near the frontiers.

<u>May 13, 1841.</u> From the Governor's Letter Book of the Communications Sent
by This Government to the Ministry of War and Navy, 1841.

The Governor asks permission of the President, through the Minister of
War and Navy, to make an expedition to explore the watering places and the
places where the Navajos retire with their families when they are at war and
also to find their <u>haciendas</u>.

<u>August 30, 1841.</u> Juan Garcia, Juzgado de Paz of Cebolleta, to the Prefect of
the First District, Don Antonio Sandoval.

"Today there appeared at this place, the Navajo Jose Largo and two Navajo
Indians with 8 horses and 80 sheep to pay for the death of a Cochiti Indian.
They desire to make the exchange at Cubero or Laguna and do not want to go to
Jemez because they fear meeting with Ute Indians."

/A note added to the letter and dated September 1, 1841, advises that he should
be assured of the recompense and upon accepting it bring it to the Justice at
Cochiti where it may be returned to the family of the dead Cochiti Indian./

<u>February 17, 1842.</u> Jose Andres Sandoval, Juzgado de Jemez, to the Secretary
Don Guadalupe Miranda.

/The letter is labeled on the outside fold with the words "with news of the
Enemy"/

Sandoval advises that the Navajos who were thought would live in peace
and work their fields are planning another war. He received this news from
the inhabitants of the Jemez Pueblo and from one of the nearby ranches where
a Navajo had visited.

110

October 18, 1842. Juan Andres Archuleta, Prefect of the First District, to
                   the Secretary of the Government, Don Guadalupe Miranda.

On the 17th the Justice of Abiquiu informed Archuleta that the Citizen
Miguel Antonio Romero came in search for horses stolen from him by the Navajos.
He was unable to get them back and asks of the Governor the necessary aid to
reclaim them. Archuleta claims not to have sufficient troops to undertake
such a course.

/In a note to Archuleta, dated October 19, 1842, the Governor informs him
that any Navajo caught stealing should be killed./

June 1, 1843. J. Sarracino, Inspector of Militia, to the Governor and
               Comandante General Don Juan Andres Archuleta.

Yesterday, received by mail the notice from Captain Sandoval that the
Navaje Chieftains Juan Chaves, Sarcillos Largos, el Facundo, and other
leading Navajos do not want war and that they are collecting in the Zuni
Mountains, el Oso, and the Chusca Mesa in order to separate themselves from   111
the "thieves" and that they are willing to accompany us in a campaign against
them, and that Your Excellency concede the land which they solicit, they come
in good faith and do not associa te with the others, for example, they have
been working with the Cebolletas to search for the Indians who robbed Jose
Chaves of some cattle. . . .

June 4, 1843. J. Sarracino, Inspector of Militia, to the Governor and
               Comandante General Don Juan Andres Archuleta.

Yesterday, during the morning, on the frontier of Jemez Navajos
appeared who stole some 50 horses and cows and it was impossible to follow
them because of the lack of mounts, according to the Justice of the Frontier
of Jemez. He warned the Jurisdiction of Cochiti and Bernalillo to furnish

12 men from each in order to guard the various passages. On June 1, the same Navajos attacked Los Chaves, Jurisdiction of Belen, and took from Don Jose Chaves cows and other animals amounting to the number of 500. The Chieftain Juan Cristoval Chaque was one of those who participated in the raids. From June 7, he is forming a guard composed of citizens from the area of Cebolleta to Socorro in order to stop the entering and leaving of the Navajos.

July 19, 1843. Comandancia to the Inspector, D. J. A. S.

.Received the official notices of the 12th and 18th of July and those of the Justice of Ojo Caliente, and I am fully informed of the deaths and robberies committed by the Navajos at the cited place. Advises that they guard all the points as best they can.

December 11, 1843. Noriega, Minister of War and Navy, to the Comandante General of New Mexico.

The President of the Republic extends his thanks to all who cooperated in the two victorious expeditions against the Navajos during which the Mexicans killed 15 braves, imprisoned 13 of both sexes, took 300 animals, two captives, and 13,000 sheep.

January 14, 1844. Letter Book of the Comandancia General of the Department of New Mexico, 1844. To the Military Commander at Jemez.

The Navajo Indians who are in the vicinity of Tome with any others you will not permit to celebrate a treaty with the residents, meanwhile, the treaties which have been made, because with such frankness they will never conclude the treaties, that they say they are now at peace and enjoying peace which can only be arranged on a secure and enduring basis, and on the

38

contrary they will be attacked by our arms.

Concerning the method which up to now they have bought from the Indians the same animals which they have robbed, I assure you that the same will continue even if there is celebrated the peace which they solicit."

__January 15, 1844.__ Letter Book of the Comandancia General of the Department of New Mexico, 1844. To the Commanders of the First and Second Districts.

"The peace treaties which the Navajos solicit of the Department are closed, never can they enjoy the benefits which the peace would apportion them, in which intelligence you will scrupulously guard that the commerce that they would have with the Indians in your district is prohibited as well as importing goods into the settlements."

__January 22, 1844.__ Letter Book of the Comandancia General of the Department of New Mexico, 1844. To the Military Commander at Jemez.

"You will arrange that the Captain Navajo named el Lucero present himself 113 in this Capital together with the Chieftain Sandoval in order to celebrate the peace which the Tribe solicits: charging you that the subscription be made directly with the Inspector of the District in order that this official make it with the Comandante General.

__January 23, 1844.__ Letter Book of the Comandancia General of the Department of New Mexico, 1844. To the Military Commander at Jemez.

"Advised of your note of yesterday which they have robbed the Navajos of some animals; those which are already in charge of the Comandante General of the Second District will be taken where they were found; and in order to avoid having to pay for them this same is repeated and you will watch that they do no harm to the Indians whatsoever."

<u>January 23, 1844.</u> Letter Book of the Comandancia General of the Department of New Mexico, 1844. To the Commanders of the First and Second Districts, Juan Andres Archuleta and Francisco Sarracino.

"About the Navajos in hopes of establishing the peace which they solicit there have been stolen from them 12 animals which they had in the vicinity of Jemez, of which they have recovered four and in order to retrieve the remainder they are proceeding in the directions of the first and second districts in order to do what is necessary, you are charged to return them, and charged to pay and to do no harm whatsoever to the said Indians . . ."

<u>January 27, 1844.</u> Letter Book of the Comandancia General of the Department of New Mexico, 1844. To the Commander of the Second District.

I am informed of yours of the 25th about the Navajo Jose Largo who has settled ranching in the vicinities of Agua Azul, and how in order to attack the settlement you need agreement for this, it will not be an obstacle in order that the Tribe to which he belongs verify the peace which they solicit, I advise of this that you may know of the matter and work what is best for the good of the Department, requesting that if you should consider it necessary to fight them, to inform me of the moment.

114

<u>January 27, 1844.</u> Letter Book of the Comandancia General of the Department of New Mexico, 1844. To the Inspector of the Second District.

I approve of the methods you have dictated and described in your note of the 25th to the end to verify if any of the residents took part in the surprise attack suffered on the rancherias of the Navajos on the outskirts of the Pueblo of Jemez, whom you will deal with to destroy suspicions fomented respective to the residents of those points where they are situated.

<u>February 12, 1844.</u> Letter Book of the Comandancia General of the Department of New Mexico, 1844. To the Commander of the First District, Colonel Don Juan Andres Archuleta.

I am informed of yours, passing on the information from the Justice of Ojo Caliente and dated February 5, describing that the citizen Pedro Herrera came to that place and with his people, killed 19 Navajos, took 18 of both sexes, captured 200 animals, and 1,600 sheep and one captive, all of which merits my approval.

February 21, 1844. Letter Book of the Comandancia General of the Department of New Mexico, 1844. To the Inspector of the Second District, Colonel Don Francisco Sarracino.

Unofficially there has arrived the notice [a rumor or report is not clear] that in spite of the prohibition against making peace treaties with the Navajos, issued on January 15, in that Demarcation, this has been done in some of them, and again he advises that Sarracine make careful cognizance of the aforesaid orders

February 24, 1844. Letter Book of the Comandancia General of the Department of New Mexico, 1844. To the Inspectors of the First and Second Districts, Colonel Don Juan Andres Archuleta and Colonel Don Francisco Sarracino.

"There is to be a peace treaty celebrated with the Navajos at Santo Domingo, on March 21, and you are advised to be present with whatever forces you find convenient and to notify the important residents of your respective districts. . . ."

115

February 26, 1844. Mariano Martinez, General Commandant of the Department of New Mexico to the Esteemed Governor of this Department, Santa Fe.

[Proposed articles for the peace solicited by the Navajos and to be celebrated at the Pueblo of Santo Domingo in March.]

Esteemed Sir: The repeated solicitations of the various Chieftains of the Navajo Tribe in order to agree to a peace, have obliged me to fix the date for their celebration of the 21st of March at the Pueblo of Santo Domingo, to which act you are invited to contribute your enlightened

41

and accredited knowledge to secure it in the most enduring manner.

Also, I am sending your Excellency some of the articles which I wish to order in the said peace, for the purpose that you will tell me if they are the most convenient, and in case they are not, to indicate those which may be the most opportune for making the peace more lasting.

Treaties of peace celebrated with the Navajo Tribe at the Pueblo of Santo Domingo the day _____ by the Commandant General of the Department Don Mariano Martinez, in virtue of the repeated solicitations which the Chieftains of the said Tribe have made for peace, Narbona, el Guero, Cabras Muchas, Juan Chaves, and Archuleta; those which have agreed in the following articles:

1. Peace and commerce will be opened between the Navajo Tribe and the citizens of the Department, always and ever that the first party does not attact in any manner the villages and individuals of this country and travelers in it.

2. In proof of the good faith with which the Navajo Tribe makes peace it will return all the captives to be found in its possession, the individuals of the Department who may have captives of theirs leaving them to the Navajos the recourse of recapturing them from whomever owns them.

116

3. The commerce remain subsistant in the Department with the Navajo Tribe in the same manner as before the war.

4. All the Navajos present have the obligation to make good that which was perpetrated by their Tribe of robbery or death.

5. The Navajo Chieftains understand that if they begin hostilities against the Department, with only one deed and still solicit peace it will not be accorded them and constant war will be made against them.

6. Always that the Navajo captives succeed in escaping from their masters and arrive at their lands they shall be free and without responsibility the Tribe.

7. When the enemies of the Mexican Republic and those of the Navajo Tribe attempt hostilities, the contracting parties are obligated to stop the aggression or give immediate notice, in order to free ourselves of the aggression.

8. If any dependent rancheria of the Navajo Tribe wishes to settle in the immediate vicinities of our villages, there will be sent to the Commandant General in order that he may consider acceding to this request.

March 7, 1844. Letter Book of the Comandancia General of the Department
of New Mexico, 1844. To the Inspector of the First District,
Colonel J. Andres Archuleta.

"In preparation for the celebration of the treaties, the Navajos have
given up our captives, that in order that it may be done likewise the
Captain Don Francisco Vigil should remit, without fault, the four Navajo
Captives which he has to this Commandant General before the date of the
treaties. . . ."

March 11, 1844. Inspector of Arms of the First District, to the Commandant
General, Don Mariano Martines.

Colonel Archuleta has been told by the Justice at Abiquiu that "on the
3d of March the Navajos took 14 oxen and 3 cattle from the Plaza del Barranco,
and they were followed by 14 men to the place called las mesas de Chaca and
that they were Navajos and not Utes. . . ."

March 18, 1844. Letter Book of the Comandancia General of the Department   117
of New Mexico, 1844. To the Governor of the Department,
Don Mariano Chaves.

"The Comandante Militar of Jemez has advised me that the Navajo
chieftains who have arrived at the Pueblo have made it clear to him that
they want to celebrate the peace treaties at Jemez and not in Santo Domingo,
for fear of the Jicarillas, and have postponed the celebration until March 24.
. . ."

March 23, 1844. Letter Book of the Comandancia General of the Department
of New Mexico, 1844. To the Inspectors of the First and
Second Districts, Colonel Don Juan Andres Archuleta and
Colonel Don Francisco Sarracino.

"The peace treaties were celebrated today with the Navajo Tribe and you will permit them to trade in the villages of the Department according t custom."

/For a translation of the articles of the treaty see supra, 42./

April 20, 1844. Letter Book of the Comandancia General of the Department of New Mexico, 1844. To the Military Commander at Jemez.

Your note of the 19th informs me of the malicious claims of the various Navajo chieftains made for the captives and horses taken from them by the Sahuanos during their last expedition, leaning on the pea in which the Commandant General promised to rescue them and return the this assertion being entirely false, since my answer to the distinct requests made over this matter was that they should look for and resc them as they were able and you make them understand that the Commandar which has superabundant recourses to make them suffer a war, to exter- mination, which they have never experienced, and that if they claim claim the captives unde r a pretext to break the peace which I accorde them, they can be assured I will not concede another time without mak them live in villages, guarded by a military force, and subject to an authority.

April 24, 1844. Letter Book of the Comandancia General of the Department of New Mexico, 1844. To the Inspector of the First Distri Don Juan Andres Archuleta.

Being indispensable to conserve the peace with the Navajo Tribe, there should be returned to them three captives they claim which were taken during the campaign of Portalam, that they are one maiden and two children, which makes it necessary that you inquire as to where they are and for how much they were sold, to the end that you make satisfactory what it was to those who have them without injury as they were before, taking them and remitting them to me: being alerted that the said Indians say the woman is at Abiquiu.

April 24, 1844. Notebook of Letters Sent by the Governor of the Department to the Authorities Within and Outside of same. Year of 18

There is an expedition ready to leave Santa Fe on the following day an it is headed by the Vicar Juan Felipe Ortiz. The Governor orders an escort to accompany him from Jemez to Zuni Pueblo because of the raids and trouble committed by the Navajos. /Directed to the Prefect of the Second District/

April 25, 1844. Notebook of Letters Sent by the Governor of the Department to the Authorities Within and Outside of Same, Year of 1844. To the Justice at Jemez.

Tells the Justice of the necessary trip of the Vicar and that when this note is in his hands he will furnish an escort of 25 well-armed men who will accompany the Vicar to Laguna and to where another escort is kept which will accompany the Vicar on to Zuni.

April 28, 1844. Record Book of the Departmental Treasury of New Mexico, Beginning on the First of January 1844.

/On this day/ the Commandant General, Don Mariano Martines, orders 297 pesos and 2 reales to be spent on the following:

111 pesos for the return of 3 captives from the Navajos in accordance with the treaties which were celebrated with that Nation.

175 pesos for gratification to Chieftains for the same Nation.

21 pesos and 2 reales for the troops.

May 8, 1844. Letter Book of the Comandancia General of the Department of New Mexico, 1844. To the Inspector of the First District, Colonel Don Juan A. Archuleta.

119

"I am in possession of the letter of the Citizen Jose Ramon Vigil, dated the 7th, relative to the latest robbery committed by the Navajos; and I answer that when the said Indians should make a raid those who are persecuted should give an immediate accounting to this Commandant."

July 11, 1844. Letter Book of the Comandancia General of the Department of New Mexico, 1844. To the Prefect of the First District. Don Juan Andres Archuleta.

Received yours of the 10th relative to the notice from the Justice at Jemez through Santa Clara that the Navajos and Utes aspire to unite and renew armed conflict, and that under this principle they have begun

a campaign; I am obliged to tell you to circulate this news to the
inhabitants so that they may be prepared to punish the enemy with
all possible brevity, accordingly now that I am disposed when they
fight with the Department.

July 11, 1844. Letter Book of the Comandancia General of the Department of
New Mexico, 1844. To the Military Commander of the First
District, Colonel Don Juan Andres Archuleta.

The Colonel is ordered to enlist 500 men from his district for the

purpose of marching to Cubero de la Laguna. From there they will march

against the Navajos, not in order to give them battle but to round them up

/To discuss further matters relative to the peace/ and he will place himself

at the head of these forces and at Cubero, Colonel Don Francisco Sarracino,

will be in charge of all the forces.

July 17, 1844. Letter Book of the Comandancia General of the Department of
New Mexico, 1844. To the Inspector, Don Francisco Sarracino,
and to the Inspector of Militia, Colonel Don Juan Andres
Archuleta.

Notifies the Colonels of the murders and robberies being committed by

the Navajos throughout the Department even after the peace treaty celebrated

on March 23 at Santo Domingo, and asks that he be informed of others as they

are committed within the demarcations.

July 20, 1844. Letter Book of the Comandancia General of the Department of
New Mexico, 1844. To the Military Commander, Colonel Don
Juan Andres Archuleta.

I am entirely satisfied with your note of the 17th in which you
describe that the robbery of 13 animals made in the vicinity of La Mesa
were retrieved at the Laguna de los Caballos by the Justice and eight
men without having killed and Indian. The Justice and the eight men
were from Ojo Caliente. . . ."

October 6, 1844. Notebook of Letters Sent by the Secretary of the Supreme
Government of New Mexico to the Authorities and Persons as
Designated Within, Year of 1844. To the Justice at Jemez.

The Governor is informed of yours of October 3 in which you describe
that the Navajo Chieftains Narbona and Cayetano have withdrawn their
obedience and joined with the Utes for a possible attack on that point.
The Governor answers that he has informed the Prefect of that District
that he prepare the pueblos for defense and to avoid a surprise attack
and that for the moment the Governor is unable to supply aid because the
troops are being occupied on the frontiers to the north.

October 10, 1844. Letter Book of the Comandancia General of the Department of
New Mexico, 1844. To the Inspector of Arms of the Third
District, Colonel Francisco Sarracino.

"You should verify the activities of the Navajo Indians in company with

the Utes at the Salida de Fray Cristoval and the attack made today on the

Real de la Caballada. I order that a hundred men be gathered in a party and

a pursuit led against the Indians to take what they have stolen and to punish

them if possible. . . ."

November 8, 1844. Notebook of Letters Sent by the Secretary of the Supreme
Government of New Mexico to the Authorities and Persons as
Designated Within, Year of 1844. To the Justice at Jemez.

"The Governor has been given your letter of November 4 in which you describe

that Gregorio Mestas has stolen a horse from the Navajos and that in their

disgust they have threatened to attack that point. The Governor orders that

the criminal be apprehended and the horse returned. . . ."

121

November 16, 1844. Letter Book of the Comandancia General of the Department of
New Mexico, 1844. To the Inspector of Militia of the
Third District at Pajarito.

Commends him highly for the pursuit of the barbarians in which they were

able to retrieve 16,000 sheep which they had stolen.

February 10, 1845. Notebook of Letters sent by the Secretary of the Supreme Government of New Mexico to the Authorities and Persons a Designated Within, Year of 1844. To the Prefect of the Third District, Don Francisco Sarracino.

The Governor grants permission to the Chieftain Jose Sarracino of the Navajos to plant at the Punto de San Mateo.

February 16, 1845. Notebook of Letters sent by the Secretary of the Supreme Government of New Mexico to the Authorities and Persons as Designated Within, Year of 1844. To the Prefect of the Third District, Don Francisco Sarracino.

The Governor is informed of yours of January 28, describing a robbery committed by the Navajos. The Governor is unable to send aid in the form of troops and explains that they are on other frontiers. . . .

February 20, 1845. Notebook of Letters sent by the Secretary of the Supreme Government of New Mexico to the Authorities and Persons as Designated Within, Year of 1844. To the Prefect of the Third District, Don Francisco Sarracino.

122 "The Governor advises that he send a detachment of 50 men to the Canon de Tafoya to stand off the raiding Navajos." /The other troop arrangements are meaningless without a previous letter of Sarracino's./

April 3, 1845. Letter Book of the Comandancia General of the Department of New Mexico, 1844. To the Militia Commander of the Pueblo of Jemez.

H e is informed of the robberies committed by the Navajos and that these turned back the 100 men who went in pursuit at the point of /Illegible in the manuscript/ and that as soon as possible the forces must march against these Navajos under an experienced commander.

3, 1845. Letter Book of the Comandancia General of the Department of
New Mexico, 1844. To the Inspector of Arms of the Second
District and the Military Commander at Jemez.

The Governor warns the inhabitants of the Second District to be prepared
surprise attacks and that the auxiliary troops should be prepared for
eventuality.

2, 1845. Letter Book of the Comandancia General of the Department of
New Mexico, 1844. To the Inspector of Arms of the Second
District.

The Commandant General advises that the auxiliaries will retire only
the enemy's [presumably Navajo in the Second District] and then retiring
the points of Cebolleta and Plaza of Ojo Caliente.

22, 1845. Letter Book of the Comandancia General of the Department of
New Mexico, 1844. To the Prefect of the First District,
Captain Don Antonio Sena.

With satisfaction I am informed of your note of yesterday
describing that of the Justice of Jemez in which he tells of a robbery
made by the Navajos against the Indians of the Pueblo of Santa Ana. And
that the latter gave them pursuit and killed two Navajos and retrieved
that which was stolen. You should tell the Justice to extend to the
Indians of Santa Ana my personal gratitude.

123

31, 1845. Letter Book of the Comandancia General of the Department of
New Mexico, 1844. To the Military Commander at the Pueblo
of Jemez, Captain Don Francisco Sandoval.

I am informed of your note of yesterday covering the pretentions
of the Chieftain el Guero of the Navajo Tribe, referring to the payment
for the two warriors killed by the Indians of the Pueblo of Santa Ana,
and the rest which in consequence he indicated: I must answer that in
accordance with the Governor of the Department I have arranged that you
should ask the said Chieftain to come to the Capital where he will
speak of the solicitation of which he treats . . . and thus exhibit on
our part the peace is never broken . . .

<u>July 15, 1845</u>. Letter Book of the Comandancia General of the Department of New Mexico, 1844. To the Military Commander at Jemez, Captai Don Francisco Sandoval.

I have received the official which you sent on the 13th in which you describe the happenings with the Navajos, and I advise you to urge all interested parties in the vicinity of those points to prevent the damages which the enemy can cause.

<u>July 31, 1845</u>. Letter Book of the Comandancia General of the Department of New Mexico, 1844. To the Frontier Commanders of Jemez and Laguna.

The Bishop will leave for Laguna on August 1, 1845, and will require an escort of 30 men to that place, because of the risk of the enemy, and from Laguna the Bishop will require 60 men from militia and residents to march on to the Pueblo of Zuni, where these men will remain until the Bishop returns.

<u>September 3, 1845</u>. Letter Book of the Comandancia General of the Department of New Mexico, 1844. To Captain Don Francisco Sandoval, at Jemez.

124

By your note dated yesterday, I am advised of the misfortunes the Navajo Indians have caused at that place, all of which I have informed the General and Chief, that for the moment you will take all methods necessary in order to find out who were the Navajos that caused those deaths to which end I am sending you the interpreter of the Navajos, the soldier Jose Lopez, . . . and that they should be informed with clarity of the evil they have worked having celebrated the peace in the Department. . . .

<u>September 6, 1845</u>. Letter Book of the Comandancia General of the Department of New Mexico, 1844. To Captain Don Francisco Sandoval, at Jemez.

I had not been informed concerning the Navajos in my last, however, now I advise that you entreat with the Indians what they claim by virtue of the peace; also the General has asked me that upon his return to Santa Fe, which will be within eight days, you will attempt to remit to him the Chieftain Sandoval in order that he can agree with him on various points of interest to the Department, reiterating to you the great vigilance necessary and to take the possible methods to guard those frontiers.

<u>March 18, 1846</u>. /The Governor's Letter Book, 1845/ to the Prefect Don
M. A. y Maestas.

Navajos have declared war, are killing and stealing sheep from the
Magdalena Mountains and the Governor advises the justices of the District
to retaliate with full force and that the Governor is appointing the
Inspector, Don Juan Perea, to lead the forces when he should arrive there.

<u>April 28, 1846</u>. /The Governor's Letter Book, 1845/ to the Prefect of the
District of the Southeast.

Sixty men from Cebolleta have asked permission to enlist in the enterprise proposed by the Navajo Chief Sandoval, to fight the enemy Navajos. The
Governor concurs providing they ask permission of the Messrs. Don Antonio
Sandoval, Don Jose Chaves y Castillo, and Don Vicente Otero, and that they
count as payment for their services the booty and spoils of war taken from
the Navajos. The Governor gives his blessing because "the war with the
Navajos is slowly consuming the Department, reducing to very obvious misery
the district of the Southwest."

125

<u>June 22, 1846</u>. /Governor Armijo's Letter Book, 1846/ to the Justice at
Jemez.

Governor sends gratifications over the successful journey against the
rebellious Navajos who have doubled their forces.

<u>July 4, 1846</u>. /Governor Armijo's Letter Book/ to the Prefect of the Third
District, n. n.

The Governor praises the Justice for the negotiations he has finished with
the Captain Sandoval. The Navajos are still in rebellion. The Governor advises
them to extend his appreciation for Sandoval's faithfulness and that his wages

will be promptly paid in full. Further advises that since the Department
awaits invasion from the United States there can be no movement of forces
against the Navajos.

July 8, 1846. /Governor Armijo's Letter Book, 1846/ to the Prefects of
 the Central, Northern, and Southeastern Districts.

Notice has been received of the coming war threatened by the Navajos
against the frontiers of the Third District. The Governor orders that they
divide the District into three military sections:

 1st section - Don Julian Perea, commanding the areas of Bernalillo,
 Corrales, Alameda, Ranchos, and Alburquerque.

 2d section - Colonel Don Ramon Luna, commanding the areas of Padillas,
 Valencia, Tome, and Laguna.

 3d section - Colonel Don Jose Chaves, commanding the areas of Belen,
 Sabinal, and Socorro.

These commanders are to lead the fight against the Navajos in case they attack
at any one of these places. They are to be given necessary support by the
citizens.

126

＊　　　　＊　　　　＊　　　　＊　　　　＊　　　　＊

SUMMARY:

Accompanying the continual movement of the Navajos, 1822-1846, there
are found no specific boundaries for them either described in records or
recognized by Mexican officials; neither are there boundaries mentioned in
treaty negotiations, see, pp. 3-4, 9-10, 17, 26, 33, 41-42. The same may

be said for the "peaceful settlements" of the Navajos, of which there appear
to be none acknowledged or described which would be in conflict with Acoma
and Laguna claims. During this time, the officials in Santa Fe, Chihuahua,
and Mexico City considered themselves at continuous war with the Navajos and
if not in actual conflict or conducting expeditions, they expected raids at
any moment and on any frontier, east or west of the Rio Grande River, and
quite often within the settled limits of the Territory itself. Therefore, the
feel of raids and expeditions for both the Mexican troops and the Navajos,
along with the places the Navajos were invited to plant and also areas forbidden
to them by the Mexican authorities, are an indication in historical records
for defining lands of the old Navajo Nation during the Mexican Period. For
the purposes of this report, landmarks are limited to those which help to
delineate claim areas between the Navajo Nation and the Acoma and Laguna Pueblos.

L. Navajo Country and the Acoma-Laguna Area as Defined in the Mexico Military
   Expeditions.

127

Retaliatory expeditions from the Rio Grande followed the Navajos generally
north and westward, sometimes to the south and west. Records of official
expeditions, either led or sanctioned directly by the Governors, often did not
mention destinations but rather the numbers of Indians killed or captured and
the booty taken. The same often occurs in the militia records. However, the
expedition led by Governor Jose Antonio Vizcarra during the summer months of
1823 spent much of the time around the Canyon de Chelly, (pp. 4-5). The
expedition of 1829 under Vizcarra proceeded probably to the same area while

the campaign under Governor Francisco Sarracino was staged out of Siete Lagunas
Jemez, and Rito de Laguna (San Jose River area). Where the operations actually
took place was not given (pp. 12-13). Likewise, the official campaign of
October 13 - November 17, 1834, was without description as was that of February
March 1835 (p. 15). The campaign conducted by Governor Albino Perez during
September and through the winter of 1836 mentioned skirmishes around Zuni, a
special detachment sent to give battle to the Navajo rancherias at Chusca and
Ose, with a final expedition against the Navajos at the Tunicha Mountains
"center of the Navajo country where they have their most secure refuge distant
from this city (Santa Fe) a little more than 200 leagues," and the Canyon de
Chelly (pp. 17-21). The commanders of the expedition had been instructed by
Governor Perez not to disturb the rancherias of the peaceful Navajos of the
Chieftains Narbona, Sandoval, Jose Tapia, Caballada Mucha, and el Negrito,
"who have been at Zuni offering the Governor their cooperation. . . ." (p. 17).
Ojo del Gallo was a place cited in the orders from which the troops belonging
to the company of Facundo Aragon would direct themselves against the Navajos
at Chusca and Ose (p. 19).

The campaign against the Navajos of September and October 1838, under the
Governor Manuel Armijo, had Jemez as its base of operations and the troops
moved from Jemez marching four days into the vicinity of the Tunicha Mountains,
thence to a more "habitable place" called Tres Lagunas. A part of the campaign
was to be devoted to making a map of Navajo country which, if accomplished,
does not seem to exist, (pp. 22-23). Another expedition against the Navajos,
October - December 1839, under Armijo, moved through the northwestern part of
New Mexico, around Canyon de Chelly and where the Canyon meets the San Juan

128

River, also Calabasa Mesa and el Carriso (pp. 27-28), returning by way of
Abiquiu. During the campaign of October 1840, the Mexican troops marched
from Abiquiu and Jemez in two companies. One of these met the Navajos at
Laguna Colorado "on the rancheria of the Chieftain Cebolla," where they gave
the Navajos battle, made captives and put the Indians to flight (pp. 29-30).
The second company besieged a mesa 600 varas high where they killed 20 warriors,
captured 6 Navajos of both sexes, 31 horses and more than 200 fanegas of corn.
And while this would not have been considered an unusual haul by the Mexicans,
the Mesa was guarded with wooden parapets on top, could only be scaled on foot,
and had caves and permanent water on top. Unfortunately, the name was not given
but in relation to the battle at Laguna Colorado and Jemez and Abiquiu, the
above mesa would correspond more nearly to the mesa country west of the Puerco
River within the Mesa Blanca and Cabezon area (pp. 30-31). This was the last
formal expedition before the arrival of the United States troops in 1846.

129

The Governors expected the "rurales" or local militia to handle many of
the Navajo raids and, according to the treaties, it was understood the captured
thieves were to be punished (pp. 9-10, 11, 33, 37, 42), the Navajo Nation should
pay for damages and losses of property (pp. 3, 11, 33), and it was common
practice that any booty taken from marauding Indians could be divided among the
militia members. It should be significant that in the reports of pursuit made
by the militia, no where was it recorded that the Navajos sought refuge in
Acoma or Laguna Pueblo lands. The places that were cited by the existing
reports as where the Navajos had been chased: the Puerco River (p. 2), Puerto
de los Ojos de Toribio (p. 3), Rito Quemado (p. 5), Mesa Azul (p. 8), Cerro
Cabezon (p. 10), Mesa Prieta (p. 14), Ojo de la Culebra (p. 16), Ojo de la Jara

(p. 29), and _Laguna de los Caballos_ (p. 46).

Acoma and Laguna Indians were enlisted to serve in the militia against the Navajo and other invaders, such as the Utes, (pp. 5, 25). How many specific instances and in what years could not be indicated with any certainty. However, there were two militia lists submitted for these Pueblos, dated August 4, 1828, and March 1839, and the latter report included the number of horses, arrows, and guns furnished by each Indian (Acoma Exhibits _____ and _____, and Laguna Exhibits _____ and _____). These Pueblos were called upon for escort duty, to guard delivery of the mails, to protect the Vicar Juan Felipe Ortiz from possible attack in April 1844 and the Bishop in August 1835 (pp. 44-45, 50). It should be noted that on one occasion, at least, the Mexican authorities met with resistance at Acoma and Laguna when trying to enlist their assistance for guard duty at Cebolleta against surprise attacks from Navajos (pp. 21-22).

130 II. Some of the settlements along the San Jose, Puerco, and Rio Grande rivers Reportedly Subject to Attacks, Raids, and Thievery from the Navajo.

While it would appear that the raids were more frequent from the Pueblo of Acoma eastwards to the Rio Grande River, the fragmentary reports were not conclusive enough to establish whether settlements to the east in reality suffered more or whether the Pueblos of Acoma and Zuni received fewer notices because of their isolated distances. Also, there was nothing in the documents to show how much the Pueblos of Acoma and Laguna may have feared the Navajo during this period or may have been trading with them, as encouraged by peace treaty.

The settlements most subject to Navajo raids: Abiquiu (pp. 6, 7, 10, 37,

56

Albuquerque (p. 16), Atrisco (p. 2), Belen (pp. 2, 5, 6, 7, 38), Cebolleta (pp. 11, 27, 37), Jemez (pp. 2, 7, 8, 11, 12, 13, 15, 29, 31, 37, 40, 48, 49), Lemitar (p. 16), Ojo Caliente (pp. 22, 38, 46), Pueblo of Acoma (pp. 28, 47, 49), Pueblo of Cochiti (p. 36), Pueblo of Isleta (p. 6), Pueblo of Laguna (pp. 5, 12, 24, 28, 47, 49), Pueblo of San Felipe (p. 21), Pueblo of Santa Ana (pp. 6, 10, 13, 49), Pueblo of Zia (p. 13), Pueblo of Zuni (p. 21), Sabinal (p. 29), Santa Cruz de la Canada (p. 6), and Socorro (pp. 12, 16).

III. Peaceful RANCHERIAS and Settlements of the Navajos in the Acoma-Laguna
Area, Mexican Period.

The Mexican Government, as late as 1835, acknowledged no peaceful settlements of Navajos within the Territory, although it had been encouraged. Almost
without exception the monthly rep_orts of the military carried a column
entitled, "Rancherias Settled in Peace." The entries did not describe a single
settlement and read, typically: 131

        There are none, and if in the class of allies who only come to this
    Capital /Santa Fe7 at different times of the year for gifts these are
    given them from the account of the Public Treasury, the Nations recog-
    nized with the names of Comanches, Utes, Jicarillas, and Navajos; who
    live in the countries to the north and west.

/From the Monthly Report of the Permanent Company at Santa Fe, July 1, 1835, in

the Mexican Collections of the New Mexico Records Center and Archives./

Mexican officials often reported the Territory to the Supreme Government
as depressed and subject to ever increasing attacks from the Navajos and
other "barbarous tribes" including the Utes. The raids of the Navajos "have
become each day more terrible with their frequent incursions for the past
five years," the Commandant General wrote the Minister of War in 1838 (p. 22).

The idea of reducing the Navajos to peaceful settlements continued from
the Spanish Period, as witness Article 4 of the treaty of February 5, 1823,
Article 7, treaty of July 15, 1829, and Article 8 of the treaty of March 1844
(pp. 3, 10, and 42). In 1843, Father Antonio Jose Martinez, long outspoken o
public affairs in New Mexico, asserted in a pamphlet to the President of Mexi
that the key to solving these problems was to be found in settling them in
boundaries, to raise crops, and participate in other industries, but they liv
by hunting and pillaging. "They do not work the lands and participate in
raising animals, except for the Navajo, which tribe, unfortunately, is the
most rapacious, the most inconstant, unfaithful in their peace, when they
are in need."[*] Father Martinez blamed the marked increase in restless activi
of these Indians on the diminishing herds of buffalo, and game in general,
since they had been encouraged to slaughter wastefully in order to trade at
the Anglo forts, mostly for liquor and for other supplies.

132   Nevertheless, the Navajo interpreter, Miguel Garcia, wrote from Jemez
on March 7, 1829, the Navajos had stolen 130 sheep in the Jurisdiction of
Jemez and were pursued to the Mesa Azul "where they have their rancherias at
San Lucas and Rincon del Vizente, and the sheep were taken to el Carriso" (p.
These sites were to the west of Acoma lands. WOur

Probably in response to Governor Sarracino's inquiry into the activities
of the Navajo Francisco Baca did Ambrosio Culaque write from Jemez in August
1834 that Baca had taken his family away from Cebolleta to parts unknown but

[*]Esposicion que el Presbitero Antonio Martinez Cura de Taos en Nuevo Mexico,
Dirije al Gobierno del Exmo. Sor. General D. Antonio Lopez de Santa-Anna.
Proponiendo la Civilisacion de las Naciones Barbaras que son al Contorno del
Departamento de Nuevo Mexico. Taos Ano de 1843. Imprenta del mismo a cargo
de J. M. B. passim.

"far away."[*]

In January 1835, Miguel Garcia reported from Jemez again that the Utes had developed close relations with the Navajos and the "rich Navajos have settled their rancherias in the Silver and Datil Mountains for that year." (p. 15)

During the expedition of 1837, the troops met no Navajos at Ojo del Gallo but four rancherias were described at Chusca and Oso (p. 19). These settlements were considerably west of Acoma lands.

During June 1839, Governor Manuel Armijo ordered the Captain Jose Francisco Chaves y Baca to "reorganize a company composed of the useful men of the Pueblos of Isleta, Laguna, and Acoma. These troops will be used to open vacant plazas and to reoccupy any useless lands there might be." (p. 25) The results of this order were nowhere to be found but presumably the order was meant to apply to abandoned lands and the said "vacant plazas" were abandoned settlements.

133

An entry for October 3, 1840, indicated that the Chieftain Cebolla had a rancheria at Laguna Colorado (p. 30). During the campaign of this same year, the friendly Navajo Chieftain Jose Largo moved his family and belongings to Encinal (p. 31), but as the government appeared unhappy with this move explained finding the Chieftain Largo and his rancheria in April 1841 "separated and in the land of the Apaches" (p. 35). By 1844, Jose Largo had settled at Blue Water (p. 40), west of Acoma lands. wm

---

[*]For the Francisco Baca – Laguna Pueblo land problem, see Jenkin's Report for the Pueblo of Laguna, pp. 78-82.

In January 1841, the Chieftain Narbona was living on <u>Mesa Azul</u> with 30 Navajos and some women (p. 32). During the unsuccessful peace negotiations of March of this year, the Navajos asked that their herds be allowed on the road between Jemez and Laguna, and that they be allowed to watch and guard them from harm (Statement Four, p. 34). However, the tenor of subsequent correspondence would indicate the Governor ignored this request. The Navajos were allowed to "dedicate themselves to planting along the margins of the Puerco River, very near the frontiers." (p. 35)

In February 1842, the Justice at Jemez reported that the Navajos who were thought would live in peace and work their fields were planning another war (p. 36), and in June 1843, the Navajo Chieftains Juan Chaves, Sarillos Largos, el Facundo, and other leading Navajos who did not want war collected in the Zuni Mountains, Oso, and the Chusca Mesa in order "to separate themselv from the thieves" and they were willing to accompany the Mexicans in a campaig against renegade Navajos (p. 37).

134

Governor Mariano Martinez granted the Chieftain Jose Sarracino permission to plant at the <u>Punto de San Mateo</u> in February 1845 (p. 48). This has been claimed by the Pueblo of Acoma to be one of its northern landmarks.

The Navajo raids continued increasing in 1845 and 1846. The authorities in Santa Fe sent no expeditions against them because of the possible invasion from the United States. However, it should be noted the Governor ordered a detachment of 50 men into the Canyon of Juan Tafoya "to stand off the raiding Navajo." (p. 48) By summer of 1846, the Navajo threat of war had caused Governor Armijo to prepare for another expedition and to divide the Third

District in New Mexico, including the Acoma-Laguna area, into three sections
under independent military leaders with orders to lead a battle against the
Navajos in case they attacked any one of the settlements of the District (p. 52).

135

1846 - 1848

Reports of military and exploring expeditions into
Navajo country between 1846 and 1850 mention no peaceful or
settled Navajos in the area from the Puerco River on the
east to beyond the Ojo del Gallo on the west, and from north
of Mount Taylor to a region some thirty miles south of the
pueblos of Acoma and Laguna. One 1846 account speaks of a
small temporary settlement west of the village of Cubero
which had apparently been recently abandoned by a few
Navajos. These reports do, however, frequently mention
Navajo raiders in the above delimited region.

The first expedition after United States occupation was
that made by forces of Colonel Alexander W. Doniphan, sent by
136 Brigadier-General Stephen S. Kearny to negotiate a treaty
with the Navajos in the fall of 1846. On September 18,
Lieutenant-Colonel Cosgrove Jackson with three companies
under Captains M. M. Parsons, John W. Reid and James A. De
Courcey left Albuquerque for the village of Cebolleta, north
of Laguna, to stop Navajo depredations, and sent runners westward into Navajo country to persuade the chiefs to come into
Santa Fe and sign a treaty.[1] As a result of the contacts
made by this group, Doniphan signed a treaty with the Navajos

---

[1] A copy of this order is in Connelley, Doniphan's
Expedition and the Conquest of New Mexico, p. 250.

at Ojo del Oso, near new Fort Wingate, south of Gallup, November 17. The troops under Jackson marched down the Rio Grande to Pajarito, thence west, crossed the Puerco River and continued through the northern Antonio Sedillo grant, then up the San José River to Laguna, passing the settlement of El Rito which had been recently abandoned because of Navajo raids.[2] Four contemporary accounts of this expedition exist, one written by Doniphan's historiographer, John T. Hughes and three by actual participants in the first Navajo reconnoissance: Privates Jacob Robinson and Meredith Moore who went with Captain Reid into the heart of the Navajo country as an advance unit, and Private Marcellus Ball Edwards who remained with Captain Jackson at the camps near Cebolleta and Cubero until the arrival of Doniphan. All agree that no Navajos, other than raiders, were to be found any where near the pueblos of Laguna and Acoma. The most graphic description of that of Robinson, A Journal of the Santa Fe Expedition under Colonel Doniphan.[3]

137

It is on this expedition that United States officials first became acquainted with the Navajo chieftain Sandoval who had, however, long been a familiar figure to Mexican military leaders as guide on Navajo expeditions. For the

---

[2] Many contemporary accounts speak of the abandoning of El Rito. According to a chart in #196, "Ambrosio Pino et al. vs. the United States," Court of Private Land Claims, five residents of El Rito were killed in the early part of 1846.

[3] The accounts of Moore and Hughes are in Connelley, Doniphan's Expedition, pp. 293-296, 123-124. The Journal of Edwards is in Bieber, Marching with the Army of the West 1846-1848, Vol. IV, pp. 173-211.

next fifteen years Sandoval figures prominently in reports
of army officers, representatives of the Indian Superintendency in Santa Fe, and other travelers, giving rise to the
false assumption that he and his band were natives of the
region around Cebolleta. The evidence clearly indicates,
however, that while Sandoval probably lived further east
than the other Navajos, his homeland was still west of Mount
Taylor and that he was permitted to come into the Cebolleta
area by Indian Superintendent James S. Calhoun in 1849 or
1850. Nor did he then remain in this region, but roamed all
over the area, sometimes remaining briefly at the eastern
edge of the Navajo country northwest of Mount Taylor, and
often encroaching on Laguna and Acoma lands. Due to the
fact that this chieftain frequently served as guide for the

138   military into Navajo country, as he had previously for Mexican
troops, he continued to be unpopular with many of his own
tribesmen. At times he was on friendly terms with the
pueblo Indians of Laguna and Acoma and traded with them; at
other times he raided the two pueblos, and out of the territory as well. He was friendly with the Mexican settlements
of Cubero and Cebolleta and used this position to barter
Navajo prisoners which he captured from the more recalci-
trant bands. Sandoval's actions were often under suspicion
from some officials, and there is concrete evidence of many
depredations committed by his band.

According to the account of Hughes, the troops first
heard of Sandoval at their September 27 camp some fifteen
miles east of Laguna:

> While at this camp, Don Chavez, a wealthy proprietor
> of the Laguna Pueblo [probably José Francisco Chavez of
> Los Padillas], well disposed towards the Americans came
> and made an offer of all his possessions. . . . Being
> requested, Don Chavez promised to use his endeavors to
> induce Sandoval, a chief of one branch or canton of the
> Navajo tribe, to bring his warriors into Cebolleta, and
> there conclude a treaty of friendship with the Ameri-
> cans. In this he partially succeeded.[4]

This statement would indicate that Sandoval lived at some
distance from Cebolleta.

Although no Navajos were seen in the area by the
troops, and no Navajo habitations, a raiding party had
recently attacked Laguna. On September 28, the soldiers
witnessed a dance over Navajo scalps at Laguna which had
been taken by members of that pueblo who had just returned
from a successful pursuit of the Navajos who had plundered
the village four days previously, killed one man and two
children and driven off a herd of sheep.[5]

After leaving Laguna, the soldiers turned north and
marched to the Spanish village of Cebolleta,[6] noting Laguna
fields and houses along the way:

> In the winding way of the valley as we came up, were
> numerous cornfields, with here and there an Indian hut,
> high onnthe hill top or beneath the mountain cliff.[7]

139

------

[4] Hughes Reprint, p. 285.

[5] Hughes Reprint, p. 284; Robinson, Journal, pp. 35-36.

[6] Edwards, Journal, p. 185, says the camp was near
Moquino, west of Cebolleta; Hughes and Robinson that it was
near Cebolleta, two miles distant.

[7] Robinson, Journal, p. 37; Edwards Journal, p. 184.

The purpose of this expedition, according to Hughes, was "to put an end to the unjust exactions and contributions, (such as loss of life and property,) which the Navajoes were perpetually levying upon the frontier Mexican and Pueblo villages."[8] The troops remained about two weeks near Cebolleta while Sandoval was sent into Navajo country to arrange a meeting with the other chiefs. That the Navajos were a long way from Cebolleta is obvious from the Hughes report:

> It was from this place [Cebolleta] that Sandoval, a noted chief of one of the Navajo cantons, who had a friendly intercourse with the New Mexicans on the frontier, was dispatched by Lieutenant-colonel Jackson to see the principal men of his tribe, and ascertain if they were of a disposition to make an amicable arrangement of existing differences. Sandoval, after an absence of about two weeks, returned and reported "that he had seen all the head men of his nation, and that they were chiefly disposed for peace; but that they were unwilling to trust themselves among the New Mexicans, unless they should be furnished with an escort of white men" whose protection would ensure their safety. And further, that before coming into the American camp, they wished to see some of the white men among them, that they might talk with them and learn what they desired. Sandoval further reported, "That the principal habitations or rather haunts of the Navajos, were two hundred miles west of Cebolleta, in the neighborhood of the great Tscheusca [Chusca] mountain, the grand dividing ridge between the Atlantic and Pacific waters, and upon the borders of the noted Laguna Colorado or Red Lake." [9]

140

On October 11, orders were received for a portion of the troops to proceed immediately into the Navajo country.

---

[8] Hughes Reprint, p. 285.

[9] Hughes Reprint, p. 287; Navajo Exhibit 42.

Accordingly, Captain Reid with ten men from each of the
three companies set out the next day, led by Sandoval.
Private Jacob Robinson, fortunately, kept a detailed diary
of this trip of thirty-one American soldiers into the heart
of one of the wildest and least known regions of New Mexico,
inhabited by one of the most formidable of Indian tribes.
The soldiers marched up the narrow canon of the Cebolleta
stream northwestward until they came to an extremely steep
mountain which they climbed with great difficulty. Although
Robinson thought: "The range of mountains over which we
passed, is the principal ridge separating New Mexico from
California," this mountain was obviously Mount Taylor rather
than the Continental Divide. After reaching the summit the
men marched westward "over an elevated plain completely
covered with loose, black, heavy, porous rocks" for some distance before "we descended into a valley, which is the
residence of Sandeval."[10]

141

Sandoval was also a man of means as Robinson noted:

> Sandeval, (who was our guide in the late expedition,)
> is rich. He has 5000 sheep, and 100 horses. His situa-
> tion is one of the most beautiful, being on an elevated
> plain, 3000 feet above the level of the country, and
> the mountain rising to snowy peaks behind it. . . . A
> view of the green grass and fine trees, with his beau-
> tiful fields of corn and wheat, make one almost forget
> that it is the abode of an untutored Indian.[11]

After leaving Sandoval's home, the small detachment

---

[10] Robinson, _Journal_, pp. 39-41.

[11] Robinson, _Journal_, p. 56.

began to see herding camps, but covered nearly a hundred miles before they met any Indians.[12] After six exhausting days they met with the Navajos under the venerable chief, Narbona, apparently near the Ojo del Oso, and the leaders promised to meet with Doniphan to discuss peace terms. The soldiers then returned to the camp, now near Cubero, where they met Doniphan who set out for the Ojo del Oso to con- clude, on November 17,[13] the first of many treaties to be made with the Navajos only to be broken within a matter of days.

In Reid's absence, a Navajo raiding party had driven off Jackson's horses from the San José camp near Cubero, and another small detachment of troops had been sent into the Navajo country to recover them. An account of Jackson's movements after the departure of Reid to the arrival of Doniphan, including the search for the missing horses, is that of Private Marcellus Ball Edwards. According to him, Jackson decided to move the camp from Cebolleta because of the scarcity of forage and water to a spot where there were

142

> some fields of corn fodder deserted by the Navajo Indians. This settlement of Indians was friendly to the Mexicans. But when they heard we were coming, the Mexicans told them it was our intention to kill every one we met with, and by these means induced the penniless and harmless Indians to quit their lodges and cornfields, and when they [had] done so, the Mexicans gathered it.[14]

---

[12] Robinson, Journal, pp. 41-56; Hughes Reprint, pp. 288-297; Meredith Moore in Connelley, Doniphan's Expedition, pp. 293-296.

[13] Navajo Exhibit 43.

[14] Edwards Journal, pp. 186-187; Navajo Exhibit 39.

According to Edwards, this camp, which he calls "Camp San José" and describes as five miles from Cubero, must have been located northwest of Cubero on the small tributary of the San José known as the "Rito de San Jose," just west of the western boundary of the Laguna Paquate Tract, as he describes the abundance of water and presence of oak trees, which the soldiers cut down for fuel, and an abandoned corn field.[15] The small stream flows into the San José River near the Acoma village of Acomita. According to Dr. Florence Hawley Ellis, an abundance of Acoma potsherds is to be found at this site, while Laguna pottery fragments were found slightly to the north. As events of 1851 and 1852 will show, the Lagunas cultivated the land just above the deserted cornfields. According to Acoma informants, a half-breed Navajo family living at the San José site at various times had been on friendly terms with the pueblos and permitted to farm a small plot.

143

The detachment sent out to recover the horses took a trail north over the San Mateo range, and then westward, somewhat south of that taken by Reid, and recovered most of the horses near Zuni. When they returned, they found that Jackson had again moved the camp into the mountains about five miles north of Cubero.[16]

---

[15] Edwards Journal, pp. 187-188; Navajo Exhibit 39. Compare with interpretation in Navajo Exhibit 38.

[16] Edwards Journal, pp. 190-209.

Meanwhile, another expedition under Lieutenant J. W. Abert of the Corps of Topographical Engineers had also entered the Laguna-Acoma area some twenty-five miles north of Jackson, up a favorite Navajo war trail, explored as far west as Acoma and returned to Albuquerque by a route to the south of the two pueblos without encountering any Navajos, although they crossed the trail of a large raiding party.

Abert was a member of the corps which was to map and describe the region covered by Brigadier-General Kearny on his westward march during the Mexican War, and with Lieutenant W. G. Peck was left in Santa Fe when the main body of troops left for California in October. Abert and Peck were to map the tributaries and main streams of the Rio Grande. With five other men, they marched west from Atrisco, just south of Albuquerque, on October 16, reaching the Puerco River at the edge of the "Cañoncito" about midway between the Sedillo and Montaño grants, intending to go to Cebolleta where Colonel Jackson was to provide an escort into the Navajo country. In spite of being warned in Albuquerque that one of the chief war trails came down the Puerco Valley, they determined to march up that river far enough to fix its course before continuing on to Cebolleta. The road was difficult because of heavy sand, but they went some eighteen or twenty miles northward, and camped near some abandoned corn fields. While here, they investigated

144

an ancient stone ruin on a bluff west of the river and a
more recently deserted settlement on the east side which
they called "El Poblazon." This was apparently the old
settlement on La Cueva in the northwest corner of the
Montaño grant. After crossing the river, they marched some
twenty miles southwest through the upper Cañoncito and into
the Mexican village of Moquino. They saw no one along the
route, but crossed the trail of a large number of men and
livestock,[17] which the Moquinos told them was that of a
raiding party of fifty Navajos who did not disturb the
village because they were on friendly terms with the
settlers.

From Moquino, the group pushed on to the Laguna
village of Paquate, "where we saw several large flocks of
sheep and goats. Continuing down the Rio Pojuate, we
passed through fields of corn and pumpkins."[18] From the
Pueblo of Laguna, their route took them southwest to the
Pueblo of Acoma. They then returned to the Rio Grande,
marching south of Acoma for a distance, then east,
before turning northeast through the abandoned Pino

145

---

[17] The Abert Report in Emory, Notes of a Military
Reconnaissance, pp. 465-467.

[18] Abert Report, p. 469.

settlement of El Rito, near the present Laguna village of
Mesita, and back to the Puerco at about the place where
Jackson and his troops had crossed on their march to
Cebolleta.[19] No Navajos were seen on the entire trip.
The Peck map appended to the Emory-Abert report of 1846
clearly shows the Navajo country in the San Juan valley
region.

Navajo depredations did not cease with the Doniphan
treaty of 1846. Even before the military forces were back
to the Rio Grande, the Navajos raided within twenty miles of
Albuquerque, as well as driving off Jackson's horses. This
set the pattern for the next eighteen years. Periodically,
the Navajos would sign a peace treaty promising to accept
United States jurisdiction, to cease raiding, and to restore
stolen stock, and would in turn receive presents and goods.
This usually took place in the late fall. Peace would be kept
until the crops were planted in the spring, then another
period of depredation would occur, another military force
would be sent and another treaty signed, only to be broken.

Early in 1847, Major W. H. T. Walker made an expedition
into Navajo country as far as Cañon de Chelly. In 1848,
Colonel Edward W. B. Newby conducted another campaign and
negotiated a treaty with the Navajos who promptly ignored
its terms.[20]

146

---

[19] Abert Report, pp. 465-474

[20] Navajo Exhibit 45. Apparently, this treaty was
never ratified by the United States.

<u>1849 - 1852</u>

James S. Calhoun, the first Superintendent of Indian
Affairs for the Territory of New Mexico, arrived in Santa Fe
in July, 1849. From that date until his departure in May of
1852, Calhoun's correspondence to the Commissioner of Indian
Affairs is filled with reports of Navajo raids and terrorism,
coupled with pleas that the peaceful pueblo Indians, as well
as the white settlers, be protected. The situation was so
serious on his arrival that on August 16, Military Governor,
Lieutenant Colonel John M. Washington, accompanied by Calhoun, made a full scale expedition into the northwest. The
troops entered Navajo country by way of Jémez Pueblo, marched
northwest through Chaco Canyon to the Tunicha valley, across
the Chusca mountains to Cañon de Chelly[21] where a treaty was
signed September 9, by which the Navajos agreed to accept
the jurisdiction of the United States, including laws regula-
ting trade and intercourse, cease all raiding and other
hostile activities and to surrender all captives and property
which had been stolen.[22]

After concluding the treaty, the troops returned by
way of Zuni, Inscription Rock, the Ojo del Gallo and Laguna.
The most detailed description of the route is that of Lieutenant J. H. Simpson, of the Topographical Corps of Army

147

---

[21] Simpson Report, pp. 64-101; Abel, ed., The Official
Correspondence of James S. Calhoun, p. 26; Navajo Exhibit 49.

[22] For terms of the treaty, see: Correspondence of
Calhoun, pp. 21-25; Kappler, Ed., Indian Affairs, Laws and
Treaties, pp. 525-527; Navajo Exhibit 47.

Engineers who also, with the assistance of E. M. Kern, made
a map of the region. Neither Simpson, nor Calhoun, speak of
encountering any Navajos before reaching the Tunicha valley.

As noted by Simpson, the guide for the expedition was
Sandoval, who joined the forces at Jémez. Simpson, however,
makes a very contradictory statement about Sandoval's location, calling him "a friendly Indian who lived near Cebolleta,
on the head-waters of the San José."[23] If Simpson meant the
San José River, this location would have been near the Ojo
del Gallo, some forty miles west of Laguna, and nearly that
distance northwest of Acoma. If, on the other hand, he meant
the head waters of the Rito de San José," the site would have
been on the northwestern part of Mount Taylor, which would
seem more likely in view of the Robinson description of
Sandoval's home in 1846. In either case, both streams were
some distance from Cebolleta. Sometime in late 1849 or
1850, however, Calhoun permitted Sandoval to move into the
Cebolleta region, temporarily, because of the hostility of
the rest of the Navajo tribe to this chieftain, as will be
noted later, and perhaps Simpson is referring to this
development, as his reference to Sandoval's location is in a
footnote undoubtedly added after his report was finished.
However, neither the map prepared by Simpson and Kern,[24] nor

148

---

[23] Simpson Report, footnote, p. 91.

[24] Simpson Report, appendix.

a sketch of the country prepared by Calhoun, October 15,
1849[25] show any Navajos east of the Mount Taylor area or
near the Ojo del Gallo. In fact, Simpson recommended that a
military post be established at Cebolletita, just south of
Cebolleta, to guard the pueblos and settlers from Navajo
war parties who swept down from the northwest:

> Coming from the mountains immediately to the north and
> back of Cebolleta and passing by Cebolleta and Cebolle-
> tita, is an avenue of approach from the Navajo country
> to the Mexican settlements in that and the neighboring
> quarter to the east of it. To the east of the selected
> point I was informed there was another avenue of approach,
> to the west, by the way of the valley of the Rio de San
> José and one of its tributaries there are other avenues
> to be guarded against.[26]

This would certainly indicate that the Navajos were west of
the Ojo del Gallo and north and west of Mount Taylor.

    While Simpson saw no evidence of Navajos on his
return from Cañon de Chelly, he saw ample evidence of Acoma
and Laguna cultivation:

149

> Three miles from our last drossing of the San Jose
> [down the valley of the Gallo], we crossed it again -
> the valley from this point gradually unfolding itself
> more uninterruptedly and continuing so down to Laguna,
> a distance of fourteen miles, within two miles of which
> we encamped. All along the valley, for this distance,
> the land is cultivated in corn and melons, the luxur-
> iance of their growth attesting the good quality of the
> soil. I also noticed, at different points, a number of
> circular places upon the ground where wheat had been
> trodden out by horses. . . . The cultivators of the
> soil are Pueblo Indians, and belong to the villages of
> Laguna and Acoma.[27]

---

[25] Included in Correspondence of Calhoun.

[26] Simpson Report, p. 138; Navajo Exhibit 50.

[27] Simpson Report, p. 129.

Like other travelers in the area, Simpson noted the presence and size of pueblo flocks. Before reaching the Laguna camp, he saw "a flock of two thousand sheep."[28] After leaving the pueblo, Simpson climbed the steep mesa of "Burned Ruins" and noted that the old stone corrals on its top "showed signs of having been recently used as sheep-pens."[29]

In accordance with Simpson's recommendations, Cebolleta (not Cebolletita) was made a military post in November, 1848, to guard one war trail from the Navajo country. However, raiding did not stop. The Washington-Calhoun treaty of September 9, 1849, lasted only until the Navajos had planted the following year's crops, for depredations began in the summer of 1850 and continued throughout the year.[30] In the fall, raiders drove off several thousand sheep near Cebolleta and committed other thefts in the Agua Salada region and along the Puerco River,

150

---

[28] Simpson Report, p. 130

[29] Simpson Report, p. 131.

[30] Calhoun to Brown, July 15, 1850, p. 217 and September 30, 1850, p. 260, Correspondence of Calhoun.

driving the stock north from Moquino along the route used
by Abert, in spite of the presence of troops at Cebolleta.[31]
As Commissioner of Indian Affairs, Luke Lea, noted to the
Secretary of the Interior, November 27, 1850:

> But their atrocities and aggressions are com-
> mitted, not only upon our citizens, but upon the
> Pueblo Indians, an interesting semi-civilized people
> living in towns or villages called Pueblos, whence
> they derive their names.[32]

Attacks on the pueblo Indians were so serious throughout
the spring of 1851 that on March 19, Calhoun gave these
Indians permission to attack any Navajos who came near
their lands.[33]

By 1851, Sandoval and his band had been permitted by
Calhoun to move into the Cebolleta region because of his
unpopularity with the other Navajo groups and assistance to
United States troops. One reason for this unpopularity was
that the chieftain was well liked by the residents of
Cebolleta and other villages, for he clearly used his favored

151

[31] Calhoun to Lea, November 4, 1850, Correspondence
of Calhoun, p. 283 and Navajo Exhibit 58; Sarracino to
Calhoun, January 29, 1851, p. 284.

[32] Lea to Stuart, U. S. Senate, Executive Document
No. 1, 31st Cong., 2nd Sess., 1850, p. 43.

[33] Whiting to Calhoun, February 10, 1851, p. 291;
Calhoun to Lea, March 31, 1851, p. 307, Correspondence of
Calhoun.

position with officials to engage in the lucrative business
of raiding other Navajo bands for prisoners and selling his
own people into slavery. On March 31, 1851, Calhoun wrote to
Commissioner Lea:

> Sandoval, our Navajo friend near Cebolleta, returned
> about the 20th of the month from a visit to his Navajo
> brethern with eighteen captives, a quantity of stock
> and several scalps.[34]

The Rev. Hiram Read, Baptist missionary and chaplain to the
forces of Colonel John Munroe (who had replaced Washington,
October 27, 1849) accompanied a detachment of troops to
Cebolleta through the Cañoncito area and put the incident
much more bluntly on March 11, 1851:

> A famous half-tamed Nabajo Chief named Sandoval who.
> resides in this vicinity, came into town today to sell
> some captives of his own nation which he has recently
> took [sic] prisoner. He sold one young man of 18 years
> of age for thirty (30) dollars.[35]

152

Others of the military did not share Calhoun's confidence in "Sandoval, our Navajo friend." On April 15, the
chieftain paid a visit to Calhoun, now governor as well as
Indian Superintendent, to procure arms, allegedly to fight
other Navajos, and was referred to Col. Munroe.[36] Munroe was
suspicious, and on April 17, Lieutenant L. McLaws, Assistant
adjutant-General of the 9th Military District, wrote Col. D.

---

[34] Calhoun to Lea, March 31, 1851, p. 307, Correspondence of Calhoun.

[35] Bloom, ed., "The Rev. Hiram Read, Baptist Missionary
to New Mexico," NMHR, XVII, p. 133.

[36] U. S. State Department, Territorial Papers, New Mexico
1851-1872, "Journal of Proceedings, Territory of New Mexico
Executive Department, entry of April 18, 1851.

T. Chandler, Commanding at Cebolleta, that Sandoval had
requested both arms and permission to accompany the next
Navajo expedition, and mentioned that while Chandler had
previously been of the opinion that the other Navajos were
hostile towards Sandoval, he was to investigate the chief's
activities carefully before recommending that the requests
be granted:

> You stated I believe on your last visit here that it was
> your impression Sandoval was not on friendly terms with
> the rest of the Nation on a/c of some of their depreda-
> tions on the Flocks and Herds of his people & of some
> acts of retaliation on his part.
> It is reported here that the Navajos living in and
> around the Cañon de Chelley & on the lower Rio San Juan,
> have separated from those living on the Upper San Juan. . .
> Sandoval may be ostensibly at war with the one portion
> of his tribe but at peace & in communication with the
> other & by giving information of our movements to the
> last, it will be communicated to the whole.
> It will therefore be necessary in your conversations
> with Sandoval not to allow him, to gain any information
> of our movements, but endeavor on your part to learn
> all concerning himself & his people.
> For they could be of assistance to us if they so
> desired & if otherwise might do some injury. . . . [37]

153

Chandler in reply, on April 13, mentioned Sandoval's
recent raids on his own people at Laguna Colorado and
while he was sure that Sandoval could be trusted, felt
that the chieftain's band would be apt to give the Navajos
word of the troop movements.[38]

In April, 1851, there was a conflict between
Laguna Indians and a few Navajos over land. Calhoun
dispatched John R. Tullis, an agent of the St. Vrain

---

[37] McLaws to Chandler, April 17, 1851, Correspondence of Calhoun, p. 309; Navajo Exhibit 62.

[38] See Navajo Exhibits 64 and 65.

Trading Company at Cebolleta, to investigate the matter.
Tullis wrote the following account of his survey:

> I have examined the matter in controversy between
> the friendly Navajos and Laguna Indians.
> It appears that the Navajos have possessed and cul-
> tivated the lands on which they live, for at least
> one hundred years; but never had held any Grant from
> the Mexican Government. A Laguna Indian at one time
> having planted on a portion of these lands, the whole
> Pueblo emboldened by this example, and knowing that
> the Navajos hold no written title have called in ques-
> tion the validity of the claim of the Navajos to the
> lands occupied by them.[39]

From this very general statement alone, it is
impossible to locate the area, but from other evidence
the dispute apparently involved some of the Sandoval
group in the land west of Cubero on the "Rito de San
José" where Jackson's troops had encamped in 1846, on
the extreme western edge of the Laguna Paquate Tract and
eastern boundary of Acoma land, since a similar quarrel
occurring the next year over this region is definitely
established. There is no record of the thoroughness of
Tullis' investigation in 1851. However, as he was a
merchant at Cebolleta,[40] and the residents of that village
were friendly with the Sandoval band, it is probable that
his sources of information were inaccurate and biased.

154

---

[39] Correspondence of Calhoun, pp. 340-341; Navajo
Exhibit 67. In Navajo Exhibit 70, Dr. Hammond gives quite
a different interpretation without documentation. In the
Journal entry of April 25, 1851, Ter. Papers, Calhoun
notes receipt of Tullis' report.

[40] RNMSIA, "Records of the Santa Fe Agency, 1849-
50," Tullis name as agent of the company appears on several
company vouchers. In U. S. Bureau of the Census, Seventh
Census of the United States:1850, Tullis was enumerator
for Valencia County, listed as a resident of Cebolleta,
38 years of age, a merchant, born in Maryland.

The implication is also apparent that the Lagunas had a legit-
imate right to the lands and that any Navajo alleged "rights"
had never been recognized by previous governments. Furthermore, if these Navajos had been in the area for some time,
as Tullis stated, he had certainly been careless in his preparation of the 1850 census returns as official enumerator,
for he reported no Navajos in Valencia County except a "Bautista
Navajo," age, fifteen, and another Navajo servant at Moquino.

In the spring of 1852, these Navajos and the Lagunas
were again at loggerheads and on April 13, Sandoval and others
of his group came into Santa Fe to appeal to Calhoun who was
usually favorably disposed towards them. Due to Calhoun's
illness, Agent John Greiner heard their complaint against the
Lagunas, and in his journal gave more details of the dispute
and the area involved than had Tullis. Sandoval, through interpreter Ramón Sánchez of Cubero, made his usual appeal because
of his friendship for the United States:

155

> He has his own people under his control he will answer
> for their good conduct, they do nothing without his orders,
> whenever he hears of other Navajos doing any thing wrong
> he tries to prevent it, Told him that was what I should
> expect from a good man as I supposed he was.[41]

The Navajos reported that a group of Mexicans in 1848 petitioned Colonel Washington for land around the San José
cienega (marsh) "about 5 leagues from the Pueblo Laguna" which
the Navajos had once used but which they had abandoned.

---

[41] Greiner Journal, p. 196.

According to their account. when they returned some eighteen
months later, Washington permitted them to have the region
again. However, the Lagunas held the lands above those the
Navajos claimed. and when the latter complained that their
irrigation water was being cut off, the Lagunas, led by Luis
Sarracino, said: "That they would not give up their land
without a fight. That they [the Navajos] might come to Santa
Fé and present their claims if they had a mind to."[42]

It seems clear that the Lagunas were using their own lands
and that they had confidence that the government officials
would protect their rights. In his report to Commissioner
Lea that the matter involved one of the most serious problems
for the pueblo of Laguna: This question of right to water is
one of the most difficult to settle that we meet with espec-
156 ially with the puebles."[43] He detailed Agent S. M. Baird to
investigate.[44]
In June, Baird made a trip to Navajo country and en route
stopped to settle the affair. On June 30, he reported that
Sandoval requested that he be allowed to settle west of Mount
Taylor:

---

[42] Greiner Journal, p. 196.

[43] Greiner Journal, p. 203. The same statement is
also made in Greiner to Lea, ROIA, NMS, LR; Navajo Exhibit 83.

[44] Greiner Journal, p. 203; Greiner to Baird, April
15, 1852, RNMSIA, LS.(Press Copies)

Sandoval a question between whom and the Lagunas about their lands was referred to me for settlement by the Superintendent declares himself anxious of settling at San Mateo west of Cebolleta Mountain for the purpose of farming -- I gave him a license to do so conditioned that he interfered with no prior claim. This at once settled the question between him and the Lagunas.[45]

Hence, in the summer of 1852, the roving chieftain again moved out of pueblo lands.

Depredations continued during the summer of 1851. Early in July, the raiders struck close to Laguna:

About the 1st of this month, near the Pueblo of Laguna, the Navajos killed three men, and caused everything to be burned up to be found in camp - the murdered men were Americans engaged in complying with a government contract for hay.[46]

On July 19, Colonel Edwin V. Sumner arrived in Santa Fe, replacing Munroe as Commanding Officer of the 9th Military District, and on August 17, led a punitive expedition into the Navajo country by way of Laguna, the San José Valley and Zuni. In his report to Major General R. Jones, Adjutant-General, Sumner noted that: "We saw no Navajos until we reached Cañon Bonito."[47] At Bonito, Sumner sent word to the chiefs in the area to meet with him, and when they refused, marched towards Cañon de Chelly, and then returned to Santa Fe in October without accomplishing anything more than killing a few scattered Navajos. He left Major E. Backus with some troops to establish Fort Defiance at Cañon Bonito,

157

---

45 Baird to Greiner, June 30, 1852, ROIA, NMS, LR; Navajo Exhibit 85.

46 Calhoun to Lea, July 25, 1851, Correspondence of Calhoun, p. 389.

47 Sumner to Jones, October 24, 1851, Correspondence of Calhoun, p. 418.

and Cebolleta was abandoned as an outpost.

Although the troops saw no Navajos from Albuquerque
to Bonito, raiders attacked Laguna while Sumner was in the
Navajo country. Private James A. Bennett noted that on October
8, as the forces were returning from the campaign, "At Laguna
[we] found that Navajos had been there ahead of us and had
stolen quite a large herd of cattle."[48] Likewise, P. G. S.
Ten Broeck, Assistant Surgeon in the Sumner forces, noted in
his journal on January 8, 1852, that the Governor of Laguna
had shown him scalps of three Navajes taken when Lagunas had
pursued the raiders who had driven off their stock during the
previous October.[49]

The fall of 1851 was a season of persistent raiding
both during and after the Sumner expedition. As Calhoun
wrote Indian Agent E. H. Wingfield on September 17, "The
Navaje Indians are travelling in every direction through this
Territory committing murders and depredations."[50] Several
raids on livestock near Cebolleta were made in September and
October.[51] The situation was complicated by the failure of

158

---

[48] Brooks and Reeve, eds., James A. Bennett, a Dragoon
in New Mexico 1850-1856, Bennett must have been in error as
to the date, for Sumner stated that he returned to Fort Union
on October 8, Sumner to Jones, October 24, 1851, Correspondence of Calhoun, p. 419.

[49] Schoolcraft, Information Respecting the History,
Conditions and Prospects of the Indian Tribes of the United
States, Vol. VI, p. 80.

[50] Calhoun to Wingfield, September 17, 1851, RNMSIA,
LS; a similar statement is in Calhoun to A. R. Worley,
September 8, 1851.

[51] Calhoun to Sumner, November 10, 1851, Correspondence of Calhoun, p. 451.

Calhoun and Sumner to agree on a unified policy, due partly
to Sumner's opposition to the use of territorial militia and
reliance on Fort Defiance to keep the Navajos quiet.[52] However, in December, various chiefs sent word into Santa Fe
that they wanted peace, and late in the month, Calhoun and
Sumner met with a delegation of 200 Navajos at Jémez. The
Navajos agreed to stop depredations and restore property,
and in return, Calhoun, over Sumner's protests, issued them
annuity goods.[53]

Affairs were comparatively quiet in 1852. Calhoun
left for Washington late in May, but died en route. Sumner
acted as civil governor until the arrival of William Carr
Lane on September 9, but Agent John Greiner was left in
charge of the Superintendency of Indian Affairs. Greiner
recorded various friendly visits of Navajos to the capitol
during the summer. In July, Greiner signed a treaty with
Mangas Coloradas of the Gila Apaches at Acoma. In his
report, Greiner noted that the Acomas were then on friendly
terms with the Navajos and "have probably more sheep and
cattle than any other Pueblo in the territory."[54] Again,

159

---

52 Communications concerning this difficulty are in
Correspondence of Calhoun, pp. 444-456.

53 Sumner to Jones, January 1, 1852, Correspondence
of Calhoun, p. 434; Brooks and Reeve, James A. Bennett, p. 32.

54 ROIA, NMS, LR, Greiner to Lea, July 3, 1852.

Greiner also stated that he had "made arrangements
with the Navajos not to steal their flocks."[55] These
"arrangements" lasted only until the Navajos decided that
Acoma flocks were too tempting not to be stolen.

Lane's policy was one of keeping the Navajos quiet
by issue of rations, the method used also by Calhoun when
the tribe was peaceful. However, Lane also advocated a
policy of moving the wandering Indians to reservations in
the eastern part of the territory. but was ordered by
Commissioner George W. Manypeny on April 9, 1853, to
suspend such plans.[56]

There were no major Navajo outbreaks during the
fall of 1852. However. Sandoval. now back in Navajo
country on the slopes of Mount Taylor, was under suspicion of fomenting trouble with the whites. Baptist
missionary John M. Shaw made a trip to Fort Defiance in
October and wrote Navajo Agent S. M. Baird that the
Zuni governor had told him that Sandoval was spreading
the rumor among his fellow tribesmen that Sumner had come
to Fort Defiance to begin a campaign of extermination
against them. Shaw also stated that Sumner had sent for
Sandoval to find out if he were guilty of causing trouble.[57]

160

[55] Greiner Journal, p. 227.

[56] ROIA, LS, Manypeny to Lane, April 9, 1853.

[57] Baird to Lane, October 25, 1852, enclosing
letter of Shaw to Baird, RNMSIA, LS.

<u>1853 - 1855</u>

In the spring of 1853, depredations, especially in the
Chama, Peña Blanca and Los Lunas areas began as soon as Navajo
crops were planted.[58] Lane abandoned his policy of appease-
ment and appealed to Sumner, in June, to conduct a vigorous
campaign to find the perpetrators. From Fort Defiance, Major
H. L. Kendrick reported that Sandoval was suspected of being
among the marauders and attributed much of the trouble to
"the machinations of Sandoval himself."[59] Lane requested
Sumner to apprehend Sandoval if the military commander had
reason to believe that this chief was an accomplice of the
raiders.[60] On July 12, Major Kendrick spoke of the necessity
of "driving these eastern Navajoes out of the mountains which
sooner or later must be done."[61]

David Meriwether arrived in Santa Fe, August 8, 1853,
to replace Lane and immediately requested instructions from
Commissioner Manypeny as to his policy towards the Navajos,
noting that his predecessor had attempted to handle trouble by
gifts and subsistence, but that raiding had continued anyway.[62]

----

[58] RNMSIA, LS: Lane to Baird, May 5, 1853; Sumner to
Lane, May 25, 1853; Vigil to Lane, May 25, 1853; Lane to
Manypeny, May 26, 1853; Navajo Exhibits 93, 94, 95, 96.

[59] Navajo Exhibit 95.

[60] Lane to Sumner, June 12, 1853, RNMSIA; Navajo
Exhibit 98.

[61] Navajo Exhibit 100.

[62] Lane to Sumner, June 12, 1853, RNMSIA, LS;
Meriwether to Manypeny, November 28, 1853.

On August 31, Meriwether wrote that scarcely a day had passed
without a raid since he had arrived in New Mexico and
remarked that Navajo strategy was to commit acts of aggression
until a military expedition was sent against them, then to
come in and sue for peace,

> make a treaty, the stipulations of which they never
> intend to comply with and receive our payments as a
> bribe to keep peace in [the] future.[63]

These depredations were profitable for Sandoval, for
in spite of alleged previous complicity, he now assisted in
recovering some of the stolen stock and was paid well for
his efforts. A receipt of September 30, 1853, issued by
Navajo Agent Henry L. Dodge reads:

> For services as interpreter and guide in the recovering
> of sheep stolen by the Navajo Indians during the months
> of July, August and September at $40 a month $120.00 . .
> Sebolla, his mark, Sandobal, Navajo[64]

162

In November, 1853, Lieutenant A. W. Whipple of the
Corps of Topographical Engineers made a reconnoissance trip
westward through Navajo country as a part of the War Department project of exploring and surveying routes for a railroad
to California. Whipple went about four miles south of Albuquerque, then turned west, crossed the Puerco and came up the
San José valley through El Rito, deserted for some ten years
because of raids, and into Laguna. Whipple reported that two
Navajos of "Carvajal's band" came into his camp at Laguna and

---

[63] Meriwether to Manypeny, August 31, 1853, U. S. H.
R., Executive Doc. No. 1, 33rd Cong., 1st Sess., 1853, pp.
430-431; Meriwether to Manypeny, September 17, 1853, RNMSIA,LS.

[64] RNMSIA, Miscellaneous Papers, 1851-1853.

noted that this group of Indians hovered about the settlements until a chance for plunder arose, and then informed
others of their kinsmen. After a raid was made, they put
the settlers on the trail of the raiders.[65]

From Laguna, Whipple took the usual route to Cubero,
remarking that "most of the valley along our route is cultivated by the Pueblo Indians."[66] From Cubero, he followed the
river to the Ojo del Gallo, Agua Fria and over the Continental
Divide where he met a group of Acomas returning from a hunting
trip,[67] another indication that the latter utilized lands far
from the pueblo. Except for the two Navajos of Carvajal's
raiders, Whipple and other accounts of his expedition report
no Navajos in the area from Albuquerque to near the Ojo del
Oso.[68] In another account entitled "Report on Indian Tribes,"
written by Whipple, Thomas Ewbank and William W. Turner, the
Navajo country is specifically outlined:

163

> They extend westward from our route to the San Juan,
> valley of Tuñescha [Tunicha], and Cañon de Chelle;
> occupying a region some 15,000 square miles in extent.[69]

------

[65] Whipple, "Report . . . upon the Route near the
Thirty-Fifth Parallel" in U. S. War Dept., Reports of Explorations and Surveys . . . Vol. III, Pt. 1, p. 61.

[66] Whipple Report, p. 61.

[67] Whipple Report, p. 63.

[68] Möllhausen, Diary of a Journey, II, gives another
account of this trip by a German observer who accompanied
Whipple, and reports no Navajos whom he calls "a robber race,"
p. 12. See Navajo Exhibit 108.

[69] Whipple Report, Vol. III, Pt. 3, p. 13.

The year 1854 was relatively quiet, although "our
Navajo ally," Sandoval, in spite of his protestations of
peaceful intentions and friendship, was somewhat busy raiding
Laguna herds as well as into the Pecos Valley Apache reservation. On May 13, Major Kendrick notified Acting Governor W.
S. Messervy that the chieftain Sarcillo Largo had told him
that there were rumors of stock theft west of Jémez:

> It is possible that the relation of Sarcillo Largo,
> above alluded to may have grown out of a raid made, I
> understand, near Laguna and perhaps done by Sandoval's
> Indians, of which raid the sheep, it is said, have been
> recovered. The Navajos, however, believe that the sheep
> retaken were not those lost, . . . 70

On October 16, Apache Agent Preston Beck, Jr., wrote
to Meriwether from the Pecos:

164

> On the 15th inst. Sandoval, a Navajo Indian of Cebolleta
> in this Territory with his son and twelve Navajos came to
> our grazing camp in this vicinity inquiring of our hearders
> [sic] where all the heards of sheep were which were usually
> hearded in this neighborhood, and if those were the fine
> American sheep so much spoken of, pointing to our heard
> grazing close by. His son attempted to take the hat off
> the head of one of the hearders and when resistance was
> made by the hearder, prevented him from getting his hat,
> he seized his lance and threw it at the hearder wounding
> him slightly in the arm. The party then went deliberately
> to work killing sheep, and after they had killed several
> the hearders told them that Maj. Carleton was close by
> with his company of U. S. troops, when they at once
> stopped the slaughter and left in the opposite direction
> from that they understood the troops to be. The Indian
> Sandoval we understand has property at or near Cebolleta
> where we could we presume recover damages from him, but
> not wishing to create any disturbance with them, we have
> taken this plan of submitting the matter to you & hope
> it will receive the attention it merits. 71

---

70 RNMSIA, Miscellaneous Papers, 1854; Navajo Exhibit 11.

71 RNMSIA, Miscellaneous Papers, 1854; Navajo Exhibit 12.

Contemporary observers during 1854 continued to define
the Navajo country as far to the west of the lands used by
Acoma and Laguna. Jonathan Letherman, Assistant Surgeon,
United States Army, stationed at Fort Defiance, delimited
their land as follows:

> The Navajo Indians are a tribe inhabiting a district
> in the territory of New Mexico, lying between the San
> Juan river on the north and northwest, the Pueblo of Zuñi
> on the south, the Moqui villages on the west, and the ridge
> of land dividing the waters which flow into the Atlantic
> Ocean from those which flow into the Pacific on the east.[72]

Travelers to Navajo land in 1855 did likewise. In
February, Governor Meriwether was designated by President
Pierce to negotiate a treaty with the Navajos, as well as with
the Apaches and Utes, by which the Indians would have the
right to the lands they possessed and used guaranteed by the
government in return for Navajo agreement to end raiding.
In addition, the governor was to have $10,000 at his disposal
for payment of annuities.[73] In July, Meriwether, accompanied
by the territorial secretary, W. W. H. Davis, left for Fort
Defiance, taking the usual route west from Pajarito through
Laguna and up the San José. In Davis' description of the
trip, he discussed the homeland of the Navajos as in the San
Juan region, some 200 miles from Santa Fe, and indicated that

165

---

[72] Letherman, "Sketch of the Navajo Tribe . . . " in
Tenth Annual Report . . . Smithsonian Institution, 1855, p. 83.

[73] Manypeny to Meriwether, March 16, 1855, ROIA, LS.

that their furthest eastern occupation was Chaco Canyon.[74]
According to him, no Navajos were seen out of that area
except one suspicious-looking small band which the negotiators saw near the Ojo del Gallo on their return, but this
group turned out to be Sandoval's band,[75] another indication
that Sandoval wandered in and out of pueblo territory.

Meriwether and Davis concluded a treaty with the
Navajos July 18, by which the Navajos agreed to claim no
land east of a line drawn diagonally northeast from Zuni to
Cañon Large, roughly following the Continental Divide, thus
admitting no claim to land east of Chaco Canyon in the north,
Blue Water in the center, or south of Zuni.[76] All the chieftains, except Sandoval, signed the treaty. This area was far
to the west of any lands claimed by Acoma and Laguna.

166

According to Meriwether, Sandoval had cut himself off
from the other groups some years before, and had been permitted by Calhoun to move into the Cebolleta region:

> Every band, except that of Sandoval, was fully repre-
> sented, and every chief, Captain and head man, except
> Sandoval signed the treaty willingly. . . . Sandoval's
> band numbers about one hundred souls, who separated from
> the remainder of the tribe some years since and the two
> parties are decidedly hostile to each other, which separa-
> tion and hostility grows out of the fact that this little
> band having refused to join with the remainder of the
> tribe in hostilities, a small Mexican settlement called
> Sebolleta was broken up or abandoned, and Gov. Calhoun

---

[74] Davis, El Gringo, p. 418.

[75] Davis, El Gringo, p. 424; entire report, pp. 389-432.

[76] Royce, comp., Indian Land Sessions, Pt. II, Map 44;
See Navajo Exhibit 127.

gave Sandoval and his party permission to occupy it,
which they have done up to this time. But I am informed
that the former occupants of this settlement claim the
land under a Mexican grant, which will render it necessary to provide for Sandoval and his followers in some
other quarter, unless this grant be purchased by the
government which I would strongly recommend, for if these
Indians are required to remain west of the mountains few
will survive long. 77

Meriwether was in error as to Cebolleta ever having
been abandoned by the grantees or that Sandoval had lived
there continuously. No statement of Calhoun granting these
terms to Sandoval has come to light, although he certainly
permitted the chieftain to live in the Cubero-Cebolleta area,
but in 1852, after the clash with Laguna at San José, Sandoval had moved west of Mount Taylor. It is obvious that in
spite of being favorably disposed towards Sandoval, Meriwether conceded that the Navajo had no real right in the
region.

167

1856 - 1858

Like other Navajo treaties, that of 1855 was of short
duration. On February 1, 1856, Major J. H. Carleton reported
to Major H. L. Kendrick, stationed at Fort Defiance, that
stock stolen on the Puerco was in the possession of Miguelito
then camped west of Cebolleta. Kendrick asked Agent Dodge to
use his influence with Miguelito to recover the stock and

---

77 Meriwether to Manypeny, July 27, 1855, RNMSIA,
LS; Navajo Exhibit 128.

noted that Navajo raiding was increasing.[78]   On February 8,
Kendrick reported to Carleton, "It would also be well to keep
an eye on Sandival [sic] and his band."[79]   Other raids were
made in March.[80]   On June 13, Dodge informed Meriwether:

> I have this moment received information from a Navajo
> Indian that a war party headed by the son of Jose Largo
> a rich man has left Cañon Blanco to steal and kill all
> persons who may be so unfortunate as to fall into their
> hands. 81

Meriwether thought that this group might strike in the Rio
Arriba region to the northeast.[82]   José Largo and his band
frequently raided Acoma (see Ellis report). Sandoval's group
also did its share of raiding. On June 25, Mariano and three
other members of Sandoval's band mortally wounded Juan de
Dios Vallejos of Cubero in the Encinal cañon, near the hacienda
of Marcos Baca.[83]   On June 25 and again on the 28th, raiders
struck at Cebolleta.[84]   The situation was serious enough to

168

---

[78] Carleton to Kendrick, February 1, 1856 and Kendrick
to Dodge, RNMSIA, Miscellaneous Papers, 1856; Navajo Exhibits
137, 138, 139, 141, 142, 143.

[79] Navajo Exhibit 140.

[80] Navajo Exhibits 144, 145.

[81] Dodge to Meriwether, June 13, 1856, RNMSIA, LR
from Agencies, 1856; Navajo Exhibit 149.

[82] Meriwether to Roival, June 23, 1856, RNMSIA, LS.

[83] Gorman to Dodge (Laguna), June 27, 1856, RNMSIA,
Miscellaneous Papers, 1856; also listed in #196, Court of
Private Land Claims, in chart of those killed at El Rito
by Navajos, 1837-1880.

[84] Luna (Los Lunas) to Meriwether, July 11, 1856,
RNMSIA, Miscellaneous Documents, Spanish Language,1852-1856.

warrant Meriwether to write Manypeny on June 30 that if the
depredations continued, a military campaign should be under-
taken against the Navajos,[85] but no forces were sent, and the
situation became less serious during the summer.[86]

Meriwether left New Mexico early in 1857 and W. W. H.
Davis acted as governor until the arrival of Abraham Rencher.
In April, the Superintendency of Indian Affairs was separated
from the governorship, and J. L. Collins was appointed as
superintendent.[87] The year was relatively quiet. Even
relations between Sandoval's group and Laguna were comparatively friendly. Colonel B. L. E. Bonneville, now in command
of the district, reported to Collins that on August 1, a band
of Utes had killed five of Sandoval's band "and a friendly
Pueblo Indian on a visit there from Laguna.[88]

Peace was short-lived, however, for 1858 saw increased
depredations and a full-scale campaign against the Navajos.
Attacks were made on herds near Cebolleta and in the Cañon
of Juan Tafoya, near present Marquez, in March and April.[89]

169

85 Meriwether to Manypeny, June 30, 1856, RNMSIA, LS.

86 Meriwether to Manypeny, September 30, 1856, U. S.
H. R., Exec. Doc. No. 1, 34th Cong., 3rd Sess., 1856, p. 733.

87 Collins to Manypeny, April 30, 1857 acknowledging
letter of appointment, RNMSIA, LS.

88 In letter of Bonneville to Collins, January 17, 1858,
RNMSIA, Miscellaneous Papers, 1858. See also Navajo Exhibit 164.

89 Baca to Rencher, March 25, 1858 enclosing communication of J. M. Ballejos of Cebolleta, March 11; Ballejos to
Rencher, April 24, 1858 lists depredations suffered and asks
permission for Navajo campaign, RNMSIA, Miscellaneous Documents,
Spanish Language, 1852-1859.

As usual, the pueblos suffered severe livestock losses. Major
W. T. H. Brooks, commanding at Fort Defiance, wrote Superintendent Collins, April 13, that he had recovered stolen
ponies which "may belong at Covero [Cubero] to some of the
puebles."[90] Attacks on the pueblos were so serious that
Jémez, Zía, Santa Ana and Laguna banded together for an
attack on the Navajos during the same month, but were dissuaded
from such a policy by Special Agent for the Navajos, John
Ward.[91] As Collins noted to Acting Commissioner Charles C.
Mix, "during the past spring and summer hardly a week has
passed without some theft being reported against them [the
Navajos]."[92]

On July 11, 1858, a Negro servant of Major Brooks was
killed at Fort Defiance, and when the Navajos refused to surrender the real murderer, another campaign was waged against
them. As in the past, Sandoval was able to play his usual
role of posing as friend of the United States against the
other Navajos and thus secure immunity for himself from
charges of complicity as well as of raiding and harboring
raiders. He particularly enlisted the support of Superintendent
Collins, although Navajo Agent Samuel M. Yost at Fort

170

---

[90] Brooks to Collins, April 13, 1858, RNMSIA, Miscellaneous Papers, 1858.

[91] Ward to Yost, April 9, 1858, RNMSIA, LR from
Agencies, 1858; Navajo Exhibit 167.

[92] Collins to Mix, September 27, 1858, U. S. H. R.,
Exec. Doc. No. 2, 35th Cong., 2nd Sess., 1858, p. 542; Navajo
Exhibit 174.

Defiance, in the midst of the troubles, was not convinced either of Sandoval's sincerity in helping the government or of his innocence of the charge of raiding.

When Colonel Dixon Miles, in charge of military forces at Defiance, attempted to get Sandoval to call the chiefs together for a conference early in September, Sandoval was very reluctant to undertake the mission.[93] However, several chiefs, among them Sandoval, did meet with the military authorities and at first agreed to surrender the murderer. On September 7, Sandoval reported to Yost that the murderer had been mortally wounded by loyal, pursuing Navajos and that the body would be delivered the next day. When Sandoval produced the corpse of the alleged murderer, the deception was evident, for it was that of a forty-five year old man who had been killed within the past few hours, whereas the murderer was known to have been about eighteen years old and had supposedly died of his wounds some twenty-four hours before.[94] In spite of Sandoval's actions, Superintendent Collins tried to exonerate him from any guilt in the ensuing struggle, and utilized his services in the campaign. On September 24, 1858, Collins reported to Acting Commissioner Mix:

171

---

93 Yost to Collins, September 5, 1858, ROIA, NMS, LR by OIA.

94 Yost to Collins, September 9, 1858 and report of J. Cooper McKee, Assistant Surgeon, U. S. A., in ROIA, NMS, LR by OIA.

The chief Sandobal mentioned in Agent Yost's letter
of the 9th instant is the principal chief of one band
of the Navajos that have always remained friendly with
us. He is here today [Santa Fe] by request of Col.
Bonneville who desires to consult him about the country
in which the troops will have to operate, should the war
be of long continuance. 95

On September 27, Collins also wrote Mix:

It is perhaps well to mention that one band of Navajos
under the chief Sandaval involving about four hundred
is entirely neutral in this conflict. 96

Three days later, Yost wrote Collins that Sandoval seemed

afraid to go among the Navajos, although instructed by Col-

onel Miles to gather the chiefs together.[97]

Sandeval's band was clearly encroaching on both Acoma

and Laguna during 1858. On April 9, Special Agent John Ward

noted:

Sandoval and Chino with their bands are now living
in the neighborhood of Laguna; the former has always
been our friend even against his own people who have
therefore expelled him from among the real Navajos, to
whom to give presents, agts. etc. 98

In October, Laguna was finally given permission by the com-

manding officer at Fort Defiance to defend herself against

the Navajos, but ironically enough, was not permitted to take

action against the band which was actually living on her land,

172

---

95 Collins to Mix, September 24, 1858, ROIA, NMS,
LR by OIA.

96 Collins to Mix, September 27, 1858, U. S. H. R.,
Exec. Doc. No. 2, 35th Cong., 2nd Sess., 1858, p. 543, Navajo
Exhibit 174.

97 Yost to Collins, September 30, 1858, RNMSIA, LR
from Agencies, 1858.

98 Ward to Yost, April 9, 1858, RNMSIA, LR from
Agencies, 1858; Navajo Exhibit 167.

n spite of the protests of Agent Yost.[99]

An armistice was agreed upon in November, and Colonel
Bonneville and Collins signed a treaty with the Navajos on
December 25 by which the latter were confined to an area far
east of the line decided upon by Meriwether in 1855. Over
the opposition of Yost, Collins insisted on excluding Sandoval from the reservation agreed upon and permitted him and
his band to remain, temporarily at least, near Laguna. In
the armistice terms, Collins stated:

> Sandoval and his people in consideration of his and
> their past fidelity and good conduct will be permitted
> to occupy the country they now occupy, notwithstanding
> the terms of the 1st of these articles, until otherwise
> provided in future; but in all other respects they are
> to be considered as part and parcel of the Navajo
> nation. 100

Yost was incensed at this exception of Sandoval and reminded
the superintendent that Sandoval had not always acted in good
faith, for he had raided, and when he was given annuity goods
denied to the other Navajos because of their hostilities,
he permitted large numbers of them to join his group to
receive supplies. He also reminded Collins of Sandoval's
deception concerning the body of the alleged murderer of

173

---

[99] Yost to Collins, October 10, 1858, RNMSIA, LR
from Agencies, 1858. Colonel Bonneville wrote to Collins,
October 16, 1858, that he had given orders to Colonel Miles
not to molest Sandoval, RNMSIA, Miscellaneous Papers, 1858.

[100] The armistice terms are in RNMSIA, Miscellaneous
Papers, 1858.

of Major Brooks' servant:

> Sandoval's tribe is equally responsible, if not more
> so, for all such theft - if committed - with the other
> bands of the nation, and it is impossible to sustain
> your inference that these Indians [near Fort Defiance]
> are alone responsible. . .
> You proceed to say that in consideration of his past
> good conduct and fidelity to the United States, he and
> his band are permitted to remain where they are, imme-
> diately on the borders of the Rio Grande; and assume
> that he and his band have been entirely guiltless of
> thefts charging every depredation to the Indians of this
> vicinity. Sandoval admitted to you and Col. Bonneville,
> as you informed me, that he was cognizant of the fact
> that the boy murdered and brought into the post for the
> murdered was not the murderer, but that the act was
> committed to deceive the government. Is this fidelity
> to the United States? I can further inform you that he
> was a party to that deception and that he was paid by
> the Indians for his services. You excused his brutal
> deception and crime by answering that Sandoval was an
> Indian and could not be expected to think, as much as
> to say, if Sandoval would not act as we would, we
> should either act with him, or tacitly endorse his
> action.
> Sandoval's band has been guilty of many of the depre-
> dations charged to these Indians . . .
> You distributed presents this year to Sandoval's
> band which consists of about 300 souls. At that dis-
> tribution, more than half of them belong to the bands
> against which the United States was at war who were
> harbored by Sandoval. . . 101

174

Regardless of this, and over the opposition of Acoma and

Laguna, Sandoval was permitted to remain in the pueblo region

to cause further trouble. Article 8 of the treaty provided:

> It is understood that Sandoval and his people are
> for the present and until otherwise provided in future
> permitted to occupy the country they now occupy, but in
> all other respects they are to be considered as part and
> parcel of the Navajo nation.

---

101 Yost to Collins, December 18, 1858, RNMSIA, LR
from Agencies, 1858; Navajo Exhibit 205.

All the people now with Sandoval who do not properly
belong to his band are to return immediately to their
own country west of the line fixed in the first of
these articles. 102

By this time, Collins had permitted Sandoval to move
into the eastern portion of the Cañoncito region along the
Puerco River on land claimed by Laguna, and both Acoma and
Laguna were threatening action against the band. On
November 8, Lieutenant J. N. G. Whistler. commanding at Los
Lunas, reported to the Acting Assistant Adjutant-General
that Sandoval had told him of his fears of the Acomas and
Lagunas and that the Acomas had killed several of his people
near their pueblo, while the Mexican settlers had also
reported to him that the puebles were considering a joint
attack.103 On November 15, 1858, Collins explained to
Mix his reasons for letting Sandoval into the Puerco
territory in a letter regarding the killing of the chieftain's son by Isleta Indians:

175

This friendly chief has some enemies who are anxious
to force him to become a party to the war that now
exists with the other branches of the nation. I have
been a close observer of his conduct for several years,
and have confidence in his fidelity and do not intend
to let him be molested if it can be prevented. He has
moved his band to within thirty miles of Albuquerque
and a good many of the peaceably inclined Indians

---

102 The treaty is in ROIA, NMS, LR by OIA, 1858,
and in RNMSIA, Miscellaneous Papers, 1858; a map of the line
is in Royce, Indian Land Sessions, Map 44.

103Navajo Exhibit 188.

belonging to the war party of the nation have sought
protection under him, and it is the determination of
Col. Bonneville, as well as myself, that they shall not
be molested as long as they remain faithful.
The murder of his son, as I understand, was the
result of a drunken frolic but to keep Sandoval's
people quiet, it is deemed necessary to place the
murderer before the civil tribunals of the territory
for trial. 104

In December, while negotiations were being carried
on and the quarrel between Yost and Collins was at its
height, Yost reported that Sandoval was raiding along the
Rio Grande.[105]

Sandoval died early in 1859, and an older brother
was placed in charge of the band for a time,[106] but the group
continued to roam in and out of the pueblo region.

1859 - 1863

176

The Navajos had no more intention of keeping the
Collins-Bonneville treaty than they had had of keeping
previous ones, and the years 1859-1863 were ones of constant
terror, complicated by another conflict between the civil
authorities and the military. In May, 1859, two pueblo

---

[104] Collins to Mix, November 15, 1858, in ROIA, NMS,
LR by OIA. J. W. Denver, Commissioner of Indian Affairs,
acknowledged receipt of the letter to Collins, December 18,
1858, RNMSIA, LR from CIA, 1858.

[105] Clipping from Santa Fe Gazette, December 21, 1858.

[106] Collins to Denver, February 21, 1859 in ROIA, LR
by OIA, 1859, says death officially reported by band on
February 1.

Indians and two Mexican sheepherders were killed near
Cebolleta.[107] The lack of protection afforded the pueblos
and settlers prompted Collins to write to Commissioner A. B.
Greenwood on September 17, 1859, that the Navajos paid no
attention to the treaty:

> They have continued to rob and murder, as they have
> been doing for years. . . . The Indians of several of
> the pueblos have met with many losses by the Navajo of
> which they very justly complain. 108

The quarrel of Collins and Governor Abraham Rencher
with Colonel Fauntleroy, now in command in New Mexico, made
matters worse in 1859-1860. On January 7, 1860, Collins
notified Greenwood that instead of living up to the terms of
the treaty, the Navajos had committed even more robberies in
the past month, while the military did nothing.[109] On February 4, Rencher wrote Secretary of State Lewis Cass that as
depredations and lack of enforcement of treaty had continued,
the legislature had held "an angry meeting" to raise volunteers, but Fauntleroy had said that he would withdraw the
regulars if the militia were used.[110] Throughout the spring

177

---

[107] Collins to Denver, May 22, 1859, ROIA, NMS, LR
by OIA.

[108] Collins to Greenwood, September 17, 1859, U. S.
Sen., Exec. Doc. No. 2, 36th Cong., 1st Sess., 1859, pp. 707-708.

[109] Collins to Greenwood, January 7, 1860, RNMSIA, LS.
A similar statement was also made in Collins to Greenwood,
ROIA, NMS, LR by OIA, January 29, 1860.

[110] In State Department, Territorial Papers, New
Mexico, 1851-1872, hereafter cited as SD, TP, NM.

the quarrel continued, as well as a serious disagreement
between Navajo Agent Silas Kendrick and Major O. L. Shepherd
at Fort Defiance.[111] On May 15, Rencher wrote Cass that
Fauntleroy still refused to take any action, and since the
Rio Grande was so high that the white settlements would not
be attacked, the Navajos were venting their fury on the
western pueblos, with the result that many had been killed
and the peaceful Indians were "almost stripped of their
flocks."[112] Five days later, two shepherds were killed near
Cubero and a large flock driven off.[113] On July 22, Collins
reported that "The Indians are stripping the settlements,
especially on the west side of the Rio Grande of the last
vistage [sic] of stock."[114] On September 24, Collins reported
that there were "repeated and almost daily incursions upon
the settlements."[115] The official census for 1860 reported
sixteen persons killed by Navajos in Valencia County.[116]

Laguna was particularly victimized by these raids, as
Pueblo Agent Silas F. Kendrick wrote to Commissioner Greenwood on September 25:

178

---

[111] Collins to Greenwood, February 5, 1860, enclosing
letters of Kendrick of January 20 and 23, and Collins to Greenwood, March 30, 1860, ROIA, NMS, LR by OIA.

[112] SD, TP, NM, 1851-1852.

[113] Collins to Greenwood, May 20, 1860, RNMSIA, LS.

[114] Collins to Greenwood, July 22, 1860, and clippings
from the Santa Fe Gazette in ROIA, LR by OIA, 1860.

[115] Collins to Greenwood, September 24, 1860, in U. S.
Sen., Exec. Doc. No. 1, 36th Cong., 2nd Sess., 1860, p. 381.

They [the Pueblos] have, however, for months past
been subjected to much loss and suffering from the in-
roads and depredations of the Navajo Indians, who, in
their hostile incursions upon the settlements of this
Territory, made no distinction of race or origin. . .
The villages of Laguna and Zuna [Zuni] have been the
chief sufferers, in consequence of their more immediate
neighborhood to the hostile tribes. These pueblos are
situated convenient to the routes pursued by war parties of the Navajoes in their attacks upon the settlements of the Mexicans. 117

The famous European priest, Abbé Em Domenech,

reporting on Indian events in the Southwest, noted of the

Laguna region in the record of his travels published in 1860:

The Navajos often make incursions into this country
and take off all they can lay their hands on; they carry
off entire flocks and even make prisoners whom they
liberate on the payment of large ransoms. Yet the
Navajos are not always at variance with the population
of the pueblos and prairies; at times they even pay
friendly visits to some of the villages to exchange
their products for other provisions. 118

Like other travelers through the region throughout the 19th

century, he delimited the Navajo country as far to the west

of the pueblos of Acoma and Laguna:

179

The Navajo country occupies an extent of about
15,000 square miles comprised between the Rio San Juan,
the Valley of Tunesha, and the Cañon de Chelly. . . 119

Because of the raids, additional regiments were sent

into New Mexico from Utah in July, 1860, and in late August,

---

117 Kendrick to Greenwood, September 25, 1860, in
U. S. Sen., Exec. Doc. No. 1, 1860, 36th Cong., 2nd Sess.,
1860, pp. 388-389.

118 Domenech, Seven Years Residence in the Great
Deserts of North America, Vol. I, pp. 206-207.

119 Domenech, Seven Years Residence, Vol. I, p. 184.

Colonel Edward R. S. Canby of the 10th Infantry was ordered
in from Fort Garland to direct a campaign against the Navajos. During October and November, Canby marched through
Navajo country by way of Chaco Canyon, but the results were
indecisive. Some of the leaders made overtures towards
peace, and on February 15, 1861. a treaty was signed by
which the chiefs agreed to confine their people to the lands
west of Fort Fauntleroy on the Ojo del Gallo.[120]

The situation soon became even more critical, however,
as many regular army officers, among them Fauntleroy in
March, and his successor, Colonel William V. Loring, in May,
left New Mexico to join the Confederate forces and military
strength was greatly weakened. The Navajos went on other
rampages, and Colonel Canby, commander after the departure
of Loring, was powerless to act in Indian uprisings. Fort
Defiance was abandoned, and the invasion of the Texas Confederates under General H. H. Sibley in the fall forced the
recall of all troops from the northwest.[121] After the Texan
defeat at Glorietta Pass in March, 1862, the Confederates
retreated from New Mexico, and in the late summer, General
J. H. Carleton and the California Column arrived. Carleton

180

---

[120] See Navajo Exhibit 266.

[121] Connelly to Seward, October 26, 1861 and November
17, 1861, gives details of depredations, SD, TP, NM, 1851-
1872.

replaced Canby.

On September 14, 1862, Governor Henry Connelly issued a proclamation calling for the organization of territorial militia to be sent into Navajo country,[122] and Carleton arrived in Santa Fe on September 20, and concentrated his attention upon Indian affairs. Veteran fur trader and former Ute Agent, Christopher Carson, was placed in charge of a campaign against Apaches and Navajos. Carson turned his attention first to the Mescalero Apaches, and Navajo depredations continued unabated through the fall of 1862.[123] By the summer of 1863, the Apaches were subdued, and Carleton and Carson were ready to undertake the Navajo campaign. On February 1, 1863, J. Francisco Chaves was sent to old Fort Fauntleroy on the Ojo del Galle, now renamed Fort Wingate, to make an attempt to secure a meeting with the Navajo chieftains. On June 15, Carson was sent _west of_ the Ojo del Oso to establish Fort Canby as a base for operations, and on June 23, Carleton advised Chavez that if the Navajos did not agree to meet by July 20, war was to be waged against them. By July 20, Carson had established Fort Canby and was at old Fort Defiance. Since the Navajos made no effort to

181

---

[122] SD, TP, NM, 1851-1872.

[123] Labadi to Collins, September 25, 1862, U. S. H. R., Exec. Doc. No. 1, 37th Cong., 3rd Sess., 1862, p. 394.

come to terms, United States forces began the systematic
destruction of Navajo crops and confiscation of livestock.
Carleton's policy through the next two years was that the
Navajos should be rounded up and removed to the Bosque
Redondo reservation.

Although Sandoval was dead, members of his band were
certainly considered as raiders, along with other Navajos,
as is obvious in the following report of September 5, 1863,
from Superintendent Michael Steck to Lorenzo Labadi, Agent
at Bosque Redondo:

> General J. H. Carleton has sent to Fort Sumner
> 50 Navajoes, men women and children belonging to San-
> doval's band. They will be taken care of by the mili-
> tary, as they are prisoners of war and should remain
> entirely under the control of the commanding officer
> while the tribe remains hostile. 124

182

The Navajos increased their attacks on Acoma and
Laguna. In August, 1863, these pueblos, joined by Isleta,
asked permission to pursue the Navajos to recover livestock.[125]
Because of their long cooperation in carrying out the desires
of the government, and their almost constant victimization
by the Navajos, Steck granted the pueblos permission to
recover their property and defend their livestock.[126]   On

---

124 RNMSIA, LR from Agencies, 1863.

125 Luna to Steck, August 28, 1863, RNMSIA, LR
from Agencies, 1863.

126 Steck to Luna, August 30, 1863, RNMSIA, LR from
Agencies, 1863.

October 5, 1863, Pueblo Agent Ramón Luna reported to Steck
that the pueblo expedition had returned with 1200 recaptured
sheep, 40 horses and mules, 51 prisoners, and that theybhad
killed 22 Navajos.[127] This was apparently the last big raid
against the pueblos, and the battle which followed at Mangas,
some eighty miles southwest of Acoma is described by several
Acoma and Laguna informants who state that the Navajo leader,
José Largo, and most of his raiders were killed after the
Navajo attack in which much stock was stolen from Laguna,
and the entire Acoma herds, gathered in corrals just south
of the pueblo were stolen (see Ellis report).

Through the fall and winter of 1863-64, Carson struck
at the Navajos, and in January carried the campaign into the
fastnesses of Cañon de Chelly, the historic last retreat of
the Navajos in time of peril. Captured Indians were held at
Fort Canby. On March 5, some 2,400 Indians with 3,000 sheep
and 474 horses, escorted by the military, began their long
trek from Canby through Fort Wingate, Cubero, Laguna, across
the Puerco to Albuquerque and to the Bosque Redondo.
According to Laguna informants, some of the Lagunas, especially in the village of Paquate, felt so sorry for those who
had not raided them, that they secreted some Navajo children
in grain bins as the troops went through to prevent them

183

---

[127] Luna to Steck, October 5, 1863, RNMSIA, LR from
Agencies, 1863.

from being incarcerated (see Ellis report). This was the
largest group to be sent to the Bosque Redondo, but smaller
numbers continued to be captured or to come in voluntarily.
The census of Navajos on the reservation made by Captain
McCabe, January 7, 1865, listed a total population of 8,354.[128]
This was the largest figure given for the numbers at Bosque
Redondo. Manuelite and Baeboncito, the last of the important
chiefs, surrendered in the fall of 1866.[129] Periodically,
some deserted the reservation, returned to their old haunts,
or raided the settlements and into the pueblo areas.[130] Stock
was stolen and four persons were killed at El Rito, near
Laguna,[132] and two at Cubero[132] in 1866. Many of the Navajos
were never captured. Special Agent J. K. Graves, sent to

184

128 The War of the Rebellion: . . . Official Records,
Vol. XLVIII, Pt. I, p. 523. Accounts of the campaign are
to be found in: XXVI, Pt. 1, pp. 232-238; XXXIV, Pt. 1, pp.
69-80.

129 Carleton to Brevet Major C. H. deForrest, Headquarters, District of New Mexico, November 17, 1866, ROI:,
LR by OIA, 1866.

130 Annual Message of Governor Henry Connelly,
December, 1865, SD, TP, NM, 1851-1872; Steck to CIA Dole,
May 20, 1864, RNMSIA, LR from CIA, 1864; Graves to Delgado,
January 5, 1866, RNMSIA, Miscellaneous Papers, 1866.

131 List of those killed by Navajos at El Rito,
1837-1880 in #196, "Ambrosio Pino et al vs. the United
States," Court of Private Land Claims.

132 "Depredaciones Indios Informe de Manuel García
J. P.," Precinct 9, Valencia County, February, 1866, in
RNMSIA, Miscellaneous Papers, 1866.

investigate the Navajo situation, reported to Commissioner
D. H. Cooley in 1866 that there were 6,447 Navajos at the
Bosque Redondo, and an estimated 1,200 still at large and
hostile.[133]

Navajo Economic Conditions Not Real Reason for
Attacks on Pueblos

Visitors to the Navajo country from the period of
United States occupation in August, 1846, until the removal
of the Indians to the Bosque Redondo, mention the extent and
quality of Navajo cultivation in the homeland region of the
valleys of the Tunicha and Chusca mountains, the San Juan
River and Cañon de Chelly, and note the size of Navajo herds.
These reports emphasize the fact that the Navajos, therefore,
did not raid the small, peaceful pueblos from economic
necessity, but from a love of adventure and rapine. As Dr.
George P. Hammond aptly noted in summarizing Navajo history
from the period of Spanish control to the late 19th century:

185

> The Navaho were ever prone to raid the Pueblos, to rob
> their crops, and to carry women and children into cap-
> tivity. This lasted until after the return of the tribe
> from their incarceration in the Bosque Redondo in 1867.[134]

---

[133] Graves to Cooley, in U. S. H. R., Exec. Doc.
No. 1, 40th Cong., 2nd Sess., 1866, p. 135.

[134] Frederick Webb Hodge, Agapito Rey and George
P. Hammond, eds., Fray Alonso de Benavides' Revised Memorial
of 1634, Vol. IV, p. 310.

In 1846, Charles Bent, first United States Governor
of New Mexico, gave the following report of the economic
status of the Navajos:

> The Navajoes are an industrious, intelligent, and war-
> like tribe of Indians who cultivate the soil and raise
> sufficient grains and fruit for their own consumption.
> They are the owners of large flocks and herds of cattle,
> sheep, horses, mules and asses. It is estimated that the
> tribe possesses 30,000 head of horned cattle, 500,000
> head of horses, mules and asses, it not being a rare
> instance for one individual to possess 5,000 to 10,000
> sheep, and 400 to 500 head of other stock. Their horses
> and sheep are said to be greatly superior to those raised
> by the New Mexicans. A large portion of their stock has
> been acquired by marauding expeditions against the
> settlements of this territory. 135

Superintendent James S. Calhoun, on the Washington
expedition of 1849, described the extensive cultivation by
the Navajos, remarking that they did not need to steal:

> The Navajoes commit their wrongs from a pure love of
> rapine and murder. They have extensive fields of corn
> and wheat - fine Peach orchards, and grow quantities of
> melons, Squashes, Beans and Peas, and have immense flocks
> of sheep, a great number of mules and horses of a super-
> ior breed; they have nothing of the cow kind. 136

On the same expedition, Lt. J. H. Simpson also noted that
in the Tunicha valley, "we passed along the route some very
extensive and luxuriant cornfields."[137]

Lt. Whipple noted in 1853: "Within the fertile valleys

---

[135] Paul A. F. Walter, "The First Civil Governor of
New Mexico," NMHR, VIII, pp. 112-113.

[136] Calhoun to Medill, October 1, 1849, Correspondence of Calhoun, p. 32; similar statement is Calhoun to
Medill, October 15, 1849, p. 55.

[137] Simpson Report, p. 53.

186

they cultivate wheat, corn and vegetables; and upon the grassy
plains graze numerous flocks and herds."[138]   Agent E. A. Graves
made a similar statement in a report to Commissioner Manypeny
on June 8, 1854:

> They possess more wealth than all the other wild tribes
> of New Mexico combined. . . . They raise, by the cultiva-
> tion of the soil, a sufficiency of grain for all purposes
> of consumption. . . . These Indians have an excellent
> country on the waters of the San Juan, and in and beyond
> the Cañon de Chille. 139

Governor David Meriwether in 1854 likewise noted that
the Navajos did not raid from economic necessity:

> The Navajo country is represented to be one of the finest
> agricultural regions within New Mexico. . . . With very
> rude and primitive implements of their own construction,
> the Navajos manage to raise an abundance of corn and wheat
> for their own subsistence. They have numerous herds of
> horses and sheep, and some horned cattle and mules, and,
> on the whole, live in a degree of comfort and plenty unknown
> to other wild Indians of this section of the Union. 140

As a result of his trip into Navajo country to sign the
treaty of 1855, Meriwether reported:

> . . . and this season [they] have almost five thousand
> acres of corn under cultivation, together with a small
> quantity of wheat, some potatoes, and other vegetables.
> They have a large number of sheep and horses, some mules
> and cattle, and are manufacturing blankets and other
> articles of clothing in increased quantities. 141

Governor Rencher noted much the same thing in a letter to
Secretary of State Lewis Cass on October 16, 1858:

187

---

138 Whipple Report, Vol. III, Pt. III, p. 13.

139 Graves to Manypeny, June 8, 1854, U. S. H. R.,
Exec. Doc. No. 2, 33rd Cong., 2nd Sess., 1854, p. 387.

140 Meriwether to Manypeny, September 1, 1854, U. S.
H. R., Exec. Doc. No. 2, 33rd Cong., 2nd Sess., 1854,
p. 380.

141 Meriwether to Manypeny, September 1, 1855, in
U. S. H. R., Exec. Doc. No. 1, 34th Cong., 1st Sess., 1855,
p. 507.

Except the Pueblo Indians the Navajoes are more advanced
in civilization than any of our Indian tribes. They cultivate the soil and have large flocks of horses, cattle
and sheep, the desire for gain, and often perhaps the
spirit of retaliation make them very troublesome to our
frontier settlements. 142

On May 7, 1859, Captain John Pope of the Army Topo-

graphical Corps wrote concerning the Navajoes:

They have places of permanent abode, own large herds of
sheep, horses & mules & cultivate extensive fields of
grain & fine orchards of fruit. 143

Alexander Baker, Agent at Fort Defiance, notified Superinten-

dent J. L. Collins in September of the same year:

Their herds of animals - horses, sheep and goats are
immense; some of their herds of horses contained four
and five hundred head of as fine animals as I ever saw. 144

Baker saw these herds on a trip from the San Juan to Cañon de

Chelly. He also described excellent fields of corn in the

Tunicha valleys.145

188

Commissioner of Indian Affairs, William P. Dole, wrote

the Secretary of the Interior in the fall of 1863, as the

campaign against the Navajos was starting:

They are represented as an ingenious and skilful people
in manufacturing blankets and other fabrics, in the cultivation of wheat and corn, and as being in all other
respects far in advance of all other tribes within the
Territory. 146

---

142 SD, TP, NM, 1851-1872.

143 Capt. John Pope, "A Military Memoir," Records of the
Office, Chief of Engineers, Topographical Engineers.
                            September 1, 1859
144 Baker to Collins, U. S. Sen., Exec. Doc. No. 2,
36th Cong., 1st Sess., 1859, p. 718.

145 Baker to Collins, August 8, 1859, RNMSIA, LR from
Agencies, 1859.

146 CIA report of October 31, 1863, U. S. H. R., Exec.
Doc., No. 1, 38th Cong., 1st Sess., 1863, p. 136.

In fact, it was more the destruction of Navajo fields
and orchards and the confiscation of livestock that enabled
Carson to subdue the Navajos in 1863-64 than actual combat.
Carson's dispatches, and those of other officers, constantly
speak of the amounts of crops destroyed and livestock captured. Captain Joseph P. Hargraves reported 1,500 sheep taken
on August 22, 1863;[147] Captain Rafael Chacón listed an additional 1,500 sheep captured on August 28;[148] men under Carson
captured 500 animals on November 25;[149] and Major Henry D.
Waller reported that his group had confiscated 9,859 sheep on
December 17.[150] However, Superintendent Steck estimated late
in the same month that the Navajos still "own many thousands
of horses and more than 500,000 sheep."[151]

This number was soon reduced as the campaign was carried
into the Cañon de Chelly in January, 1864. Corn crops were
destroyed and wheat fed to the army horses.[152] The Navajos
who surrendered or were captured and sent to the Bosque Redondo
were permitted to take some livestock with them. Captain

189

---

147 O. R., Ser. I, XXVI, Pt. 1, 259.

148 O. R., XXVI, Pt. 1, 258.

149 O. R., XXVI, Pt. 1, 256.

150 O. R., XXVI, Pt. 1, 260.

151 Steck to Dole, December 10, 1863, ROIA, NMS, LR
by OIA, 1863.

152 O. R., XXVI, Pt. 1, 232-238.

Francis McCabe wrote in his report of January 7, 1865, concerning the census which he had recently taken:

> They have for a long time bestowed great care in the breeding of sheep and were formerly owners of large flocks of these valuable animals, and the tables herewith show them as still owners of no inconsiderable numbers. 153

The tables referred to listed the reservation Indians as possessing 3,038 horses; 143 mules; 6,962 sheep; 2,757 goats.[154] This number diminished rapidly as Agent Theodore H. Dodd reported in June, 1867, that the Navajos had 550 horses; 20 mules; 940 sheep; and 1,025 goats, and asked that they be furnished additional sheep so that they could become self-sufficient.[155]

While few historians would care to defend the treatment of the Navajos at Bosque Redondo, their past activities would indicate that some punishment was merited.

Post Bosque Redondo

As time went on, it became clear that the Bosque Redondo reservation was no lasting solution to the Navajo problem. Navajos and Apaches were at constant swords-points, crops failed year after year, wood supplies were soon depleted, much of the livestock died and government subsistence was insufficient to keep the Indians clothed and fed. In September,

190

---

[153] O. R., XXVI, Pt. 1, 527.

[154] O. R., XXVI, Pt. 1, 523.

[155] Dodd to Norton, June 30, 1867, U. S. H. R., Exec. Doc. No. 1, Pt. 2, 40th Cong., 1st Sess., 1867, pp. 198-199.

1867   several of the chieftains, led by Barboncito, pleaded
with Major General George W. Getty and Supterintendent A. B.
Norton that they be permitted to return to their homes.[156]   On
November 1, 1867, the Navajos were transferred from the Army to
the Indian Department and Major Charles J. Whiting turned over
to Navajo Agent, Theodore H. Dodd, 7,111 Navajos.[157]   Although
Governor R. B. Mitchell was opposed to permitting the Indians
to leave the Bosque Redondo,[158] Indian officials favored the
transfer.[159]   In late May, 1868, General William T. Sherman
and Samuel F. Tappan were sent to the Bosque Redondo to investigate conditions and decide on future policies for the Navajos.   On May 28, the commissioners met with Barboncito, Delgadito, Manuelito and four lesser chieftains.   Barboncito and
his band had originally come from the Cañon de Chelly and
Chasca mountain area; Manuelito had lived north of the Ojo
del Oso; Delgadito and Armijo were from the Tunicha mountains,
all in the heart of the Navajo country.[160]

191

        Barboncito begged that his people be allowed to return

    [156] Norton to Commissioner Taylor, September 15, 1867,
RNMSIA, LR from CIA, 1867.

    [157] Statement of Whiting, Major 3rd U. S. Cavalry,
November 1, 1867, in RNMSIA, LR from Agencies, 1867.

    [158] SD, TP, NM, 1851-1872, Annual messages of December,
1867 and 1868.

    [159] Davis, Clerk and Acting Superintendent to Taylor,
February 18, 1868. The later superintendent, A. B. Norton, who
had died in January, also favored the transfer, RNMSIA, LS.

    [160] Norton to Taylor, September 15, 1867, RNMSIA,
Miscellaneous Papers, 1867. An unsigned memorandum in the
same collection also gives these locations of the bands.

to their homeland and promised that if permitted to do so,
his tribesmen would keep the peace and stay on their own
lands. Sherman agreed to permit the Navajos to return if the
Indians would agree to stay within their designated area and
not let the young men leave the reservation or steal, and
told the chieftains to gather together the entire tribe and
have them choose ten men to settle the reservation line. On
the 29th, the Navajos selected Barboncito as spokesman, as
well as Delgadito, Manuelito, Largo, Herrera, Armijo, Chiquito,
Muerte del Hombre, Hombro and Narbono. Cañada Mucho was
added the next day.

Sherman informed the Navajos that they must obey Barboncito when they returned to their homes, that they must keep
together on the way back and not scatter or drop out, and that
they must remain upon the reservation. Barboncito, speaking
for the tribe, requested that they be allowed to return by the
same route they had taken to the Bosque Redondo, back to Cañon
de Chelly, from which center he would then settle them

> between the San Mateo Mountains and San Juan River. I
> said yesterday this was the heart of the Navajo country.
> In this place there is a mountain called the Sierra
> Chusque [Chusca] or mountain of agriculture from which
> when it rains the water flows in abundance creating large
> sand bars on which the Navajos plant their corn; it is a
> fine country for stock or agriculture - there is another
> mountain called the Mesa Calabasa where these beads which
> we wear on our necks have been handed down from generation
> to generation, and where we were told by our forefathers
> never to leave our own country. 161

161 This and subsequent quotations of the treaty negotiations are to be found in the Papers of William T. Sherman, Vol.
23, 1868, Manuscript Division, Library of Congress, entitled,
"Proceedings of a Council between General W. T. Sherman and
Samuel F. Tappan, Commissioners on the part of the United States

The "Calabasa Mesa" lay north of the Hopi villages, but was
denied to the Navajos by Sherman. Barboncito thus clearly
indicated that the lands the Navajos claimed lay far to the
west and north of lands used and claimed by Acoma and Laguna.
The head chief, however, was not sure that one group of his
people could be depended upon to abide by the agreement, and
said:

> There is one family whose intention I do not know (the
> Saviettas) [Cebolletas]. I do not know whether or not
> they want to go back to their own country.

He thus indicated that only one family was involved in the
Cebolleta-Cubero-Laguna-Acoma area. Sherman answered:

> If the 'Saviettas' choose they can go and live among
> the Mexicans in this Territory, but if they do they
> will not be entitled to any of the advantages of the
> Treaty.

Barboncito, however, wanted no misunderstanding about this   193

group:

> I merely wished to mention it for if they remain with
> the Mexicans I cannot be held responsible for their
> conduct.

This oral statement given by Sherman in answer to
Barboncito's query about the Sandoval people is important in
view of the fact that no special provisions for them were
written into the subsequent treaty. Furthermore, groups of
Navajos did drop off in the Laguna-Acoma region, in spite of

---

and the chiefs and head-men of the Navajo Tribe of Indians,
held at the Reservation known as the Bosque Redondo, at Fort
Sumner in the Territory of New Mexico on the 28th day of
May, 29th day of May, and 30th day of May, 1868.

Sherman's warning that they were not to do so, and later
they claimed that they had a right to live in the area since
Sherman had specifically permitted them to do so. There is
no authority for this claim in the records of the proceedings
at Bosque Redondo, for the status of this band of Indians was
never mentioned again. Moreover, Navajo chieftains who turn
up periodically in the Cubero, Cebolleta and Cañoncito area,
and claimed and received annuity goods although they lived off
the reservation, signed the treaty of June 1, 1868, agreeing
to live on the new reservation as delimited, namely: on the
north by the 37th parallel north latitude; on the south by an
east and west line through the site of Fort Defiance; on the
east by the parallels of longitude which if projected south
would pass through old Fort Lyon on the Ojo del Oso (renamed

194

Fort Wingate later in the year); and on the west by the parallel of longitude of about 109° 30' west of Greenwich, but
including the Cañon de Chelly. Among the chiefs who signed
the treaty, but turned up in the Laguna area were: Delgadito,
for a brief time; Guero; and Chino. According to Article 13,
the Navajos as a tribe were not to settle elsewhere, and if
any left the reservation, they were to forfeit all rights and
privileges under the treaty.[162]

Violation of the terms of the treaty in the Laguna and
Acoma area began almost immediately. On June 15, 1868, the

---

[162] Kappler, Indian Affairs, Laws and Treaties, pp.
527-533.

Navajos began their trek back to the western homeland, but some
dropped out along the way.

A large number of the Navajos, under the chief Delgadito, of the old Sandoval tribe, have taken up their
residence near Cubero and Cebolleta, their former home.
This faction numbers over four hundred. The people complain in that section of many recent losses of stock, and
charge the Indians with being the perpetrators of the
thefts. 163

Both Laguna and Acoma informants relate various episodes of
individual Navajos stopping briefly at Paquate and Acoma, and
because of their destitute condition, asking for work, or
exchanging bundles of firewood, which they had gathered, for
food. In these cases, the pueblos took pity on the stragglers
and fed them, and these Navajos stayed around the pueblo
villages for a short time. After a few months, however,
large numbers attempted to come into the region in spite of
the treaty.

195

When the Navajos returned to their homeland, old Fort
Defiance was made into the Navajo Agency and Fort Lyon [Canby] on the
Ojo del Oso was reactivated as new Fort Wingate for control of
the Indians. The Navajos were subject to the agent, but the
military was responsible for rounding up those who wandered off
the reservation.

Veteran Indian Agent, John Ward, formerly friendly to
Sandoval, was requested to submit a report on Navajo history
and background and make recommendations for Navajo control

---

163 The Santa Fe New Mexican, August 10, 1868. Dodd
Weber, Fort Wingate, August 5, 1868, stated that from 700 to
1,000 Navajos failed to show up at Fort Defiance and were
running at large, U. S. H. R., Exec. Doc. No. 1, 40th Cong.,
3rd Sess., 1868, p. 623.

to the Indian Peace Commission headed by Sherman and Tappan.
After long experience with the Navajos, Ward proposed that
the best way to keep the peace would be to ring the Navajo
country with a series of forts to keep the Navajos within the
land agreed upon in the treaty and whites out of the region.
Ward strongly recommended that one of these forts should be at
the settlement of San Mateo west of Mount Taylor to keep the
Navajos out of the pueblo area.[164]

Complaints against the Navajos refusing to abide by the
treaty soon came from the Acoma-Laguna region. On February 1,
1869, Superintendent J. M. Gallegos wrote to Navajo Agent, J.
Carey French:

> I understand from citizens of Bernalillo and Valencia
> Counties, that there are a number of Navajos, who belong
> to your agency, who have settled at or near the town of
> Cubero. You will at once take the necessary action to
> have these Indians placed on the reservation. 165

Apparently, by this time, Navajos other than the family
mentioned by Barboncito to Sherman at Bosque Redondo as not
wanting to return to the homeland were attempting to live where
they pleased, regardless of having signed the treaty, and
were trying to convince the agent that Sherman had actually
given them permission to do so, for Agent French answered
Gallegos on March 26:

196

---

[164] Ward to Tappan, August 4, 1868, ROIA, NMS, LR
by OIA.

[165] RNMSIA, LS, Gallegos to French, February 1, 1869.

I understand that when Genl. Sherman was out here he told
many of them that they might live off the reservation and
around the settlements. One chief called Peno with a
band of 140 has written to reside at Cubero – another at
Cebolleta with his band. I have called them in. Peno
came with his people and I have located him on lands near
the Agency where he is now prepairing [sic] to plant. 166

Although French seemed to have believed the Indians, he
obviously did not feel that he had the authority to permit
these groups to live off the reservation.

Throughout the spring, the superintendent continued to
notify the commander at Fort Wingate, and the agents, to keep
the Navajos on the reservation as depredations continued to
be committed.[167] Some joined the Apaches. In July, Navajo
Agent French reported that he had recovered a stolen mule
from a reservation Navajo who said that he had bought it "from
a party of Navajos and Apaches who live together south of
Acoma."[168]

Both the Superintendent of Indian Affairs and the military authorities in 1868 clearly interpreted the treaty to
mean that all Navajos, with the exception of a very small
group using some land around new Fort Wingate, were bound by
the treaty to remain on the reservation. Acting Assistant

197

---

166 French to Gallegos, March 26, 1869, RNMSIA, LR from
Navajo Agency, 1869.

167 Gallegos to French, March 2, 1869; Catanach to Ward,
March 4, 1869, RNMSIA, LS.

168 French to Gallegos, July 10, 1869, ROIA, NMS, LR
by OIA.

Adjutant General William A. Kobbe notified Lieutenant Col-

onel V. K. Evans at Wingate on July 14:

> to strictly enforce its provisions [general orders pre-
> viously sent] and instructions as far as the Navajo tribe
> of Indians are concerned.
> All Navajoes found outside the well defined limits of
> their reservation "unless accompanied by a military
> guard" will be considered as hostile as authorized in
> Par. 3 of the order . . . The above instructions are
> not intended to apply at present to those Navajoes who
> are cultivating land on the Military Reservation at
> Fort Wingate. 169

On August 2, 1869, Governor Mitchell issued a proclam-

ation declaring that all Navajos and Apaches off the reser-

vation, unless accompanied by soldiers, to be outlaws and

authorized New Mexico citizens to use force when necessary

to protect their property.[170] Both military and Indian

officials opposed this step,[171] and it was modified by Gov-

198 ernor William A. Pile on September 15, when he replaced

Mitchell.[172] Pueblo Agent Charles S. Cooper was particularly

aroused because many of the depredations were upon the

pueblos, and notified Superintendent William Clinton on

August 31, 1869:

---

169 Kobbe to Evans, July 14, RNMSIA, LR from Headquarters, District of New Mexico (U. S. Army), 1869.

170 SD, TP, NM, 1851-1872

171 Parker to Clinton, August 14, 1869, RNMSIA, LR
from CIA, 1869.

172 SD, TP, NM, 1851-1872.

A few months ago the Navajoe Indians made a dash on one or two Pueblos and carried off twenty-one (21) horses. Such depredations are of frequent occurrence lately, and so according to the proclamation by the President and also one by Governor Mitchell of this Territory, calling upon all good citizens to defend themselves against the Navajoes, I have given the Pueblo Indians permission to defend themselves against the Navajoes, in case they are again molested, and in all cases to endeavor to defend or recover their stock. 173

In another letter to Clinton on September 8, Cooper made a caustic comparison of the treatment of the peaceful pueblos then suffering from white encroachment as well as Navajo depredations.

These are the most honest, peaceable, kind-hearted, industrious and christianized Indians upon the continent, but as they say they have received nothing. If they were a warlike people fighting against the government, they would receive presents of every kind; as they remain at home, however, endeavoring to obey the laws, etc. they are forgotten. 174

In spite of officers and the pueblo agent, however, the Navajos continued to stay off the reservation. In his annual report of 1869 to Secretary of the Interior J. D. Cox, Commissioner E. S. Parker estimated that there were "about two thousand [Navajos] living with other tribes or roaming at large."175   In September, Navajo Agent F. T. Bennett, who replaced French during the summer, reported that

199

---

173 Cooper to Clinton, August 31, 1869, RNMSIA, LR from Pueblo Special Agency, 1869.

174 Cooper to Clinton, September 8, 1869, RNMSIA, LR from Pueblo Special Agency, 1869.

175U. S. H. R., Exec. Doc. No. 1, 41st Cong., 2nd Sess., 1869, p. 464.

Cubero citizens had killed two Navajos who had settled west of Cubero, apparently in about the same site on the Rito of San José where the struggle with Laguna had taken place in 1850 and 1851. The Cubero residents had lured the Navajos some distance east to the Cañada de Pedro Padilla, about seven miles northeast of the Laguna village of Paquate, killed them, stole their stock and then drove some fourteen other Navajos from the San José site and appropriated their property.[176] Although Bennett was justifiably incensed at this treatment of the Navajos and quite properly wanted action against the Cubero residents, he did not seem to realize that both the Navajos and the Cuberos were trespassing on lands, the lower part of which belonged to the Pueblo of Acoma and the upper portion to the Pueblo of Laguna.

200

Guero, the principal leader of the group in the Cubero-Laguna-Cebolleta area, like his predecessor, Sandoval, moved in and out of the region. Late in 1869, he was back in the reservation country, according to Agent Bennett:

> From opinions I hear expressed by those living down about the Mexican settlements and those living with other Indians (some of whom have not been living with the Navajo nation for the last ten or twelve years) I am of the opinion that before the time for commencing planting arrives, great numbers will move into the

---

[176] Bennett to Clinton, September 9, 1869, RNMSIA, LR from Navajo Agency, 1869, says the dispossessed Navajos had appealed to Delgadito, now back in his own land, and that Delgadito had appealed to the agent. See also: Evans to Kobbe, January 20, 1869, in LR from Headquarters, 1869.

agency and will want to be assigned to homes on the reservation. I have an instance of one chief "Juero" who has been living in the vicinity of Cabelletta [sic] who has just moved here with his band (numbering about 120) and intends farming here next summer. It is my intention to offer every inducement in my power to have all Navajos move onto the Reservation and live. 177

Depredations began anew in 1870. In February, Navajos raided Acoma and stole several horses and cattle. Major A. W. Evans at Fort Wingate, to whom the Acomas appealed for assistance, notified Agent Bennett at Fort Defiance of the theft and requested action. Bennett answered that the horses had been recovered, but that the cattle had been killed and eaten, and the Acomas should prepare an affidavit of their loss for investigation; then reimbursement could be made from Navajo tribal funds.[178] Evans was irritated at the treatment of Acoma, reminding the agent that the pueblo Indians knew nothing about preparing affidavits, and again requested reimbursement from the Navajo herds.[179] The records do not reveal that any action was taken. As Major Evans said in reporting the matter to Pueblo Agent, Charles S. Cooper:

201

Of course the Acoma people want restitution rather than revenge; and I need hardly say to you to whom I now beg leave to refer this matter, that a more quiet, honest, and deserving people does not live in New Mexico. 180

---

177 Bennett to Clinton, December 30, 1869, ROIA, LR by OIA.

178 Bennett to Evans, February 9; Bennett to Clinton, February 1, 1870, RNMSIA, LR from Navajo Agency, 1870.

179 Evans to Bennett, February 10; Bennett to Evans, February 14, 1870, RNMSIA, LR from Navajo Agency.

180 Evans to Cooper, February 10, 1870, RNMSIA, LR from Abiquiu Agency, 1870.

Ironically enough, before the year was out, an Acoma
Indian was accused by Barboncito of stealing two horses, but
the treatment of the culprit was far different, for the Acoma
governor, on being informed, immediately took from the thief
the goods which he had received for selling the horses at Los
Lunas. The governor then notified Barboncito that he could
either have the confiscated goods or that Acoma would recover
the horses. A military detail was sent from Fort Wingate to
bring back the articles, but three members of the detail
deserted, taking the goods with them.[181]

Guero soon moved back into the Cebolleta region,
accompanied by his band, and when challenged, this group again
used Sherman's statement early in the Bosque Redondo proceedings, but never incorporated into the 1868 treaty, that
the "Cebolleta family" could remain in the settlements. This
band, 160 in number, according to Superintendent Clinton,
both expected to live off the reservation and receive treaty
advantages as well. Clinton reported their actions to Commissioner Parker on March 31, 1870, as follows:

> I have the honor to report for the information and
> action of the Hon. Com. that a party of Navajoes [sic]
> Indians known as Guero's Band called at this Superinten-
> dency yesterday for the purpose of having a talk with me
> and getting my advice as to their future course.
> This Band resides at or near Cebolleta and are Chris-
> tians. They say that they have always resided there,

202

---

[181] Bennett to Pope, January 1, 1871, RNMSIA, LR from
Navajo Agency, 1871.

that most of them have been born there, and that they do
not wish to go on the reservation, with the other Navajoes. They give as a reason that they are not now, nor
never have been on good terms with other bands of their
tribe, owing to the fact that they had been raised amongst
the Mexicans, and being Christians they have taken part
with the Mexicans, when disputes occurred between them
and the Navajoes.

This band numbers about 160 souls, and support themselves by farming. They say that they have received
nothing from their agent, neither sheep, goats, seeds,
nor implements, all of which they stand very much in need.

These Indians have impressed me very favorably as they
are very reasonable in their demands, or rather requests.

They say that if the government will only give them
tools such as hoes, spades, axes etc. and the Lord will
only give them good crops they will try to supply their
other wants themselves. 182

These statements by the Navajos bear some examination.
That some of them had been in the Cebolleta area was possible,
since Sandoval had been permitted to come into the region in
1850 or 1851, and his band had moved in and out of the area.
Census reports for 1850 and 1860, however, do not reveal
their presence in Valencia County. The reasons for the hostility towards them because of their friendship with the
whites had been true since Sandoval had guided the troops
and raided his own people for captives. Neither of these
claims, however, indicated any right to be in the region or
any continuous occupation.

The statement that they were Christians is most interesting. If this were true, the question arises, where were
the records of their baptisms, marriages and burials. Church

203

----

182 Clinton to Parker, March 31, 1870, RNMSIA, LS.

records do not bear out the Navajo claim. Baptismal records are relatively complete for Laguna and Cebolleta for the years 1846 -1890, and record a few scattered instances of Navajo baptism, only, usually of small children. In every instance these baptized had either white or pueblo Indian godparents, indicating that they were undoubtedly captives. In 1847, a five-year-old child and a twenty-nine year old Navajo were baptized at Laguna. A Navajo child was baptized in the chapel at Paquate on March 15, 1851. and another at Laguna, May 3 of the same year. On July 25, 1853, a three-year-old Navajo "of the house of Jesus Apodaca" was baptized at Laguna. On November 10, 1858, the "infidel Navajo Leonardo" was baptized at Laguna. On April 18 and June 19, 1860, Don Marcos Baca and his wife of Cubero were godparents to small Navajo children baptized at Laguna. A fifty-year-old Navajo and the eleven-year old son of Gañada Negra were baptized at Cebolleta in 1887.[183] These few instances would indicate that there were few Christian Navajos in the region over a period of forty years.

204

Commissioner Parker was reluctant to permit the band to live off the reservation and still collect goods.

It is not known by this office whether the Indians in question are or are not parties to the treaty made with

---

[183] Church records for these years are in the Diocese of Gallup, Cathedral of the Sacred Heart, Gallup, New Mexico.

the Navajoes in 1868. If they are, they should go to the
reservation provided for them in said treaty; and if they
are not, they cannot claim any rights or privileges under
the treaty without joining their brethern at their new
home. 184

In responding on May 5, 1870, Clinton admitted that
Guero had signed the treaty, but apparently misled by the
statements or Guero and influenced by white traders of
Cebolleta, who wanted the Navajos to remain in the region, the
superintendent replied that Sherman had given them permission
to live in the area, [185] and to support his request that Guero
and the others be given goods, he enclosed letters from
Simon Bibo and José Gonzales praising these Indians. [186] Both
Bibo and Gonzales were traders at Cebolleta. If the Navajos
stayed nearby, they would be customers for the purchase of
supplies and furnishing of blankets for sale.

205

Commissioner Parker reluctantly gave his provisional
permission that some supplies be given Guero's band, but made
it clear that the Navajos were not entitled to them nor were
they given permission to live off the reservation:

> You will advise the Indians when the issue is made,
> that these implements, etc. are given to them as a gra-
> tuity by the government and not in accordance with the
> terms of the treaty made with the United States in 1868;
> also, that they are not entitled to any of the benefits
> to be derived under the treaty, unless they go to the
> reservation therein set apart for their occupancy. 187

---

184 Parker to Clinton, April 15, 1870, RNMSIA, LR from
CIA, 1870.

185 Clinton to Parker, May 11, 1870, RNMSIA, LS.

186 Bibo and Gonzales to Clinton, May 11, 1870, RNMSIA,
LR from Headquarters, District of New Mexico (U. S. Army),
1870.

187 RNMSIA, LR from CIA, 1870, Parker to Clinton,
May 28, 1870.

On June 6, 1870, Clinton informed the Navajos through trader
Gonzales that their supplies had arrived,[188] and Nathan Bibo,
brother of the Cebolleta trader, stated that he was selected
by Clinton to distribute the supplies.[189]

Special Agent W. F. M. Arny, sent out by Clinton in
June, 1870, to make an investigation of the pueblos as well
as the Navajos and to take a comprehensive census of all
Indians, noted one activity of these Navajos in the Laguna
area which was not so peaceful:

> The Navajos at Cubero and Sebbittita [sic] who are off
> their reservation made a campaign against the Coyotero
> Apaches, destroyed a ranche and brought away 11 children
> whom they refuve to give up. 190

A raid near Los Lunas in December, 1870, was also the
work of this group. The attack was reported to Superintendent Nathaniel Pope, who had replaced Clinton in the fall,
by Beneceslado Luna, Probate Judge of Valencia County, on
December 25.[191] Special Agent J. A. Manley, sent to investigate the situation, stated on March 10, 1871, that the
culprits lived "mostly about Cubero and Sevietta [sic] to

206

---

188 RNMSIA, LS, Clinton to Gonzales, June 22, 1870.

189 Bibo, The Albuquerque Evening Herald, June 11,
1922, says he was appointed sub-agent, but no record of such
appointment has come to light.

190 In Arny's Journal, ROIA, NMS, LR by OIA, 1870,
entry made October 8, while Arny was taking the Laguna census
at El Rito.

191 Luna to Pope, December 25, 1870, RNMSIA, LR from
Headquarters, District of N. M. (U. S. Army), 1870.

which places they migrate every spring from the Reservation after being fed over winter."[192]

    Some of those Navajos involved in this raid seem to have been held in servitude by residents of Cubero and Cebolleta.[193] This factor of servitude also explains the presence of some Navajos in the area both before and after Bosque Redondo, dating back into the Spanish period. It had long been the practice for New Mexicans to use captured Navajos as domestics. The custom was for a bride to be presented with a Navajo serving girl about her own age.[194] By coincidence, both the young wife and the Navajo servant often bore their first child at about the same time, and frequently the half-breed children of the Navajo union were allowed by their Spanish fathers to live on small tracts of land, even though the land belonged to the pueblo Indians. A "Francisco Baca, Navajo," from whom the Cubero residents originally purchased land in 1832, was probably one of these and was closely related to the descendants of the Baca family, members of whom were alcaldes of Laguna in the late 18th and first half of the 19th centuries.

207

---

[192] Manley to Pope, March 10, 1871, RNMSIA, LR from Abiquiu Agency, 1871.

[193] Parker to Pope, January 28, 1871; RNMSIA, LR from CIA, 1871; Manley to Pope, March 23, 1871, LR from Abiquiu Agency, 1871; Pope to Manley, January 16, 1871, RNMSIA, LS.

[194] Twitchell, Leading Facts, Vol. II, pp. 303-304, note 228.

Acoma informants relate that a half-Navajo who lived
in the disputed San José region west of Cubero on Acoma and
Laguna lands before Bosque Redondo was "Dimas" Pino, son of
Pablo Pino of Cubero. According to official census reports
of 1860-1880, Pablo Pino of Cubero had a Navajo servant,
Guadalupe, the same age as his wife, Petra.

The sale of captive members of his own people, as
shown before, was one of the reasons for Sandoval's unpopularity with the rest of the Navajes. Cebolleta and Cubero
were centers for the trade in captives throughout the 19th
century. At Cebolleta, in the period before Bosque Redondo,
there was a group of young men who called themselves the
"Cebolleteños," or "Seboyetaños," whose chief occupation was
to raid the Navajo country to fill orders for particular types
of servants desired by purchasers.[195] A descendant of one of
this band has written:

> If the captives were of average age, or young and could
> be domesticated and taught, then their capture bore
> rich fruit. 196

In describing this trade, Superintendent Michael Steck wrote
to Commissioner William P. Dole in 1864:

> They are usually adopted into the family, baptized and
> brought up in the Catholic faith, and given the name of
> the owner's family, generally become faithful and trust-
> worthy servants, and sometimes are married to native New
> Mexicans. 197

208

---

[195] Twitchell, Leading Facts, II, pp. 303-304, note 228.

[196] C. C. Marin, "The Seboyetanos and the Navahos,"
Reeve and Duncan, eds., NMHR, XXIX (January, 1954), p. 11.

[197] Steck to Dole, January 13, ROIA, NMS, LR By OIA, 1864.

None of the official United States census reports
from 1860 to 1890 listed Navajos living in Valencia County,
except those who were servants, thereby seeming to indicate
that at the time the censuses were taken, at least, no groups
were residing in the region. The census of 1850 listed two
Navajo servants at the village of Moquino near Cebolleta; that
of 1860 listed many in both Cebolleta and Cubero. On May 16,
1862, William Need, a soldier who frequently reported on
Indian affairs in New Mexico, told Superintendent Collins
that one of the reasons for depredations was that white raiding
parties from the Rio Grande and Cebolleta had been kidnapping
and selling Navajos in Cubero.[198] Nathan Bibo, white trader
in the area during the late 1860's and 1870's, in discussing
the successes of Román A. Baca of Cebolleta, who had led a
company of volunteers against the Navajos in the 1862-63 campaign, stated that the reason for frequent victories was due
to the fact that:

209

> They became familiar with the country and the Indian
> hiding places and they took hundreds of prisoners, who,
> as was the custom in those early days, were sold as
> domestics all over the territory, sometimes at very high
> prices. [199]

Although Congress passed a law prohibiting peonage in New
Mexico, March 2, 1867, and Governor Mitchell on April 14,

---

[198] Need to Collins, RNMSIA, Miscellaneous Correspondence and Accounting Papers, 1862.

[199] Bibo, The Albuquerque Evening Herald, June 11, 1922.

issued a proclamation declaring the practice ended, some Navajos continued to be held as captives. Superintendent Norton, on November 10, 1867, ordered that Navajo children held as captives at Cubero be released.[200] On January 14, 1870, several chieftains asked Superintendent Clinton to have their people returned to them.[201] The 1870 census, however, revealed fourteen Indian servants at Cubero and thirteen at Cebolleta. In 1880, there were still nine at Cebolleta and the Navajo servant of Pablo Pino at Cubero.

Throughout 1871 and 1872, James H. Miller, Agent at Fort Defiance who replaced Bennett in February, 1871, attempted to persuade the Navajos in the Cebolleta-Cubero area to return to the reservation, for as he stated:

210

> I am of the opinion that it would be a good thing for the tribe to move them as nearly all of the stealing is done by those outside, and blamed on those who are on the reservation. [202]

Agent Miller and other authorities had little success in returning the Navajos from the Laguna region to the reservation at that time, and depredations continued. On March 9, 1872, Guero and twenty-four others from his band again appealed to Superintendent Pope and again put forth the old allegation that Sherman had expressly given them permission

---

[200] RNMSIA, LS, 1867.

[201] Clinton to Parker, January 18, 1870, RNMSIA, LS.

[202] Miller to Pope, December 11, 1871, RNMSIA, LR from Navajo Agency, 1871. A similar statement was expressed to Pope in a letter of April 5, 1871.

to live off the reservation. The members of the "Cebolleta
family" had certainly increased from Bosque Redondo days.
Whereas there were 160 who claimed the right in 1870, Guero
now reported 215 who should be allowed to remain, and stated:

> That they were contented with their present location and
> lived on good terms with the Mexicans and they requested
> me to take the necessary steps to secure lands for their
> use, and to furnish seeds - implements - clothing that
> they might be able to take care of themselves. 203.

Pope, however, realized that Guero was not entitled to land,
but asked the Commissioner of Indian Affairs that he and his
band be given provisions and allowed to remain temporarily:

> I informed them that in view of the existing treaty
> with the Navajos, no land could be awarded to them out-
> side of the reservation; that if they were acting in
> good faith and would pledge themselves to prevent the
> young men from stealing I would state their case to the
> Hon. Commr. and ask that they be furnished with limited
> quantities of seeds - agricultural implements - plants -
> clothing etc and that they be permitted to remain where
> they are for the present.
> During the Navajo war these Indians served the govern-
> ment faithfully and fought with the U. S. troops against
> the Navajo tribe;which is another reason for their
> reluctance to live on the Reservation. As yet I have
> heard no complaint against this portion of the tribe,
> and therefore recommend the favorable consideration of
> their case. The season is advancing and if the Depart-
> ment decided favorably I request that I be authorized by
> telegraph to make the necessary provision for them. 204

211

The statement that "As yet I have heard no complaint against
this portion of the tribe" is difficult to understand in view
of the many past complaints against Guero's band. Before

---

203 Pope to Voller, CIA, March 9, 1872, RNMSIA, LS.
204 Pope to Voller, March 9, 1872, RNMSIA, LS.

the year was over, there were others. On September 18,
Agent A. J. Curtis of the Mescalero Apaches reported the
theft of stock by Navajo marauders.[205] Special Agent at
Fort Defiance, Thomas V. Keams, reported to Pope of the
depredations near Fort Stanton:

> I would state that nearly all of these thefts, were
> committed by Indians living in the Mexican and Pueblo
> Indian settlements, but being Navajoes, they sometimes
> drive the stock on to the reservation, and the blame is
> attached to the whole tribe. [206]

This was an all too frequent tactic of Guero's band. A few
days later, Keams again reported to Pope that the Navajos
responsible lived near Cubero, but had brought the stolen
stock into the reservation where it had been recovered.[207]

Late in May, 1872, traveler J. H. Beadle and his party
stopped at El Rito en route to Fort Defiance and while there
met a delegation of Laguna Indians who had come "to complain
of the Navajos who had been stealing their stock."[208]

During 1873, more complaints, especially by the
Lagunas, against the Navajos in the Cubero-Cebolleta area
increased. Navajo Agent W. F. M. Arny at Fort Defiance was
aware of the activities of this group of his charges and,
like several of his predecessors, attempted to persuade the

212

---

[205] Curtis to Pope, September 18, 1872, RNMSIA, LR
from Mescalero Agency, 1872.

[206] Keams to Pope, September 1, 1872, RNMSIA, LR
from Navajo Agency, 1872.

[207] Keams to Pope, September 7, RNMSIA, LR from
Navajo Agency, 1872.

[208] Beadle, The Undeveloped West ..., p. 498; Beadle,
Western Wilds, p. 240.

Superintendent of Indian Affairs at Santa Fe, now Colonel
L. Edwin Dudley, to enforce treaty obligations on the Navajos and stop their encroachment. On November 4, 1873, he
wrote Dudley:

> At Cubero-Cebollita [sic] and other places in New
> Mexico there are several hundred Navajoes who never come
> to this reservation except to get their annuity goods.
> I have sent several messengers to them to come here but
> they decline doing so. They are a pest to the settle-
> ments and aid Navajoes and other Indians to information
> in regard to stock that can be stolen, and in many cases
> steal stock themselves which they trade and exchange to
> the pueblos, Mexicans Utes and Southern Apaches and
> thus give more trouble to this whole region of country.
> At the same time they have heretofore managed to find
> out when the issues are to [be] made. They then come,
> draw annuity goods, and return to Valencia County New
> Mexico, and as it is difficult for the agent to distin-
> guish them when mixed up with several thousand Indians,
> they have heretofore been supplied the same as those who
> are living on the reservation in compliance with the
> treaty. I will use every endeavor to get them here and
> give nothing to those who refuse to come. "Delgadito"
> who formerly lived with them informs me that they still
> refuse to come here to live. I will see him to distin-
> guish them if possible, and as soon as I can know the
> result of my present effort to get them on the reserva-
> tion I will report more fully. 209

213

Arny was particularly displeased with the Navajos
living in the Cubero-Cebolleta region without right, because
Pueblo Agent Edwin C. Lewis had notified him on September 15,
1873, that the Navajos were continuing to trespass on Laguna
crops near the village of Paquate. Lewis had written:

> Laguna Indians cultivating lands at Pojuate complain
> that the Navajoes at that place trespass upon their
> fields, and allow stock to injure their crops.

---

209 Arny to Dudley, November 4, 1873, RNMSIA, LR
from Navajo Agency, 1873.

I would respectfully ask that measures be taken to
prevent these outrages, and remunerate the Laguna Indians
for damages already sustained by them. 210

In transmitting Lewis' letter to Superintendent Dudley

Arny wrote on November 11:

I have the honor herewith to enclose a copy of letter
from Agent Lewis in regard to Navajoes who are trespassing upon Laguna Pueblo Indians; the Navajoes complained of are the same of whom I allude in my communication dated Nov 4th as living off the reservation and
in the neighborhood of Cubero, Cíbollito [sic] etc. and
they have invariably refused to live in this reservation.
They evidently come under the head of such Indians as
are contemplated in the circular of the Hon Commissionr
of Indian Affairs dated June 12[,] 1869, and October 21st
1873, and in my judgement should be placed in charge of
the Military in conformity with such circulars, and
should be compelled to move on to this reservation in
conformity with the treaty of 1868. I have done all I
can with the assistance of Chief Delgadito and other
Indians to induce them to locate here but they still
refuse, and I respectfully refer the matter to you with
the request that you will instruct me in regard thereto. 211

214 Superintendent Dudley, however, was reluctant to use force

to make these Indians live up to their treaty obligations

and wrote to Commissioner of Indian Affairs, Edward P. Smith:

I do not believe it wise to call upon troops to com-
pel the return of the Navajos who live in the vicinity
of Lagunia [sic], at least until some attempt has been
made to ensure their return by peaceable means. 212

Early in 1874, however, Guero was back on the

---

210 Lewis to Arny, September 15, 1873, RNMSIA, LR from
Navajo Agency, 1873.

211 Arny to Dudley, November 11, 1873, RNMSIA, LR
from Navajo Agency, 1873.

212 Dudley to Smith, December 11, 1873, ROIA, LR by
OIA, 1873.

reservation. The Navajos were then petitioning for an
enlargement of their boundaries. At a council meeting of
February 11, they authorized their chiefs to sign the petition for increasing the limits, and at this meeting, Navajo
Agent, W. F. M. Arny made it clear that there was no provision in the treaty of 1868 and no authorization from General
Sherman for them to live off the reservation. The chiefs,
among them Guero, signed the petition and agreed to remain on
the reservation if it were increased. In transmitting the
petition and a letter from the chiefs asking for permission
to visit Washington, Arny wrote to Commissioner Smith that the

> letter and petition were adopted and signed in full
> Council of the Indians living on this reservation and
> other Navajo Indians who have heretofore lived off the
> reservation all of whom in Council held on the 11th
> instant authorized the chiefs to sign the same, and as
> they also request me to explain to you the reason why
> they should visit Washington I will do so as briefly
> as possible.
> The Navajoes claim that General Sherman at the making
> of the treaty in 1868 gave permission to certain Indians
> to live off the reservation. And this claimed privilege
> has been a source of constant trouble ever since that
> treaty was made, I have told the Indians that no such
> provision is in the treaty and that they misunderstood
> General Sherman, and I have called their attention to
> Article 13 of the treaty and had it fully and clearly
> translated to them, and they now consent to discontinue
> to roam off the reservation and in the settlements pro-
> vided an addition is made to their reservation in the
> south in exchange for which they propose to give the
> north portion of their reserve which includes the San
> Juan river country, and for this purpose they desire that
> a delegation should go to Washington.
> Until within six months they have never had their
> treaty fully explained to them. . . 213

215

---

213 Arny to Smith, February 18, 1874, ROIA, NMS, LR
by OIA.

In May of 1874, however, Guero's group again raided the Southern Apache reservation.[214] Arny promised Apache Agent B. M. Thomas to do what he could, but admitted that he had little success in controlling these Indians:

> Huero and the party who visited your place are Indians who claim that they have permission of Genl. Sherman to live off the reservation and I cannot control them. I have been some time making efforts to have them compelled to come to the reservation but have so far failed. Next week I expect to visit the region where they live (which you know is over a hundred miles from here) and will do all I can to find out about the stolen horses, and have them returned. 215

Guero apparently soon gave up the struggle to remain in the Cebolletta-Cubero-Laguna area and returned to the reservation. On October 27. 1874, with other chieftains, he signed another request for a Navajo delegation to visit Washington,[216] as well as a petition against Arny as Agent on May 5, 1875.[217]

216

Cañoncito Navajos

Meanwhile, two Navajos in 1869, and seventeen others from 1870 to 1881, wandered into the rugged Cañoncito region wast of the Laguna Paquate tract, settled, and later

---

[214] Thomas to Arny, RNMSIA, LR from Navajo Agency, May 30, 1874.

[215] Arny to Thomas, June 18, 1874, RNMSIA, LR from Navajo Agency, 1874.

[216] In ROIA, NMS, LR by OIA, 1874.

[217] In ROIA, NMS, LR by OIA, 1875.

homesteaded, lands over which the Lagunas had grazed for many
years. The only mention of Navajos, except for raiding parties, in the Cañoncito prior to Bosque Redondo, was the November 15, 1858 letter of Superintendent J. L. Collins to
Commissioner J. W. Denver that he had permitted Sandoval to
move his band temporarily "within thirty miles of Albuquerque."
This was possibly the eastern edge of the Cañoncito, but the
Navajos remained there for only a short time. As noted
before, the Sandoval band was incarcerated at Bosque Redondo
in 1863. Some Navajos dropped off in the Cubero-Cebolleta-
Laguna-Acoma region on the return from exile in 1868. Laguna
and Acoma informants relate how these Navajos asked for food,
sold firewood or worked for the pueblo Indians briefly. After
1869, Guero and the remnants of the Sandoval group moved in
and out of the area. Lagunas also state that a Navajo who
dropped out in their vicinity lived for a few months north
of the Baca holdings in the Paquate, and then moved over into
the Cañoncito (see Ellis report).

According to homestead entries in the U. S. General
Land Office, Juan Padilla and José Castillo settled in Township 10 north, Range 3 west, in 1869. Apparently, the latter
was the same Castillo mentioned by traders Bibo and Gonzales
as being near Cebolleta in 1870. Some ten other Navajos
settled in the same township and range in 1870 and 1871.
Seven more joined them from 1875 to 1881. These nineteen, in
1886, filed under the Indian Homestead Act of July 4, 1884

217

for lands in Township 10 north, Range 3 west. Patents were
later issued to at least ten of them. This was undoubtedly
the beginning of Navajo occupation of the region which was
later made into the Cañoncito reservation. The twelve who
claimed they had settled in 1869-1871 gave the village of
San Mateo as their post office, while the seven who claimed
that they had settled in 1875-1881 listed Albuquerque as
their post office. The homestead entries are as follows:[218]

Name	Location T10N, R3W	Date Settled	Date Filed	Later History
Juan Padilla	W½SE¼ Sec.25 W½NE¼ Sec. 36	1869	1886	no patent
José Castillo	S½NW¼ Sec.3 S½NE¼ Sec.3	1869	1886	patent 1905
Vicente Castillo	SW¼NE¼ Sec.10 NW¼NE¼ Sec.15	1870	1886	no patent
Vicente Chaves	N½NE¼ Sec.3 N½NW¼ Sec.3	1871	1886	patent 1905
Julian Chaves	E½SW¼ Sec.11 NE¼NW¼ Sec.14	1871	1886	patent 1905
José Chaves	S½NE¼ Sec.22	1871	1886	cancelled 1889
Gregorio Cordova	NE¼NE¼ Sec.15 E½SE¼ Sec.10	1871	1886	patent 1905
José Chenchor	E½SE¼ Sec.26 E½NE¼ Sec.35	1871	1886	no patent
Delgadito	E½SW¼ Sec.26 E½NW¼ Sec.35	1871	1886	patent 1905

218

---

[218] This and subsequent information concerning home-
steads is taken from U. S. General Land Office, Register of
Homestead Entries, Santa Fe, N. M.

Name	Location T10N, R3W	Date Settled	Date Filed	Later History
Julian Picado	W½SW¼ Sec.11 NW¼NW¼ Sec.14	1871	1886	no patent
José Turnino	N½NW¼ Sec.10 N½NE¼ Sec.10	1871	1886	cancelled 1893
José Antonio	W½NW¼ Sec.26 W½NW¼ Sec.35	1871	1886	patent 1906
María Aragón	SE¼SE¼ Sec.14 E½NE¼ Sec.23 NE¼SE¼ Sec.23	1875	1886	no patent
José María Chavez	SE¼NE¼ Sec.11 E½SE¼ Sec.11 NE¼NE¼ Sec.14	1877	1886	patent 1905
Juan Chavez	E½SE¼ Sec.25 E½NE¼ Sec.36	1877	1886	patent 1905
José Chiquite	SW¼SE¼ Sec.26 W½NE¼ Sec.35	1877	1886	patent 1905
Clemente	W½NW¼ Sec.25 W½NW¼ Sec.36	1877	1886	died ca. 1888
Platero	W½SE¼ Sec.11 NW¼NE¼ Sec.14	1880	1886	patent 1905
Barboncito	NW¼SE¼ Sec.23 SW¼SE¼ Sec.14	1881	1886	no patent

Of these homesteaders, Juan Padilla, age 91, Hoalin [Julian] Chavez, age 75 and Pah Platero, age 75, appear in the 1910 census of the 191 Navajos then living in the Cañoncito. From the similarity of names, others on the 1910 census would appear to be the sons of the original homesteaders. These include: Jose Chirchul [Chenchor?], Vicente Costero [Castillo?], Antonio Delgadito, and several with the last name of Platero, Chaves and Padilla. The name of <u>Antonio Sandoval</u>, age, 31, possibly a descendant of the old chieftain also appears.[219] Nathan Bibo, who pleaded with Superintendent Clinton in 1870 that supplies be given to José Castillo's band around Cebolleta, later stated that he had been instrumental in helpi 3 <u>Castillo</u>, <u>Huero Patolero</u> [<u>Platero</u>] and <u>Conejo</u> secure land in the Cañoncito.[220] No other reference to <u>Conejo</u> appears. Whether <u>Huero Patolero</u> was the <u>Guero</u> frequently mentioned in the Cebolleta-Cubero-Laguna area after Bosque Redondo by agents and superintendents is unknown.

These homesteaders were followed by others into the same township and range in 1912-1914.[221]

Thus, by 1874, the "Sandoval band" of Navajos who had wandered in and out of Laguna and Acoma lands since 1846, sometimes on peaceful terms with the pueblo Indians, and often raiding, had either returned to the Navajo reservation or moved east into the Cañoncito. But the latter they claimed by right of homestead.

220

---

[219] This information is taken from "Census of Canon City Navajos by Reuben Perry, Supt., July 1, 1910," in the office of the United States Indian Service, Albuquerque, New Mexico. The list was obviously prepared by someone unfamiliar with Spanish spellings of proper names. Some of the names listed are Navajo phonetically spelled, and gence difficult to compare with those used by agents and superintendents.

[220] Bibo, The Albuquerque Evening Herald, June 11, 1922.

[221] These names are on a list called "Navajo Fee Patents in Canoncito Navajo Community, March 1, 1945," in office of the United States Indian Service, Albuquerque, New Mexico.

INDEX OF CITATIONS

Page of Report	Date of Document	Document	Source
1	9/18/1846	Orders to Doniphan	Connelley, Doniphan, p. 250
2	1846	List of residents killed at El Rito	#196, Court of Private Land Claims
4	9/27/1846	Hughes Reprint	Connelley, Doniphan, p. 285
4	9/28/1846	Hughes Reprint Robinson Journal	Connelley, Doniphan, p. 284 Robinson, Journal, pp. 35-36
4	9/29/1846	Robinson Journal Edwards Journal	Robinson, Journal, p. 37 Marching with the Army, p. 184
5	10/1846	Hughes Reprint	Connelley, Doniphan, p. 285
5	10/11/1846	Hughes Reprint	Connelley, Doniphan, p. 287 Navajo Exhibit 42
6	10/12/1846	Robinson Journal	Robinson, Journal, pp. 39-41
6	10/20/1846	Robinson Journal	Robinson, Journal, p. 56
7	11/12/1846	Treaty	Navajo Exhibit 43
7	9/10/1846	Edwards Journal	Marching with the Army, pp. 186-187 Navajo Exhibit 38
8	10/12-13/1846	Edwards Journal	Marching with the Army, pp. 187-188 Navajo Exhibit 39
8	10/22 - 11/21/1846	Edwards Journal	Marching with the Army, pp. 190-209
10	10/16-17/1846	Abert Report	Emory, Notes of a Reconnoissance, pp. 465-467
10	10/24/1846	Abert Report	Emory, Notes of a Reconnoissance, p. 469
11	10/16-24/1846	Abert Report	Emory, Notes of a Reconnoissance, pp. 465-474
12	8/16 - 9/8/1847	Simpson Report	Journal of a Military Expedition, pp. 64-101 Navajo Exhibit 49
12	9/9/1849	Treaty	Navajo Exhibit 47
13	8/31/1849	Simpson Report	Journal of a Military Expedition, p. 91
13	9/1849	Simpson Report	Journal of a Military Expedition, Appendix
14	10/15/1849	Calhoun Map	Abel, Correspondence of Calhoun
14	10/10/1849	Simpson Report	Journal of a Military Expedition, p. 138 Navajo Exhibit 50
14	9/19/1849	Simpson Report	Journal of a Military Expedition, p. 129

Page of Report	Date of Document	Document	Source
15	9/19/1849	Simpson Report	Journal of a Military Expedition, p. 130
15	9/20/1849	Simpson Report	Journal of a Military Expedition, p. 131
16	7/15/1850	Calhoun to Brown	Abel, Correspondence of Calhoun, p. 217
16	9/30/1850	Calhoun to Brown	Abel, Correspondence of Calhoun, p. 200
16	11/4/1850	Calhoun to Lea	Abel, Correspondence of Calhoun, p. 283 Navajo Exhibit 58
16	1/29/1851	Sarracino to Calhoun	Abel, Correspondence of Calhoun, p. 284
16	11/27/1850	Lea to Sec. of Int.	U. S. Sen., Ex. Doc. 1 31st C., 2nd S., p. 43
16	2/10/1851	Whiting to Calhoun	Abel, Correspondence of Calhoun, p. 291
16-17	3/31/1851	Calhoun to Lea	Abel, Correspondence of Calhoun, p. 307
17	3/11/1851	Read's Journal	NMHR, XVII, p. 133
17	4/18/1851	Calhoun's Journal	NA, SD, TP. NM
18	4/17/1851	McLaws to Chandler	Navajo Exhibit 62
18	4/19/1851	Memorandum of a Talk	Navajo Exhibit 64
18	4/23/1851	Chandler to McLaws	Navajo Exhibit 65
19	4/25/1851	Calhoun's Journal	Navajo Exhibit 67
19	5/4/1851	Tullis to Calhoun	Navajo Exhibit 70 but misinterpreted
19	1849 & 1850	St. Vrain Trading Co. vouchers	NA, RNMSIA, Records of Santa Fe Agency, 1849-50
19	1850	7th U. S. Census	Census Enumeration
20	4/13/1852	Greiner Journal	Abel, Old Santa Fe, III p. 196
21	4/30/1852	Greiner Journal	Abel, Old Santa Fe, III p.203 Navajo Exhibit 83
21	4/15/1852	Greiner to Baird	NA, RNMSIA, LS
22	6/30/1852	Baird to Greiner	NA, ROIA, NMS, LR Navajo Exhibit 85
22	7/25/1851	Calhoun to Lea	Abel, Correspondence of Calhoun, p. 389
22	10/24/1851	Sumner to Jones	Abel, Correspondence of Calhoun, p. 418
23	10/8/1851	Bennett Journal	Brooks and Reeve, James A. Bennett, p. 30
23	1/8/1852	Ten Broeck Journal	Schoolcraft, Information, Vol. VI, p. 80
23	9/17/1851	Calhoun to Wingfield	NA, RNMSIA, LS
23	9/8/1851	Calhoun to Worley	NA, RNMSIA, LS
23	11/10/1851	Calhoun to Sumner	Abel, Correspondence of Calhoun, p. 451

222

Page of Report	Date of Document	Document	Source
24	1/1/1852	Sumner to Jones	Abel, Correspondence of Calhoun, p. 434
24	1/1852	Bennett Journal	Brooks and Reeve, James A. Bennett, p. 32
24	7/3/1852	Greiner to Lea	NA, ROIA, NMS, LR
25	7/11/1852	Greiner Journal	Abel, Old Santa Fe, III p. 227
25	4/9/1853	Manypeny to Lane	NA, ROIA, LS
25	10/25/1852	Baird to Lane	NA, RNMSIA, LS
26	5/5/1853	Lane to Baird	NA, RNMSIA, LS
26	5/25/1853	Sumner to Lane	NA, RNMSIA, LS
26	5/25/1853	Vigil to Lane	NA, RNMSIA, LS Navajo Exhibit 94
26	5/26/1853	Lane to Manypeny	NA, RNMSIA, LS
26	5/25/1853	Kendrick to Sturgis	Navajo Exhibit 95
26	6/12/1853	Lane to Sumner	Navajo Exhibit 98
26	7/12/1853	Kendrick to Sturgis	Navajo Exhibit 100
26	11/28/1853	Meriwether to Manypeny	NA, RNMSIA, LS
27	8/31/1853	Meriwether to Manypeny	U. S. H.R., Ex. Doc. I, 33rd C., 1st S.,1853, pp. 430-431
27	9/17/1853	Meriwether to Manypeny	NA, RNMSIA, LS
27	9/30/1853	Receipt to Sandoval	NA, RNMSIA, Misc. Papers, 1851-53
28	11/14/1853	Whipple Report	Reports of Explorations, III, Pt. I, p. 61
28	11/14/1853	Whipple Report	Reports of Explorations, III, Pt. I, p. 63
28	1853	Möllhausen	Diary of a Journey, II. p. 12
28	1853	Whipple, Ewbank and Turner	Reports of Explorations, III, Pt. 3, p. 13
29	5/13/1854	Kendrick to Manypeny	NA, RNMSIA, Misc. Papers, 1854 Navajo Exhibit 113
29	10/16/1854	Beck to Meriwether	NA, RNMSIA, Misc. Papers. 1854 Navajo Exhibit 120
30	1854	Letherman Report	10th Annual Report, Smithsonian Institute, 1855, p. 83
30	3/16/1855	Manypeny to Meriwether	NA, ROIA, LS
31	1855	Davis Account	El Gringo, p. 418
31	7/19/1855	Davis Account	El Gringo, p. 424
31	7/18/1855	Meriwether Treaty	Royce, Indian Land Sessions, Pt. II, Map 44 See Navajo Exhibit 127
32	7/27/1855	Meriwether to Manypeny	NA, RNMSIA, LS Navajo Exhibit 128

Page of Report	Date of Document	Document	Source
33	2/1/1856	Carleton to Kendrick	NA, RNMSIA, Misc. Papers, 1856 Navajo Exhibit 137
33	2/6/1856	Kendrick to Dodge	NA, RNMSIA, Misc. Papers 1856 Navajo Exhibit 139
33	2/8/1856	Kendrick to Carleton	Navajo Exhibit 140
33	4/8/1856	Davis to Dodge	Navajo Exhibit 144
33	4/9/1856	Davis to Manypeny	Navajo Exhibit 145
33	6/13/1856	Dodge to Meriwether	NA, RNMSIA, LR from Agencies, 1856 Navajo Exhibit 149
33	6/23/1856	Meriwether to Rolval	NA, RNMSIA, LS
33	6/27/1856	Gorman to Dodge	NA, RNMSIA, Misc. Papers 1856 #196, Court of P. L. C.
33	7/11/1856	Luna to Meriwether	NA, RNMSIA, Misc. Docs. Sp. Lang., 1852-56
34	6/30/1856	Meriwether to Manypeny	NA, RNMSIA, LS
34	9/30/1856	Meriwether to Manypeny	U.S.H.R., Ex. Doc. 1, 34th C., 3rd S., 1856, p.73
34	4/30/1857	Collins to Manypeny	NA, RNMSIA, LS
34	1/17/1858	Bonneville to Collins	NA, RNMSIA, Misc. Papers 1858 Navajo Exhibit 164
34	3/25/1858	Baca to Rencher	NA, RNMSIA, Misc. Doc. Sp. Lang., 1852-59
34	4/24/1858	Ballejos to Rencher	NA, RNMSIA, Misc. Doc. Sp. Lang., 1852-59
35	4/13/1858	Brooks to Collins	NA, RNMSIA, Misc. Papers 1858
35	4/9/1858	Ward to Yost	NA, RNMSIA, LR from Agencies, 1858 Navajo Exhibit 167
35	9/27/1858	Collins to Mix	U.S.H.R., Ex. Doc. 2 35th C., 3rd S., 1858, p. 542 Navajo Exhibit 174
36	9/5/1858	Yost to Collins	NA, ROIA, NMS, LR by OIA
36	9/9/1858	Yost to Collins	NA, ROIA, NMS, LR by OIA
36	9/1858	Report of J. Cooper McKew	NA, ROIA, NMS, LR by OIA
37	9/24/1858	Collins to Mix	NA, ROIA, NMS, LR by OIA
37	9/27/1858	Collins to Mix	U.S.H.R. Ex. Doc. 2, 35th C., 2nd S., 1858, p. 543 Navajo Exhibit 174
37	9/30/1858	Yost to Collins	NA, RNMSIA, LR from Agencies, 1858
37	4/9/1858	Ward to Yost	NA, RNMSIA, LR from Agencies, 1858 Navajo Exhibit 167

224

Page of Report	Date of Document	Document	Source
38	10/10/1858	Yost to Collins	NA, RNMSIA, LR from Agencies, 1858
38	10/16/1858	Bonneville to Collins	NA, RNMSIA, Misc. Papers, 1858
38	11/1858	Armistice Terms	NA, RNMSIA, Misc. Papers, 1858
39	12/18/1858	Yost to Collins	NA, RNMSIA, LR from Agencies, 1858 Navajo Exhibit 205
40	12/25/1858	Treaty	NA, ROIA, NMS, LR by OIA, 1858
40	12/25/1858	Map of Treaty	Royce, Indian Land Sessions
40	11/18/1858	Whistler to Williams	Navajo Exhibit 188
40	11/15/1858	Collins to Mix	NA, ROIA, NMS, LR by OIA
41	12/18/1858	Denver to Collins	NA, RNMSIA, LR from CIA, 1858
41	12/21/1858	Santa Fe Gazette	
41	2/21/1859	Collins to Denver	NA, ROIA, LR by OIA, 1859
42	5/22/1859	Collins to Denver	NA, ROIA, NMS, LR by OIA
42	9/17/1859	Collins to Greenwood	U.S. Sen. Ex. Doc. 2, 36th C., 1st S., 1859, pp. 707-708
42	2/4/1860	Rencher to Cass	SD, TP, NM
43	2/5/1860	Collins to Greenwood	NA, ROIA, NMS, LR by OIA
43	3/30/1860	Collins to Greenwood	NA, ROIA, NMS, LR by OIA
43	5/15/1860	Rencher to Cass	NA, SD, TP, NM
43	5/20/1860	Collins to Greenwood	NA, RNMSIA, LS
43	7/22/1860	Collins to Greenwood	NA, ROIA, LR by OIA
43	9/24/1860	Collins to Greenwood	U. S. Sen. Ex. Doc. 1, 36th C., 2nd S., 1860, p. 381
44	9/25/1860	Kendrick to Greenwood	U. S. Sen. Ex. Doc. 1, 36th C., 2nd S., 1860, pp. 388-389
44	1860	Domenech Report	Domenesch, Seven Years' Residence, I, 184, 206-07
45	2/15/1861	Treaty	Navajo Exhibit 266
45	10/26/1861	Connelly to Seward	NA, SD, TP, NM
45	11/17/1861	Connelly to Seward	NA, SD, TP, NM
46	9/14/1862	Connelly Proclamation	NA, SD, TP, NM
46	9/25/1862	Labadie to Collins	U.S.H.R., Ex. Doc. 1, 37th C., 3rd S., 1862. p. 394
47	9/5/1863	Steck to Labadie	NA, RNMSIA, LR from Agencies, 1863
47	8/28/1863	Luna to Steck	NA, RNMSIA, LR from Agencies, 1863

Page of Report	Date of Document	Document	Source
47	8/30/1863	Steck to Luna	NA, RNMSIA, LR from Agencies, 1863
48	10/5/1863	Luna to Steck	NA, RNMSIA, LR from Agencies, 1863
49	1/7/1865	Capt. McCabe	O.R., XLVIII, Pt. 1, p. 523
49	11/17/1866	Carleton to deForrest	NA, ROIA, LR by OIA
49	12/1865	Connelly message	SD, TP, NM
49	5/20/186	Steck to Dole	NA, RNMSIA, LR from CIA, 1864
49	1/5/1866	Graves to Delgado	NA, RNMSIA, Misc. Papers, 1866
49	1866	List of those killed at El Rito by Navajos	#196, Ct. of P. L. C.
49	2/1866	Garcia, "Depredaciones"	NA, RNMSIA, Misc. Papers, 1866
50	1866	Graves to Cooley	U.S.H.R., Ex. Doc. 1, 39th C., 2nd S., 1866, p. 135
50	1945	Benavides' Revised Memorial, 1634	Hodge, Rey, Hammond, p. 310
51	9/1846	Bent	Walter,"First Civil Governor," NMHR, VIII, 112-113
51	10/1/1849	Calhoun to Medill	Abel, Correspondence of Calhoun, p. 22
51	10/5/1849	Calhoun to Medill	Abel, Correspondence of Calhoun, p. 85
51	8/30/1849	Simpson Report	Journal of a Military Expedition, p. 53 ...
52	1853	Whipple, Ewbank, Turner	Reports of Explorations, III, Pt. 3, p. 13
52	6/8/1854	Graves to Manypeny	U.S.H.R., Ex. Doc. 2, 33rd C., 2nd S.,1854, p. 387
52	9/1/1854	Meriwether to Manypeny	U.S.H.R., Ex. Doc. 2, 33rd C., 2nd S., 1854, p. 380
52	9/1/1855	Meriwether to Manypeny	U.S.H.R., Ex. Doc. 1, 34th C., 1st S., 1855, p. 507
53	10/16/1858	Rencher to Cass	SD, TP, NM
53	5/7/1859	Pope, Military Memoir	Records of the Office, Chief of Eng., Top. Eng.
53	9/1/1859	Baker to Collins	U.S.Sen., Ex. Doc. 2, 36th C., 1st S., 1859, p. 718
53	8/8/1859	Baker to Collins	NA, RNMSIA, LR from Agencies, 1859

226

Page of Report	Date of Document	Document	Source
53	10/31/1863	Dole to Sec. of Int.	U.S.H.R., Ex. Doc. 1, 38th C., 1st S., 1863, p. 136
54	8/22/1863	Hargraves Report	O. R., Ser. I, XXVI, pt. 1, p. 259
54	8/28/1863	Chacon Report	O. R., Ser. I, XXVI, pt. 1, p. 258
54	11/ 25/1863	Carson Report	O. R., Ser. I, XXVI, pt. 1, p. 256
54	12/17/1863	Waller Report	O. R., Ser. I, XXVI, pt. 1, p. 260
54	12/10/1863	Steck to Dole	NA, ROIA, NMS, LR by OIA, 1863
55	1/7/1865	McCabe Report	O. R., Ser. I, XXVI, Pt. 1, pp. 523,527
55	6/30/1867	Dodd to Norton	U.S.H.R., Ex. Doc. 1, 40th C., 1st S., 1867, pp. 198-199
56	9/15/1867	Norton to Taylor	NA, RNMSIA, LR from CIA, 1867
56	11/1/1867	Whiting Statement	NA, RNMSIA, LR from Agencies, 1867
56	12/1867	Gov. Mitchell message	SD, TP, NM
56	12/1868	Gov. Mitchell message	SD, TP, NM
56	2/18/1868	Davis to Taylor	NA, RNMSIA, LS
56	9/15/1867	Norton to Taylor	NA, RNMSIA, Misc. Papers, 1867
56	9/1867	Memorandum	NA, RNMSIA, Misc. Papers, 1867
57	5/29/1868	Treaty Negotiations	Sherman Papers
59	6/1/1868	Treaty	Kappler, Indian Treaties, pp. 527-533
60	7/10/1868	Santa Fe New Mexican	
60	8/5/1868	Dodd to Weber	U.S.H.R., Ex. Doc. 1, 40th C., 3rd S., 1868, p. 623
61	8/4/1868	Ward to Tappan	NA, ROIA, NMS, LR by OIA
61	2/1/1869	Gallegos to French	NA, RNMSIA, LS
62	3/26/1869	French to Gallegos	NA, RNMSIA, LR from Nav. Agency
62	3/2/1869	Gallegos to French	NA, RNMSIA, LS
62	3/4/1869	Catanach to Ward	NA, RNMSIA, LS
62	7/10/ 1869	French to Gallegos	NA, ROIA, NMS, LR by OIA
63	7/14/1869	Kobbe to Evans	NA, RNMSIA, LR from Hq., Dept. of N.M. (U.S.A.), 1869
63	8/2/1869	Mitchell Proclamation	SD, TP, NM

227

Page of Report	Date of Document	Document	Source
63	8/14/1869	Parker to Clinton	NA, RNMSIA, LR from CIA 1869
63	9/15/1869	Gov. Pile Proclamation	SD, TP, NM
64	8/31/1869	Cooper to Clinton	NA, RNMSIA, LR from Pueblo Special Agency, 1869
64	9/8/1869	Cooper to Clinton	NA, RNMSIA, LR from Pueblo Special Agency, 1869
64	1869	Parker to Cox (Report)	U.S.H.R., Ex. Doc. 1, 41st C., 2nd S., 1869, p.464
65	9/9/1869	Bennett to Clinton	NA, RNMSIA, LR from Nav. Agency, 1869
65	1/20/1869	Evans to Kobbe	NA, RNMSIA, LR from Hq. U. S. A., 1869
66	12/30/1869	Bennett to Clinton	NA, ROIA, LR by OIA
66	2/9/1870	Bennett to Evans	NA, RNMSIA, LR from Nav. Agency, 1870
66	2/1/1870	Bennett to Clinton	NA, RNMSIA, LR from Nav. Agency, 1870
66	2/10/1870	Evans to Bennett	NA, RNMSIA, LR from Nav. Agency, 1870
66	2/14/1870	Bennett to Evans	NA, RNMSIA, LR from Nav. Agency, 1870
66	2/10/1870	Evans to Cooper	NA, RNMSIA, LR from Abiquiu Agency, 1870
67	1/1/1871	Bennett to Pope	NA, RNMSIA, LR from Nav. Agency, 1871
68	3/31/1870	Clinton to Parker	NA, RNMSIA, LS
69	1846-1890	Baptism Records	Diocese of Gallup, Cath. of Sacred Heart, Gallup
70	4/15/1870	Parker to Clinton	NA, RNMSIA, LR from CIA, 1870
70	5/11/1870	Clinton to Parker	NA, RNMSIA, LS
70	5/11/1870	Bibo to Clinton	NA, RNMSIA, LR from Hq. U. S. A., 1870
70	5/11/1870	Gonzalez to Clinton	NA, RNMSIA, LR from Hq. U. S. A., 1870
70	5/28/1870	Parker to Clinton	NA, RNMSIA, LR from CIA, 1870
71	6/22/1870	Clinton to Gonzalez	NA, RNMSIA, LS
71	6/11/1922	Bibo	Albuquerque Evening Herald
71	10/8/1870	Arny's Journal	NA, ROIA, NMS, LR by OIA, 1870
71	12/25.1870	Luna to Pope	NA, RNMSIA, LR from Hq. U.S.A., 1870
72	3/10/1871	Manley to Pope	NA, RNMSIA, LR from Abiquiu Agency, 1871
72	1/28/1871	Parker to Pope	NA, RNMSIA, LR from CIA, 1871
72	3/23/1871	Manley to Pope	NA, RNMSIA, LR from Abiquiu Agency, 1871

228

Page of Report	Date of Document	Document	Source
72	1/16/1871	Pope to Manley	NA, RNMSIA, LS
72	1914	Navajo slavery	Twitchell, Leading Facts, II, 303-304, note 228
73	1954	Navajo slavery	Marin, "Seboyetanos," NMHR, XXIX, p. 11
73	1/13/1864	Steck to Dole	NA, ROIA, NMS, LR by OIA, 1864
74	5/16/1862	Need to Collins	NA, RNMSIA, Misc. Corresp. & Acctg. Papers, 1862
74	6/11/1922	Bibo Account	Albuquerque Evening Herald
75	11/10/1867	Norton order	NA, RNMSIA, LS
75	1/18/1870	Clinton to Parker	NA, RNMSIA, LS
75	4/5/1871	Miller to Pope	NA, RNMSIA, LR from Nav. Agency, 1871
75	12/11/1871	Miller to Pope	NA, RNMSIA, LR from Nav. Agency, 1871
76	3/9/1872	Pope to Voller	NA, RNMSIA, LS
76	9/18/1872	Curtis to Pope	NA, RNMSIA, LR from Mescalero Apache Agency, 1872
77	9/1/1872	Keams to Pope	NA, RNMSIA, LR from Nav. Agency, 1872
77	9/7/1872	Keams to Pope	NA, RNMSIA, LR from Nav. Agency, 1872
77	5/1872	Beadle	Undeveloped West, p. 498
77	5/1872	Beadle	Western Wilds, p. 240
78	11/4/1873	Arny to Dudley	NA, RNMSIA, LR from Nav. Agency, 1873
79	9/15/1873	Lewis to Arny	NA, RNMSIA, LR from Nav. Agency, 1873
79	11/11/1873	Arny to Dudley	NA, RNMSIA, LR from Nav. Agency, 1873
79	12/11/1873	Dudley to Smith	NA, ROIA, LR by OIA, 1873
80	2/18/1874	Arny to Smith	NA, ROIA, LR by OIA, 1874
81	5/30/1874	Thomas to Arny	NA, RNMSIA, LR from Nav. Agency, 1874
81	6/18/1874	Arny to Thomas	NA, RNMSIA, LR from Nav. Agency, 1874
81	10/27/1874	Navajo petition	NA, ROIA, LR by OIA, 1874
81	5/5/1875	Navajo petition	NA, ROIA, LR by OIA, 1875
83-84	1886	Homestead entries	U.S. Gen. Land Office, Register of Homestead Entries, Santa Fe
84-85	7/1/1910	Canoncito census	U. S. Ind. Service, Albuquerque
85	6/11/1922	Bibo	Albuquerque Evening Herald
85	3/1/1945	Navajo fee patents, Canoncito	U. S. Ind. Service, Albuquerque

229

BIBLIOGRAPHY

I. PRIMARY SOURCES (and Abbreviations)

A. National Archives Collections

ROIA, NMS - Records of the Office of Indian Affairs,
          New Mexico Superintendency

LR by OIA ⊕ Letters Received by Office of Indian Affairs,
          1849 - 1875

LS - Letters Sent, 1846-1875

RMMSIA - Records of the Superintendency of Indian Affairs,
          1849-1880

Records of the Santa Fe Agency, 1849-50

LS - Letters Sent, 1851-1872

Miscellaneous Documents, Spanish Language, 1852-1859

Miscellaneous Papers, 1851-1867

LR from CIA - Letters Received from Commissioner of
          Indian Affairs, 1854-1872

LR from Agencies, 1854-1868

Miscellaneous Correspondence and Accounting Papers, 1861-
          1873

Letters Received from Pueblo Special Agency, 1869

Letters Received from Navajo Agency, 1869-1875

Letters Received from Headquarters, District of New
          Mexico (U. S. Army), 1869-1870

Letters Received from Pueblo Agency, 1871

Letters Received from Abiquiu Agency, 1871

Letters Received from Mescalero Apache Agency, 1872

SD, TP, NM - United States State Department, Territorial
          Papers, New Mexico, 1851-1872

230

I.   PRIMARY SOURCES (Continued)

B.   Secretary of the Interior and Commissioner of Indian
     Affairs Reports - Congressional Documents

          29th Cong., 2nd Sess., 1846 - 41st Cong., 3rd Sess.,
          1870

C.   Miscellaneous Collections

     United States Bureau of the Census, 1850 - 1890

     "Census of Canon Cito Navajos by Reuben Perry, Supt.,
          July 1, 1910," Office of the U. S. Indian Service,
          Albuquerque, New Mexico

     #196, "Ambrosio Pino et al vs.the United States," Court
          of Private Land Claims, General Land Office, Santa Fe,
          New Mexico

     Diocese of Gallup, Cathedral of the Sacred Heart,
          Baptismal Records of Cubero, Cebolleta, Laguna,
          Acoma, 1846-1890, Gallup, New Mexico

     U. S. General Land Office, Register of Homestead Entries,
          Santa Fe, New Mexico

     "Navajo Fee Patents in Canoncito Navajo Community,
          March 1, 1945," Office of the U. S. Indian Service,
          Albuquerque, New Mexico

     O. R. - The War of the Rebellion: a Compilation of the
          Official Records of the Union and Confederate Armies,
          Washington: Government Printing Office, 1896, XXVI,
          Pt. 1; XXXIV, Pt. 1; XLVIII, Pt. 1.

     Papers of William T. Sherman, Vol. 23, 1868, Manuscript
          Division, Library of Congress, "Proceedings of the
          Council between General W. T. Sherman and Samuel F.
          Tappan, Commissioners on the part of the United
          States and the chiefs and head-men of the Navajo
          Tribe of Indians, held at the Reservation known as
          the Bosque Redondo, at Fort Sumner in the Territory
          of New Mexico on the 28th day of May, 29th day of
          May, and 30th day of May, 1868.

D.   Miscellaneous Primary Accounts

     Abel, Annie H., ed., "The Journal of John Greiner," Old
          Santa Fe, III (July, 1916), 189-243.

     Abel, Annie H., ed., The Official Correspondence of James
          S. Calhoun . . . Washington: Government Printing
          Office, 1915.

231

I. PRIMARY ACCOUNTS (Continued)

D. Miscellaneous Primary Accounts (Continued)

Beadle, J. H., The Undeveloped West; or Five Years in the Territories. Philadelphia: National Printing Co., 1873.

Beadle, J. H., Western Wilds and the Men who Redeem them. Cincinnati: Jones Brothers and Company, 1878.

Bibo, Nathan, "Reminiscences of Early Days in New Mexico," The Albuquerque Evening Herald, June 11, 1922.

Bieber, Ralph P., ed., Marching with the Army of the West 1846-1848. Vol. IV of Southwest Historical Series; Glendale, California: The Arthur H. Clark Company, 1936. Contains account of Marcellus Ball Edwards.

Bloom, Lansing B., "The Rev. Hiram Read, Baptist Missionary to New Mexico," New Mexico Historical Review, XVII (April, 1942), 113-147.

Brooks, Clinton E. and Frank D. Reeve, eds., James A. Bennett, a Dragoon in New Mexico 1850-1856. Albuquerque: The University of New Mexico Press, 1948.

232

Connelley, William Elsey, Doniphan's Expedition and the Conquest of New Mexico. Topeka: Privately Published, 1907. Contains John Hughes and Meredith Moore accounts.

Davis, W. W. H., El Gringo; or New Mexico and her People. New York: Harper and Bros., 1857, pp. 389-443.

Domenech, Abbé M., Seven Years' Residence in the Great Deserts of North America. London: Longman, Green, Longman, Roberts, 1860, Vol. I, pp. 199-215.

Emory, W. H., Notes of a Military Reconnoissance . . . U. S. Senate, Exec. Doc. No. 7, 30th Cong., 1st Sess., 1848. Contains Report of Lt. J. W. Abert, pp. 465-476.

Hodge, Frederick Webb, Agapito Rey and George P. Hammond, eds., Fray Alonso de Benavides' Revised Memorial of 1634. Vol. IV of Coronado Cuatro Centennial Publications; Albuquerque: The University of New Mexico, 1945, p. 310.

PRIMARY ACCOUNTS (Continued)

. Miscellaneous Primary Accounts (Continued)

Kappler, Charles J., ed., Indian Affairs, Laws and Treaties. Washington: Government Printing Office, 1913,
   pp. 525-533.

Letherman, Jonah, "Sketches of the Navajo Tribe of Indians,"
   Tenth Annual Report of the Board of Regents, Smithsonian
   Institution, 1855, U. S. H. R., Misc. Doc. No. 113,
   34th Cong., 1st Sess., 1855, pp. 283-297.

Marin, C. C., "The Seboyetanos and the Navahos," Frank D.
   Reeve and Robert Duncan, eds., New Mexico Historical
   Review, XXIX (January, 1954), pp. 8-27.

Möllhausen, Baldwin, Diary of a Journey from the Mississippi
   to the Coasts of the Pacific, Mrs. Percy Sinnett, trans.,
   London: Longmans, Brown, Green, Longman and Roberts,
   1858, II, p. 12.

Pope, Capt. John, "A Military Memoir of the Country
   between the Mississippi River and the Pacific Ocean
   with Some Account of Frontier Defenses," Records of the
   Office, Chief of Engineers, Topographical Engineers.

Robinson, Jacob, A Journal of the Santa Fe Expedition under
   Doniphan. Princeton: Princeton University Press, 1932

Royce, Charles C., comp., Indian Land Sessions in the
   United States. Eighteenth Annual Report of the Bureau
   of American Ethnology. Washington: Government Printing
   Office, 1899, Pt. II, Map 44; treaty of 1858.

Schoolcraft, Henry R., Information Regarding the History
   and Prospects of the Indian Tribes of the United
   States. Collected and Prepared under the Direction of
   the Bureau of Indian Affairs by Act of Congress, March
   2, 1847; Philadelphia: J. B. Lippincott and Co., 1856,
   Vol. VI, pp. 72-91.

Simpson, J. H., "Journal of a Military Reconnoissance from
   Santa Fe, New Mexico to the Navajo Country . . . in
   1849," U. S. Senate, Reports of the Secretary of War,
   Exec. Doc. 64, 31st Cong., 1st Sess., 1850.

Whipple, A. W., "Report . . . upon the Route near the
   Thirty-Fifth Parallel," in U. S. War Department,
   Reports of Explorations and Surveys to Ascertain the
   most Practical and Economical Route for a Railroad from
   the Mississippi River to the Pacific Ocean, U. S. Sen.
   Exec. Doc. No. 76, 33rd Cong., 2nd Sess., 1853, III, Pt. 1.

233

II. SECONDARY ACCOUNTS

Amsden, Charles, "The Navaho Exile at Bosque Redondo," *New Mexico Historical Review*, VIII (January, 1933), pp. 31-50.

Bender, A. B., "Frontier Defense in the Territory of New Mexico," *New Mexico Historical Review*, IX (July, 1934), pp. 249-272.

Heyman, Max L., Jr., "On the Navaho Trail: The Campaign of 1860-61," *New Mexico Historical Review*, XXVI (January, 1951), pp. 44-63.

Keleher, William A., *Turmoil in New Mexico 1846-1868*. Santa Fe: The Rydal Press, 1952.

Reeve, Frank D., "The Federal Indian Policy in New Mexico, 1858-1880, *New Mexico Historical Review*, XII (July, 1937), pp. 218-269; XIII (January, 1938), pp. 14-62; (April, 1938), pp. 146-191; (July, 1938), pp. 261-313.

Reeve, Frank D., "The Government and the Navaho," *New Mexico Historical Review*, XVI (January, 1939), pp. 82-114.

Twitchell, Ralph Emerson, *Leading Facts in New Mexican History*. Cedar City: The Torch Press, 1914), Vol. II, pp. 303-304, note 228.

Walter, Paul A. F., "The First Civil Governor of New Mexico under the Stars and Stripes," *New Mexico Historical Review*, VIII (April, 1933), pp. 98-129.

234

THE NAVAJO INDIANS

by

Frank D. Reeve

University of New Mexico

Albuquerque, N. M.

CONTENTS

237

238

THE NAVAJO HOMELAND 1848-1868

Summary

The Navajos, a branch of the Athapaskan linguistic Indian
family, more commonly known as Apaches, lived in the northwestern
quarter of the present state of New Mexico when the Spanish appeared
on the scene in the seventeenth century. They inhabited the canyons
that extend northwestward from the continental divide and constitute a
part of the drainage system of the San Juan River, and on Cebolleta
Mountain to the south. About the middle of the eighteenth century
they were as far east as Canon Largo and along the San Juan River
where it flows westward for a considerable distance before bending
toward the northwest to mingle its waters with those of the Colorado
River of the West. Under pressure from the Ute Indians, the influence
of missionaries and a drought, they abandoned the Largo region and
moved westward into the Chuska Range and a few southward to the
Cebolleta Mountain and the land between these two major geographical
land marks.

When the Government of the United States assumed sovereignty
over New Mexico by the Treaty of Guadalupe Hidalgo, the whereabouts of
the Navajos was well known to the New Mexicans except for details on
the western part of their land. Without doubt they occupied the Chuska
Range and the valley on each side from the San Juan River southward to
Campbell's Pass where the Atchison, Topeka & Santa Fe Railway was built
in 1880. The Zuni Mountains rise south of the Pass and afforded rich
pasturage for Navajo livestock and an abundance of water at Bear Springs
for raising corn. Some of these folks had also moved to the Blue Water

239

in the early 1840's. Farther eastward they had long competed with Pueblos and New Mexicans for land and water along the north side of the Rio San Jose and the adjacent mountain canyons. On the east side of Cebolleta Mountain they had lost ownership of Cebolleta Canyon, but still retained a foothold in the canyons farther north. The land between Cebolleta Mountain and the Rio Puerco of the East was used jointly by Navajo and New Mexican, and to a lesser extent by the Laguna Indians.

On the north side of Navajoland, these pastoral folks utilized the lower La Plata and Las Animas valleys, although the region was often referred to as Ute country. However, the Utes did not practice agriculture and sheep raising as early as the Navajos, but were more of a hunting people; consequently, both groups could reside in this region without basic conflict of interest. Their chief problem was to avoid stealing one another's livestock.

240

The Utes made occasional use of the land at the headwaters of the Rio Puerco of the East for camping, probably when on a trading expedition to the Pueblos, hunting or marauding against Navajos. At any rate, references to Utes being in the Navajo country appear in eighteenth and nineteenth century documents. One site was sometimes referred to as the Alto Utah and lay north of present-day Cuba along the continental divide which customarily was thought of as marking the eastside beginnings of Navajoland in the eighteenth century.

On the south, the Navajos customarily ventured into Apache country to trade, visit or fight; and the Apaches came northward for the same purposes, seeking their kinsmen in the canyons of Cebolleta

Mountain and the Chuska Range. There is little evidence of Navajo occupation, other than under duress, south of the Rio San Jose and its headwaters prior to the American occupation.

When Navajo raiders struck at New Mexican livestock and settlements in the valley of the Rio Grande, they invariably fled westward or northwestward toward their haunts in the above-cited places. On one occasion prior to the American occupation they fled southward into Apacheland when pursued by New Mexican forces too strong to cope with in their home mountains. Flight to the south became common during the Carleton campaign of 1863 when they were rounded up for resettlement in the Pecos Valley of eastern New Mexico.

Westward from the Chuska Range, the Navajos did not live much beyond the Pueblo Colorado Wash and Steamboat ~~Bonea~~ Canyon. They grazed their sheep to some extent on Black Mesa, but their cornfields lay in the Wash and in Black Creek Canyon with a spill over into the Puerco Valley of the West near the junction of the Creek and the Puerco River. They might have grazed their stock farther southwestward along the Puerco, and perhaps even south of that river for some distance toward the Little Colorado River; but the extent is not known and probably was not significant.

241

Under military pressure from the American army in the 1860's, they did flee far to the west of the Hopi villages; but that region was not their customary homesite, nor was it needed. In the light of their estimated population and the size of their flocks and herds, the regions as described above provided ample room if they could maintain control against the continuous pressure from the expanding New Mexican population which became aggressive around the turn of the nineteenth century.

NAVAJO LOCATIONS 1800-1848

Gazing westward from Albuquerque on a clear day, the skyline of Cebolleta Mountain can be seen, dominated by Mt. Taylor on the southern end, soaring to a height of over eleven thousand feet. The Mountain extends about forty-five miles from northeast to southwest, deeply etched by the forces of nature whereby numerous canyons with running water and grass afford a living for farmer and stockman.

The Rio Puerco of the East rises in the highlands northeast of Cebolleta Mountain and flows far to the south where its waters mingle with the Rio Grande--that is, when there is water enough to travel the distance. The river marked the jumping off place for travelers to the Land of the Navajos whose realm extended to the west of Cebolleta Mountain as revealed in 1782 when Father Morfi discussed the location of the Moqui (Hopi) folks in relation to other Indians:

> This province is bounded on the east by the land of the Zuni and Navajo, on the west and north-west by the Cominas, on the north by the Utes, on the south by Apaches who in New Mexico they call Mescaleros and in Moqui the Yochies, and Tasabues; they are the same as the Gila Apaches and Pimas (Fray Juan Agustin de Morfi, Descripcion Geografica del Nuevo Mexico, Archivo General de Mexico, Historia 25, pt. 1, f113).

So, toward the end of the eighteenth century the Navajos lived between the Rio Puerco of the East and the land of the Hopi to the west, and their locations were well known to the Spanish. "In general," Governor de la Concha wrote, "they occupy rough mesas of difficult access, and pasture their livestock on the borders of the Rio Puerco and in the Canyon de Chelly" ("Advice on Governing New Mexico, 1794," Trans. by Donald E. Worcester, New Mexico Historical Review, 24:239).

242

Alternate peace and war marked the relations between Navajo and New
Mexican, with land use a prime factor in their affairs. Governor Concha's
predecessor had

> arranged with the Navajo nation that any individual
> in the Province might pasture stock, not only on the
> Puerco, where they had possession, but also among their
> own establishments, provided that the stock did not
> invade their planted fields.

> So it has been done and is still done, in such
> fashion that those /New Mexicans/ who unaided utilized
> in practice a small district of one league or at the
> most two, are found today at a distance of fifty to
> sixty leagues, without any friction or strife having
> occurred between those people and our pastors (Gov.
> Fernando Chacon, Relacion, Santa Fe, N. M., May 1,
> 1793. Archivo General de Indias, Sevilla, Mexico,
> 89-6-23. Ayer Transcript, Newberry Library, Chicago,
> Ill.).

Needless to say, the arrangement for joint land use did not
eliminate friction between New Mexican and Navajo since there had been
intermittent raiding back and forth for a generation. The focal points
of trouble were: Cebolleta Canyon, Pedro Padilla Canyon, Juan Tafoya
Canyon, Guadalupe Canyon, San Miguel Canyon, Chaco Canyon and Mesa, and
the Cubero region on the south side of Cebolleta Mountain (Cf: Antonio
Cordero, Documentos para la Historia de Durango, p. 229. Bancroft
Library, Berkeley, Calif. Also in translation by Daniel S. Matson and
Albert H. Schroeder, New Mexico Historical Review, 32:356).

Cebolleta Canyon lies on the southeastern side of Cebolleta
Mountain and contains arable land and water. At the turn of the
century, Gov. Fernando Chacon decided that it should belong to New
Mexican settlers after vigorous protest and violence from Navajos
(Federal Land Office, Santa Fe, N. M. Cebolleta Grant, R46 (F73),

243

Doc. C, January 23, 1800. Gov. Chacon to Nemesio Salcedo. Santa Fe, N. M., March 28, 1804. R. E. Twitchell, Spanish Archives of New Mexico, II, 1714).

Pedro Padilla Canyon stretches from north to south along the western side of Mesa Gigante which is a few miles east of Cebolleta Canyon. The old road from Sia to Laguna passed by the north end of the Mesa and southward through the canyon. In the interest of peace, the Spanish officials decided in 1808 that the Navajos should be permitted to occupy this canyon although it lay within the boundary of the land granted to the settlers at Cebolleta. There was an additional possibility that the Indians would serve as a buffer against attacks from the southern Apaches (Ibid., II, 2105).

Juan Tafoya Canyon is a few miles north of Cebolleta Canyon and stretches eastward toward the Rio Puerco. Today the village of Marquez lies at its head. In the olden days, Vicente and his Navajo kinsmen occupied the site, so friction developed when New Mexican sheepmen led their flocks into the canyon. In March of 1805, Gov. Chacon stipulated the conditions of peace for these Navajos and another group under Cristobal; namely, that they should not move their flocks south of three basic points: Juan Tafoya Canyon, San Mateo on the southwestern side of Cebolleta Mountain and Bear Creek, presumably the site of the present-day Fort Wingate Ordnance Depot. The terms of peace concluded in May carried a specific provision that the Navajos should not claim the lands in Cebolleta Canyon (Ibid., II, 1810, 1828).

244

Friction again occurred in Juan Tafoya Canyon in 1808, so Bartolome Baca journeyed there in June and arranged for the New Mexican stockmen to graze their animals in the lower reaches of the Canyon from Cerro Chato (Ibid., II, 2105), a volcanic neck that marks the landscape on the south side of Agua Salado which carries whatever water that escapes from Juan Tafoya Canyon.

Guadalupe Canyon stretches from the northeastern end of Cebolleta Mountain and widens out to the east where it drains into the Rio Puerco. Navajos had established a stronghold on top of the mountain and had planted corn in the canyon below for at least a century and a half before the American occupation of the Southwest.

In 1818, a few of these folks attacked a party of herders near the Rio Puerco, eastward from Laguna Pueblo. They were pursued to the top of Cebolleta Mountain and toward the north end where lay their old stronghold (Archivo General de Indias, Estado Mexico, Legajo 13, Ayer Transcript, Newberry Library, Chicago, Ill.). Captain Facundo Melgares besieged them without success in this same year, but in 1840 the place was captured by a surprise attack at night and the Navajos suffered severe losses in lives and property (New Mexico Archives, Vol. 1840, pt. 4, University of New Mexico. Hereafter cited as NMA).

245

San Miguel Canyon stems from the northwestern side of Cebolleta Mountain as a branch of the Arroyo Chico which encircles the north end of the Mountain and joins the Rio Puerco of the East. This canyon was the home of Cristobal, the Navajo involved with Vicente in peace talks with Governor Chacon and forbidden to graze his flocks south of San Mateo Spring.

In April of 1804, some Navajos attacked the New Mexicans at
Ojo del Espiritu Santo on the Southwestern side of Nacimiento Mountain
east of the Rio Puerco. They were pursued and attacked on the Rio de
San Miguel. Other Navajo aggressors were overtaken at the Agua del
Raton, a spring near Pueblo Pintado, one of the ruins in Chaco Canyon
about thirty miles airline to the northwest of Cebolleta Mountain.

Further difficulties occurred with the Navajos when New
Mexican sheepmen invaded the Canyon of San Miguel in 1816 with their
flocks and two pastors were killed. Two years later another one was
killed and three wounded; in fear of retaliation, the Navajos moved
away for the moment.

246

In the light of this dispute, peace talks were held between
the two parties whereby the Navajos retained "the land that heretofore
they had used for corn fields. . . ," and the "boundary line as
formerly established remained without change up to Canon Largo, the
mouth of Chaco Canyon and Blue Water . . ." (Instructions to Governor
Facundo Melgares, August 18, 1819. Peace terms approved by Viceroy
Conde del Venadito, October 25, 1819. Gaceta de Mexico, Tomo X,
vol. 40, pp. 1127-30).

The Blue Water site represented a concession to the Navajos
because it lies about twenty miles west of Mt. Taylor on the Rio San
Jose, or about twenty miles south and west of San Mateo Spring which
was the southern point in the treaty of 1805. Perhaps the negotiators
did not consider significant the difference in location between the
two sites when delimiting pasture land.

The Chaco Canyon and Mesa was another area of Navajo occupation
beginning at a point about fifteen miles airline north of Cebolleta
Mountain. In the spring of 1844, these folks ran off some stock from
the Plaza Barranca, a few miles upstream from Abiquiu in the Chama
Valley, and were trailed to the Chaco Mesa, but the plunder was not
recovered (NMA, 1844, pt. 4). The following year they stole two
saddle horses belonging to the pueblo of Santa Ana which is a close
neighbor of Jemez Pueblo. They were promptly pursued to the Chaco
Mesa where one was killed when fighting to retain his horse (Ibid.,
1845, pt. 4).

The Rio San Juan, far to the north of Cebolleta Mountain,
drains northwestern New Mexico, bending slowly from a southern course
to a western and then northwestern to empty its waters into the
Colorado River. The Rio Chama rises near the San Juan south of the
present Colorado State boundary, flowing southward and southeastward
to join the Rio Grande northwest of Santa Fe. The village of Abiquiu
nestles on a high point a few miles downstream from the Rio Chama
Canyon where the river begins its southeastern course. The Rio Puerco
of the North flows from the south to join the Chama at a junction site
known as the Piedra Alumbre where the main stream emerges from its
canyon. The Navajos and Utes had a common interest in the Abiquiu
region for trade and marauding, and the Jicarillas acquired a modest
interest after the American occupation of the Southwest.

As early as 1796, Spanish officials commented on the close
relationship that existed between Navajos and Utes. The latter were of
the Capote branch whose members wandered over the region both east and

247

west of the Rio Chama and the lands north of the San Juan (Pedro de Nava
to Governor, Chihuahua, July 8, 1796. Twitchell, *Spanish Archives*, II,
1366). A decade later a group of Utes and Jicarillas arranged for a
joint buffalo hunt on the eastern plains. The Utes were referred to as
"dispersed throughout the regions of Navajo, Ojo del Espiritu Santo, and
Cerro de S. Antonio" (*Ibid.*, 2304). This description, of course, embrace
other bands of Utes than the Capotes who were in closest contact with
Navajos. The first of the three localities lies westward from the Rio
Chama into the Rio San Juan Valley; Ojo del Espiritu Santo is located
east of the upper Rio Chama; and the Cerro de San Antonio marks the
valley of the Rio Grande, north of Taos, New Mexico.

The "regions of Navajo" was crossed by these folks when bent
on mischief toward their New Mexican neighbors, and likewise by the
latter when pursuing their tormentors. In 1844, for instance, some
Navajos were overtaken at Horse Lake with cattle stolen from the
village of Ojo Caliente which lies fifteen miles airline to the
northeast of Abiquiu. Horse Lake lay along the Old Spanish Trail into
Utah and was a favorite camp site for Indian and trader. It is
distant some fifty miles airline to the northwest of Abiquiu. Unfortunately for the Navajos, but otherwise for the New Mexicans,
the stolen cattle were recovered (Governor of New Mexico, July 20,
1844. NMA, 1844, pt. 2). A less successful bunch of raiders were
caught in the attractive valley of Tierra Amarilla, about ten miles
east of Horse Lake, where a few lost their lives and others were capture
(Juan Andres Archuleta to Governor, Santa Fe, November 21, 1845. *Ibid.*,
1845, pt. 7).

248

When the New Mexicans planned an expedition against the Navajos, they did not expect to find them in the region of Horse Lake, but much farther to the west in the Tunicha Valley and Chuska Range. The usual points of departure against them were three: Abiquiu, Jemez or Laguna. In October 1838, Governor Armijo marched westward from Jemez with an unusually large contingent of men, and established a base camp at three lakes. Scouting parties were dispatched to find the enemy with instructions to reunite at Tunicha, close to the Mountain of the same name which is better known as Chuska. This was the central part of Navajoland because of the rugged terrain, good water supply and adequate pasture. On this campaign, the New Mexicans drove some Navajos from "Tunicha Mountain, their temple, more than 100 leagues," into the land of the Gila Apaches who joined forces with the pursued and gave battle to the invaders (NMA, 1838, pt. 3, p. 560).

249

In December, a sizeable campaign was launched from Abiquiu under command of Pedro Leon Lujan who led his men across the headwaters of the Rio Gallinas, over the Cuesta Navajo /Alto Utah/ into Largo Canyon. About midway of the Canyon, he moved westward across the high country, crossing Canon Blanco (tributary of the San Juan), and found a Navajo rancheria in the lower Tunicha Valley near the mountain of the Hot Springs or Bennett Peak as it is known today. The Arroyo de los Ojos Calientes begins near the north side of the Peak and soon joins the Arroyo Pena Blanca which is a tributary of the Rio Chaco. The Arroyo Pena Blanca provided grass and water for Indian livestock. This arroyo is sometimes referred to as Canon Blanco and must not be confused with the one above.

On the return journey, the advance party met with the baggage train at the junction of the Rios de las Animas and San Juan. If not short on supplies and ammunition, they could have pushed farther westward and found more Navajos. When the Spanish were having trouble with these people in 1818, the rebellious ones as the invaders termed them were believed to have assembled at Carrizo, and that "some" Utes accompanied them when they sallied forth from fortified mesas to commit robberies (Vergara to Gov. Pedro Maria de Allande, July 21, 1818. Twitchell, Spanish Archives, II, 2736). The Carrizo is the mountain of that name rising from the surrounding country to the north of the Luchachukai (or Chuska Range) and south of the Rio San Juan, about forty miles northwest of Bennett Peak.

250

Navajos ventured north of the Rio San Juan to plant corn in the lower valley of the Rios de la Plata and Las Animas, and graze their flocks on the rich pastures of La Plata Range which is drained to the southwest by the Rio Mancos, and on the south and east by the Rios Salado and La Plata, all tributaries of the San Juan rising in the extreme southwest corner of the state of Colorado. In this region they mingled with Utes as was attested in 1835 when two Ute men and two women visited Jemez Pueblo to trade. They were questioned about conditions among the Navajos and replied that all the rich chiefs were in the middle of La Plata and Datil Mountains with the Utes who also have their dwellings there. They were engaged in sowing their fields (M. Garcia to Blas Hinojos, Comandante General, Jemez, January 12, 1835. NMA, vol. 1835, pt. 1, Garcia was the representative of the Mexican government whose business was to know what went on in Navajoland since he was officially the Interpreter). The Datil Mountains lay at the junction of the Rios San Juan and Las Animas, north of the former and west of the latter. La Plata Mountains lay to the northeast of the Datils (Miera y Pacheco Map of 1778. A. G. N., Historia 26. Copy in H. E. Bolton, Pageant in the Wilderness, Salt Lake City, Utah, 1951), but the name Datil has been dropped and La Plata now designates the range.

The visit of the Utes to Jemez in 1835 was typical of the status of that village in Indian affairs. It was a common meeting point for Navajo, New Mexican, and sometimes the Ute. The Spanish stationed their Interpreter at Jemez in the late eighteenth century, and in a later treaty stipulated that a Navajo "general" should live there. It is doubtful that this provision was literally observed, but it was not unusual for a few Navajos to live with the Jemez for a period of time, and shorter visits were common, especially since they lived close by--and, of course, friction was periodical.

251

One of the abortive peace treaties between New Mexican and Navajo, negotiated in 1841 at the pueblo of Santo Domingo on the Rio Grande, led to the renewal of trade and joint use of land in the Puerco valley, so the status quo ante bellum reigned once more along the frontier "and in their own lands where /New Mexican/ stock is now grazing, besides that no theft has occurred nor the least insult to the pastors; moreover, they /Navajos/ are engaged in sowing their fields on the margins of the Rio Puerco very close to the frontiers" (NMA, 1841, pt. 1, and pt. 2).

This idyllic state did not last long; moreover, trouble broke
out with the Utes. A party of New Mexicans was licensed in 1843 to plunder
the Navajos in the San Juan region. Failing to find them, the speculators
attacked a band of peaceful Utes in the Abiquiu region and their chief,
Spanish Cigar, was soon in consultation with the Governor at Santa Fe
demanding redress of grievance.

> The Governor refused to give him the desired satis-
> faction, and the Indian seized him by the throat,
> and commenced shaking him. Martines drew his sword,
> and run the Indian through the body;--he then gave
> orders to his soldiers to fire, and six of the
> Indians who had accompanied the Eutaw Chief were
> killed upon the spot (George Bent, Taos, Sept. 9,
> 1844. "Letters and Notes," _Colorado Magazine_,
> 11:226. Nov. 1934).

This same year, a small group of Navajos "in the suburbs of
Jemez Pueblo" were attacked in the winter and instructions came from
252 Santa Fe to investigate the matter (January 27, 1844. NMA, 1844, pt. 2).
The term suburb implies in the _very_ neighborhood, but the statement is
vague.

The trouble may have stemmed from the New Mexican ranchers
in the neighborhood. Diego Baca, age sixty-nine, testified in 1893
as to his knowledge of the Ojo del Espiritu Santo Grant on the west
side of Nacimiento Mountain or due west of Jemez, and he recalled
having known the locality since 1842 because in that year he accompanied
his uncle to Mesta's house _west_ of the Puerco to arrange peace with
some Navajos (Federal Land Office, Santa Fe, Court of Private Land Claims,
Case #50). A land grant had been made to Joaquin Mesta in 1768, although
occupancy had not been continuous. Gregorio Mesta in the 1840's was
accused of having stolen a horse from his neighbors and, as a result, the
Navajos were "moving some of their families away" (NMA, 1844, pt. 2).

After the fracas with Governor Martinez in 1844, Utes made
overtures for peace through Chief Narbonna of the Navajos who came to
Jemez to reconfirm his own desire for a continuing peace, and to open
talks for the Utes. They had journeyed to his home in the Tunicha
Valley to solicit aid. Narbonna was assured that all the Utes need do
was to send emissaries to Abiquiu or Jemez for talks and they need not
be afraid of harm when coming for that purpose. In February of 1846,
three Ute captains did come to Jemez--but more important for the moment
is the location of Narbonna's home. It was in the heartland of the
Navajo country, or the "temple" whence Governor Armijo had driven them
in 1838.

The glory of the heartland is the Canyon de Chelly on the
west side of the Chuska Range, a magnificent red sandstone walled canyon
with drainage westward into the Chinle Wash which extends northward to
the Rio San Juan. The Canon del Muerto, or Massacre Canyon, a branch of
the Chelly, was the site where Governor Narbonna trapped a large number
of Navajos in a cave and killed many, mostly women and children. It
was this campaign that led to the futile boundary delimitation of 1805.

253

The land along the west and east sides of the Chuska Range was
rich in grass and the streams from the mountain nourished many corn
patches. However, geographical detail westward from the Range is lacking
for the Mexican era. The south end of the Chuska fades away into the
low pass across the continental divide where the Atchison, Topeka and
Santa Fe Railroad laid rails in the 1880's that were extended on to
California. Across the pass the Zuni Mountains rise and at their northern
edge Bear Spring bubbles from the ground.

The pueblo of Zuni lies over the Mountain to the west of south
from Bear Spring and Blue Water is thirty-five miles toward the southeast. Farther eastward lies the Cubero region where a scattering of
Navajos lived. From these several vantage points they annoyed the Zuni
and ventured far to the south for trading or marauding in the country
of the Apaches.

The Apaches in southwestern New Mexico, of course, had long
been a thorn in the flesh of New Mexicans, and after the diplomatic
success of Governor Anza in the 1780's whereby he made allies of the
Navajos, they in turn were attacked by southern Apaches and retaliated--
likewise the folks of Zuni who were menaced by "Coyotero Apaches of the
Pinal, who are there called Mescaleros, and to the north /of the Pinal/
by the Apaches of the San Francisco and Mogollon Ranges. They have
penetrated inland, pursued by our arms. They are called Gilenos there
/New Mexico/" ("The Zuniga Journal, Tucson to Santa Fe." Ed., George P.
Hammond. New Mexico Historical Review, 6:63).

254

At the opening of the nineteenth century, the Escalante expedition found Navajos bartering blankets with Apaches in the Mogollon
Mountains, a home site of the latter (Nemesio Salcedo to Governor of New
Mexico, Chihuahua, July 5, 1806. Spanish Archives, II, 1998). On another
occasion, some Gila Apaches visited the Navajos in Canyon de Chelly. A
few of the latter accompanied the visitors on the homeward trip to do
some trading, but enroute their so-called friends stole the Navajo horses
at siesta time. This story was told by Chief Segundo of the Navajos
when visiting in Santa Fe (Nicholas de Almanza for the Governor,
Santa Fe, November 3, 1807. Ibid., 2089).

In 1813, two Navajos set out to steal from the southern Apaches
and reported killing one at Agua Caliente, taking a horse and a saddled
mule belonging to the unfortunate victim. His kinsmen retaliated by
stealing horses from Navajos. The Alcalde of Laguna followed their
trail, but abandoned it in the Datil Mountains, about 100 miles to the
south as the crow flies (Vicente Lopez to Governor, Laguna, September 14,
1813. Ibid., 2514). The raiders from the south reached their northern
goal by way of a trail along the west side of the McCarty lava flow
into the valley where lay the spring of El Gallo, the future side of
Old Fort Wingate after the American occupation of New Mexico.

In July of 1815, five Apaches seized some horses and one burro
from the Zuni folk. Pursuers were unable to overtake them, but found
the burro dead "a long distance from Zuni" (Ibid., 2616). Two months
later the Navajos launched an attack on the Mogollon Mountain Apaches
and seized six persons (Ibid., 2585).

255

These various episodes illustrate the fact that the Navajos
and Apaches lived far apart. The former north of the Rio San Jose and
the latter at least as far south as the Datil Mountains, although their
more common location was deeper into the southwestern mountainous
country. At first glance this viewpoint might be modified with the possession of sheep by Apaches, but on second thought it is not.

In the 1830's, the Governor granted permission to Rafael Lopez
for a raid on a flock of sheep belonging to "Apaches" on the Rio Salado,
presumably the one to the southwest of Belen, New Mexico. He set forth
with fifteen men and claimed to have started for home with 3,500 sheep,
three burros and six horses, but the Apaches attacked and recovered their

stock (J. de Madariaga to Gefe Politico y Militar del Territorio, Tome, June 26, 1836. NMA, 1836, pt. 2). The site of this foray lay southwes of a prominent landmark known as Ladron Peak which in turn is southwest of Belen, or toward the haunts of the Gila Apaches. Since the word Apache had been dropped in reference to Navajos, were these folks truly Apaches or Navajos?

The Apaches were not commonly sheep owners as was so true of the Navajos, but during the course of the nineteenth century they did occasionally steal sheep. In 1815, for instance, a band attacked the Zuni Pueblo flocks and drove away a number of ewes (Spanish Archives, II, 2585). In southern New Mexico, some Mescalero Apaches ran off a few sheep in 1824 from the neighborhood of San Elizario, a settlement on the Rio Grande below El Paso (Diary of Captain Santos Orcasitos. Secretaria de la Defensa. Operaciones Militar1824-1825. Archivo Historico Militar, Mexico, DF). About a quarter century later, Apaches raided near Santa Cruz, Sonora, and tried to steal some sheep. They failed but managed to secure cattle and horses (Santa Cruz, September 8, 1848. Documentos para la Historia de Sonora, 4:84. Bancroft Library). And after the political organization of New Mexico as a Territory of the United States, "Apaches" raided the flocks belonging to the pueblo of Cochiti (Annie Heloise Abel, The Official Correspondence of James S. Calhoun, pp. 48-58. Washington, 1915); but this is too far fetched to be taken at face value.

Navajos occasionally raided the New Mexicans downstream from Belen in the region where Apaches also felt at home in the game of hide and seek. In 1840, they stole some animals just north of Socorro and

256

were pursued to the northwest as far as Ojo de la Jara, but were not
overtaken (Juan Francisco Baca to Don Mariano Chaves, Socorro, August 24,
1840. NMA, vol. 1840, pt. 3). These marauding activities were of concern to the more responsible minded Navajos as well as to the New Mexican
officials, so representatives of Narbonna and Armijo, prominent Navajo
leaders, journeyed to the village of San Ysidro in the Jemez Valley to
discuss the matter. They stated that Armijo had traveled extensively
in Navajoland exhorting his people to remain at peace, but that /Jose7
Largo was in the "Apache country." However, he too wanted peace and
was willing to return to his "old planting fields" if it were not for
the fact that the Utes might molest him (Francisco Sandoval to M. Armijo,
San Ysidro, April 6, 1841. Ibid., vol. 1841, pt. 3). Largo's predica-
ment probably arose from the intensive campaigns launched against the
Navajos by Governor Manuel Armijo in 1838 when one party was pursued
into the haunts of the Gila Apaches. So it is far more likely that
the sheep raided by Rafael Lopez belonged to Navajos and not to Apaches.

257

When trouble between New Mexican and Navajo was brewing again
in 1843, leaders among the peaceful Navajos tried to avoid involvement;
therefore, J. Chavez, Sarcillos Largos and El Facundo let it be known
that they wanted the recognized right to settle in the Zuni Mountains
at the Bear Spring and on the Chusca Mesa. Prefect J. Sarracino approved
this request and invited the Navajo leaders to a conference when arrangements would be made for them to campaign with New Mexicans against their
own people (J. Sarracino to J. A. Archuleta, Pajarito, June, 1843.
Ibid., vol. 1843, pt. 4). Whether the Governor approved the Prefect's
decision is not known, but three years later it was rumored that Largo

had settled at Blue Water, the small canyon with arable land and water
opening into the Rio San Jose Valley from the northern side of the Zuni
Mountains that was mentioned in the treaty of 1819. This was not pleasi
to New Mexican authorities at this later date and there was the possibil
that they might try to drive the Navajos away from the site (Letter to
Commandant of the 2nd District, Pajarito, Jan. 27, 1844. Ibid., vol. 18
pt. 2).

The Cubero Region, where friction was chronic, lay east of Blue
Water. In 1806, the Spanish authorities planned an all out attack on
the Navajos with a force sent northward from Sonora by way of Zuni
Pueblo to unite with a New Mexican force assembled near Cubero. Then
they moved northwestward into the heart of Navajoland but found only
four Indians in the Chuska Valley. They killed the two men and captured
the woman and child. A second invasion led to an hours-long fight in
the Canyon del Muerto.

Military movements launched from Cubero or Laguna did not
prevent a scattering of Navajos from living around the southern end of
Cebolleta Mountain. About 1816, some of them wanted to move to the
Canyon de Chelly in fear of attacks from Comanches. They asked
Governor Pedro Maria de Allande of New Mexico to give them a certificate of ownership for holdings at Encinal, San Jose and Cubero so that
their lands would not be appropriated by New Mexicans during their
temporary absence (Spanish Archives, I, 668).

The expansion of population led a group of settlers at Cebollet
to apply for a grant of land at Cubero in 1833 which was approved by
the Governor with Cebolleta Mountain as the northern boundary. The

258

grantees were Juan Chavez and sixty-one others. Francisco Baca, "a
Navajo Indian," was a prior claimant to this land, so his holdings
were bought out by the new-comers. However, the folks of Laguna Pueblo
claimed the same land and denied the right of Baca to sell. A petition
was made to the Governor of New Mexico in August, 1835, to quiet title.
The Alcalde took the side of Laguna against the Navajo and the new
settlers but the last named eventually won out (Ibid., I, 910, 1310.
Federal Land Office, Santa Fe. Cubero Town Grant, C. D. No. 1,
File 26, doc. 3).

Another Navajo by the name of Jose Sarracino was successful
in realizing his desire when the Governor of New Mexico permitted him
in February of 1845 to plant at San Mateo, and the local Prefect was
instructed to assist with a supply of seed (NMA, Vol. 1844, pt. 2).
San Mateo lies on the southwestern flank of Cebolleta Mountain, a
few miles from the head of San Lucas Canyon which is a branch of San
Miguel Canyon. The last named canyon, of course, was or had been
occupied by Navajos. Cubero lay over the mountain to the south from
San Mateo and Blue Water was about equidistant toward the west. Other
Navajos continued to live in the canyons to the north of Cubero, prior
to the coming of the Americans, visiting, trading and sometimes
committing a theft in the settlements.

NAVAJO EASTERN FRONTIER

With the American annexation of the Southwest in 1848, the
picture of Navajo location along their eastern frontier underwent no
immediate change. A military detachment was established in 1846 near
the village of Cebolleta (most likely the site called Cebolletita) on

259

the southeastern side of Cebolleta Mountain which is topped by Mt. Taylo
"The Nebajos, as we learn, have left a corn-field, which is said to be
about ten miles from us [the military detachment], to which we think of
moving, if we can find a pass through the mountains" (Jacob S. Robinson,
A Journal of the Santa Fe Expedition under Colonel Doniphan, p. 39.
Princeton University Press, 1932). The location of the cornfield was
pinpointed by Edwards: "Colonel Jackson has concluded to move in the
morning ten miles west of this [Moquino] to a place where there is plent
of good wood, water, and grass, and some fields of corn fodder deserted
by the Navaje Indians" ("Journal of Marcellus Ball Edwards, 1846-1847."
Edited by Ralph P. Bieber. The Southwest Historical Series, 4:187.
The Arthur H. Clark Company, Glendale, California, 1936). The site
was Encinal, about five miles from Cubero, and the cornfields as Edwards
wrote were full of Indian lodges which the soldiers burned for firewood,
not realizing, of course, that the Indians would be back in season to
occupy them.

260

A detachment was sent westward from Cebolleta to contact the
leading men in the center of Navajoland. Having traveled about twenty-
five miles over the mountain, the soldiers "descended into a valley,
which is the residence of Sandoval. . . . ," a rich Navajo.

> His situation is one of the most beautiful, being
> on an elevated plain, 3000 feet above the level of
> the country, and the mountain rising to snowy peaks
> behind it. Springs of pure water gush from the
> rocks, and find their way in rivulets across the plain
> to the precipice, down which the waters leap, scattering
> their spray to the winds. A view of the green grass and
> fine trees, with his beautiful fields of corn and wheat,
> make one almost forget that it is the abode of an un-
> tutored Indian (Robinson, op. cit., pp. 41, 56).

Sandoval's valley so described by Robinson lay on the west side of Cebolleta Mountain, at the spring of San Mateo or Willow Springs, a few miles farther north, where the Old Mountain Road descended into Arroyo Chico. The upshot of this first step in American policy toward the "untutored Indian" was their understanding not to fight Americans, but a lack of understanding that they could not continue to fight Mexicans, especially since the Americans were now fighting them. After the close of the War with Mexico, the Federal Government took in hand the matter of preventing the Navajos from fighting anyone, Mexican or American. Sandoval, a Navajo leader in the Cubero region, became an intermediary between his people, who lived at Tunicha and Chusca, and the military. In January of 1849, Capt. Creghan Kerr, commander at Cebolletita, a couple of miles south of Cebolleta, sent word through Sandoval that he would agree to peace only with Navajos who were favorably disposed and would locate in a fertile valley about fifteen miles from Cebolleta (Kerr to AAAG, Cebolleta, January 29, 1849. United States Army Command, New Mexico, Letters Received, 1848-1849, Kl. The National Archives, Record Group 98. Hereafter cited in abbreviated form).

261

The distance of fifteen miles to the "fertile valley" was only approximate and could include one of several sites in relation to Cebolleta: Juan Tafoya and Guadalupe Canyon to the north; Encinal or some farther canyon on the west; or Sandoval's home valley on the west side of Cebolleta Mountain. The nearby lands at Pojuate, Cebolleta, and Cubero were occupied; they were "ordinary Mexican" villages (not Indian Pueblos) (James H. Simpson, Journal of a Military Reconnaissance, from Santa Fe, New Mexico, to the Navajo Country, p. 114. Philadelphia, 1852).

According to an early visitor in these years, Cebolleta village "is located far up among the mountains of the Nabajo country . . ." ("The Rev. Hiram Walter Read, Baptist Minister to New Mexico," _New Mexico Historical Review_, 17:133). Insofar as distance is concerned, Cebolleta village is about ten miles as the crow flies north of the pueblo of Laguna. Pojuate lies about midway of these two villages, and Cubero lies a few miles to the northwest of Laguna. Simpson recommended in October of 1849 that a military post be established at Cebolletita, specifying certain military advantages and also for protection of friendly Navajos (_op. cit._), but his recommendation was not carried out other than stationing a detachment of troops there at times.

During the decade of the 1850's, government representatives toyed with the idea that the Navajos were not a united people and that the troublesome ones could be differentiated from the peaceful ones. They detected a difference between the groups who lived west of the Chuska Mountain, far to the northwest of Mt. Taylor, and those to the east. There was a portion among the eastern group who could be accepted as peaceful and should be accorded special consideration.

Sandoval was the alleged head man of the group in the peaceful category. Through long contact with New Mexicans, and even baptism in the colonial period, they were referred to as the Christian Navajos and were sometimes at odds with their kinsmen. Sandoval even engaged in raids against those who lived on the east side of the Chuska range.

> A famous half-tamed Nabajo Chief named Sandoval, who resides in this vicinity, came into town today to sell some captives of his own nation which he has recently took prisoners. --He sold one young man of 18 years of age for thirty (30) dollars (Read, _op. cit._, p. 133).

262

However, Sandoval and his own followers were not entirely trusted by the military. The chief could serve as a guide for the white man in military operations against the Navajos, but some of his own group might warn their kinsmen that trouble was on the way (D. T. Chandler to AAAG, Cebolleta, April 23, 1851. USAC, NM, LR 1851, C37). Furthermore, it was not always possible to determine whether a Navajo from Sandoval's group had caused trouble or whether the troublemaker came from elsewhere.

In 1853, Col. Edwin Vose Sumner was of the opinion that Sandoval "with his half Pueblo, half Navajo band" had a hand in current trouble. "He is an unprincipled scoundrel" and gains from war by stealing from both sides (Sumner to Gov. Wm. Carr Lane, Albuquerque, June 10, 1853. USAC, NM, LS, Vol. 8, p. 544), that is, from his own kinsmen and from the New Mexicans.

Major H. L. Kendrick held the more favorable view that "in relation to Sandoval, I have now to say that these people [other Navajos] are anxious to get rid of him fearing him greatly, whereas we ought to sustain him and to use him as a scourge" (Kendrick to AAAG. Fort Defiance, June 14, 1853. USAC, NM, LR 1853, K15). When Sarcillos Largos, leader of a Navajo group that lived westward from Sandoval's location, reported to the military at Fort Defiance that some Navajos had run off a band of sheep west of Jemez Pueblo, Kendrick suspected that the raid was one that had been made near Laguna, and that the culprits belonged to Sandoval's band (Kendrick to Acting Governor W. G. Messervy. Fort Defiance, May 13, 1854. Office of Indian Affairs, New Mexico Superintendency, Letters Received, Misc. Papers, 1854. The National Archives Record Group 75). The matter was one of probability,

263

but serves to reveal the conflicting attitude toward Sandoval's status.
His band, at least, was not attacked when the military campaigned
against Navajos during the decade of the 1850's, although they were
never above suspicion as troublemakers.

A few months later, "On the 15th inst. Sandoval, a Navajo
Indian, (of Cebolleta in this Territory) with his Son and twelve
Navajos came to our grazing camp in this vicinity. . . ." After some
arguments and sheep killing, the Indians were scared away (Preston
Beck, Jr., to Gov. D. Meriwether. Preston, Pecos River, October 16,
1854. Ibid.). Sandoval was certainly far afield trying to steal sheep
in far eastern New Mexico, or maybe just begging for some food, because
the Beck land grant lay near Las Vegas, New Mexico.

A couple of years later, it was reported that four Navajos
on Wednesday, June 25, 1856, "said to be of Sandoval's party . . . ,
came upon Juan de Dios Ballejos of Covera, in the mountain a little
above Ensenal /Encinal/, and shot him in two places" with a rifle ball
and an arrow, "and another one /arrow/ was shot into the back of his
shepherd" (S. Gorman to Capt. H. L. Dodge. Laguna, June 27, 1856.
Ibid., Misc. Papers 1856). Encinal lies a short distance to the east
of Cubero, and the mountain referred to, of course, was the southern
slope of Cebolleta Mountain. There are several canyons there, and
the Navajos did occupy one or more of them.

Moving out of Cubero in 1859, Lieut. Freedley visited these
folks.

264

Many of the indians had left their camp the night
before, but some I was informed were still encampted
in the Canon. I met a Mexican Boy with a burro
packed with beef. he stated that the indians had
killed one Cow on their trail and that he was
returning with the portion of it that they had
left behind. he stated also that there was tracks
of only three Cows with the indians although it
was said more were missing. I also met W. Wallace
who had lost the horses. he was returning having
given up the pursuit. The remainder of the indians
who were at Canon de San Jose fled before my arrival.
I seeing only one he being high up upon the mountain
among the rocks. The Canon de San Jose is a southern
Canon of the San Mateo /Cebolleta/ Mountain and is
about six miles from Cavero. A small stream of
water runs through the Canon and empties into the Ojo
del Galla. The water here was good but the grazing
was very poor owing to the number of sheep which are
grazed in the vicinity and to the amount of stock
belonging to the Indians lately in the Canon (H. W. Freedley, to Capt.
George Sykes, Los Lumás, April 30, 1859, USAC, NM, LR, Box 12, L28).

If the incident concerning Ballejos were a matter of concern

to some people as the beginning of real trouble between the Navajos   265

and the military, there was at least one skeptic:

> So far as we can learn the Navajo war is all 'in
> my eye.' Some few of Sandoval's band under Mariano
> are cutting up their 'shindys,' and popped a Mex.
> from Cuvero who was up in their country the other
> day. The people say that Kendrick's Indians
> are all as friendly as ever and have no intention
> of fighting. So we go (Extract from Lieut. John
> Trevitt to Asst. Surgeon De Leon. Near Laguna,
> July 3, 1856, in Carleton to Nichols, July 8.
> USAC, NM, LR 1856, C26).

The theory of separating the Navajos into peaceful and hostile

groups was also illustrated in 1851 when a few Navajo families were per-

mitted to settle near Cebolleta by the common consent of the military

and Governor James S. Calhoun (Lt. L. McLaws to Chandler, June 10, 1851.

USAC, NM, LS, vol. 7, p. 168. Old Book 4). As Governor Merivether

wrote three years later:

During these Navajo hostilities, a small Mexican
settlement called Sebolleta was broken up or
abandoned, and Gov. Calhoun gave Sandoval and his
party permission to occupy it, which they have
done up to this time, cultivating the soil with
some degree of success. But I am informed that the
former occupants of this settlement claim the land
under a Mexican grant, which will render it necessary
to provide for Sandoval and his followers in some
other quarters. . . . (Meriwether to Commissioner
G. W. Manypenny, Santa Fe, July 27, 1855. OIA, NM,
LS, vol. 2, p. 580).

The settling of these migrants to the east of Cebolleta
Mountain implies that Sandoval's location on the west side has become
too "hot" for his people because of retaliatory warfare from their
kinsmen. When Governor Meriwether negotiated a treaty with Navajo leaders
in 1855, Sandoval was not present because he had separated from the tribe
at large upon refusing to fight against the white folks (Meriwether to
266 Commissioner Manypenny, Santa Fe, July 27, 1855.   Ibid., p. 581).

As of 1857, Sandoval was credited in military circles with
having aided the Americans on campaigns as far back as the arrival of
General Kearny and the American occupation of New Mexico. According
to Colonel Bonneville, he had assisted Colonel Washington against the
Navajos in 1849 and later Colonel Sumner. He assisted in the campaign
against the southern Apaches in 1857 under the command of Colonel
Bonneville. During this campaign, a band of Utah Indians from the
Rio San Juan country raided Sandoval's "town," killed several Navajos
and a Pueblo Indian "on a visit there from Laguna" (Col. B. L. E.
Bonneville to AAG, Albuquerque, November 24, 1857. USAC, NM, LR,
Box 8, B43. Col. Bonneville to Supt. J. L. Collins, Albuquerque,
January 17, 1858. OIA, NM, LR, Misc. Papers 1858).

In the spring of 1858, John Ward, Special Agent for the Navajos, visited the frontier, touching at Jemez, Cebolleta, Cubero and "two Navaho camps." He reported that many Navajos had abandoned their fields in fear of attack by a combination of Utes, Pueblo Indians, and white men.

> Sandoval and Chino with their bands, are now
> living in the neighborhood of Laguna; the former
> has always been our friend, even against his own
> people who have, therefore, expelled him from
> among the real Navajos, to whom we give presents,
> Agents, etc. (John Ward to Agent S. M. Yost (pro
> tem Supt.), Albuquerque, April 9, 1858. OIA, NM, Misc.
> Files 1858. Same letter in Ibid., Agency Letters
> 1858).

The Military campaigned against the Navajos in the summer of 1858 in Major Brook's war, but Sandoval's band continued to enjoy its usual status although they had shifted location unless "neighborhood" has a very loose meaning. They were

267

> residing on the Puerco, and towards Jemez. They have
> for years been looked upon as a separate people. The
> superintendent of Indian affairs has decided they are
> at peace; they have just received their presents and
> must not be molested (AAAG to Miles, Santa Fe,
> October 14, 1858. AGO, Old Army Records, Letters
> Sent from Santa Fe. Also printed in 35 cong., 2 sess.,
> sen ex. doc. 1, 2:329).

The agent to the Navajos was very skeptical about their co-operative relations with the whites and so informed his superior:

> You distributed presents this year to Sandobals band
> which consists of about 300 souls. At that distribution
> there were over 700 persons of the Navajoe nation. More
> than half of them belong to the bands against which the
> United States were at war, who were harbored by Sandobal
> during hostilities and paid in presents by the Indian
> Superintendent (without the knowledge of the Agent) while
> hostilities were being carried on here in the region of this
> Post (Yost to Collins, Fort Defiance, December 18, 1858.
> OIA, NM, LR, Agency Letters 1858. RG75).

When rumors developed that the folks of Laguna and Acoma planned
to cooperate in an attack on the Sandoval band living on the Puerco, they
were promptly warned by the military not to molest these Navajos because
they were at peace and helping the soldiers as informants (Lt. J. N. G.
Whistler to Wilkins, Los Lunas, Nov. 8, 1858. Record Group 98. USAC,
NM, LR, W28/1858. Cited in Navajo Land Claim Case, Pl. Ex. 188,
Dockett 229).

The fact that they had left the Cebolleta site is confirmed
by Lt. Freedley who reported in 1859 that

> Besides Sebolletta there are several pueblos
> and ranchos in this Valley, each within about a
> mile of the other. The principal ones of them
> are called Sebollettatila /Sebolletita/, Moquina
> and Pojuate. these small towns are inhabited by
> . . . Mexicans . . ." (Lt. H. W. Freedley to Capt.
> George Sykes, Los Lunas, April 30, 1859. USAC, NM,
> Box 12, S28).

268

"On the Puerco" was not a clear statement, but since a traveler
spent the night with Sandoval's band, he was near a line of travel and
therefore just below the Agua Salada where one road passed to Jemez or
father south on the Cebolleta-Albuquerque road; the latter was more probable since in this instance the traveler was enroute to Los Lunas which
lies about twenty miles south of Albuquerque and served as a junction
point for travelers.

> A clerk of Judge Watts informed me today that a
> few days since while he was returning from Cebolleta
> he camped with Sandoval on the Puerco, and that night
> one of his animals was shot with an arrow, which
> since Sandoval has acknowledged to have been done
> by one or two Indians from the Navajo country who were
> in his camp that night (Lt. J. S. G. Whistler to AAG,
> Los Lunas, Nov. 1, 1858. USAC, NM, LR, Box 11, W25).

When framing terms for another peace treaty in December of 1858, the Superintendent of Indian Affairs stipulated that

> Sandoval and his people in consideration of his and
> their past fidelity and good conduct, will be per-
> mitted to occupy the country they now occupy
> notwithstanding the terms of the first of these
> articles /in the proposed treaty/ until otherwise
> provided in future, but in all other respects they
> are to be considered as part and parcel of the Navajo
> Nation (Collins to Bonneville, December 3, 1858. OIA,
> NM, LR, I-947 & C-1829. RG 75).

This stipulation was inserted in the treaty of December 25.

A probable location of Sandoval at this time can be inferred from Lt. Abert's report when he moved westward from Albuquerque in October of 1846, exploring the Puerco for a few miles up and down stream from where he first touched it. On the northern march, he encountered the old Spanish eighteenth century settlement of San Fernando, now abandoned and known simply as Poblazon with its history already forgotten by the New Mexicans. Nearby, in the river bed, he found "a conical hut, composed of light poles covered with boughs of trees and mud; also a corral, but no recent signs of their having been used." He also found a corn field which "The ravens had right of pos-session, and had eaten much of the corn, and picked all the seeds out of the big pumpkins that were strewed around us." However, the intruders challenged the possessory right of ravens and fed some of the corn to their animals who were much fatigued from traveling in sand which at every step enfolded the fetlocks. Continuing the journey westward, the weary travelers late the next day arrived near the village of Moquino (Lt. J. W. Abert, Report of his Examination of New Mexico in the years 1846-1847, p. 466f, Washington, 1848). The description recorded by

269

Abert fits the Navajo pattern of living. They planted their fields and left them largely to the tender mercy of nature while going about their business: trading, hunting, marauding or visiting kinfolk.

The region between Cebolleta Mountain and Chaco Mesa on the west and the Rio Puerco to the east was crossed by Navajos when visiting or raiding the settlements east of the river, and by New Mexicans when in search of Navajos for trade or plunder. On one occasion a band of these folks stole some sheep from a citizen of Corrales in the Rio Grande Valley and were pursued as far as Chaco Canyon (Ferdinand Aragon, Justice of the Peace at Corrales, to the Governor, January 14, 1857. OIA, NM, LR). Major Kendrick made a reconnaissance of the Navajo country in 1853 and remarked, among other things, that the numerous depredations on New Mexican stock were made in part "by a few bad and irresponsible men living near the mesa of Chaca, the Oso, and in the vicinity of Chuska" (Kendrick to AAAG, Fort Defiance, June 14, 1853. USAC, NM, LR, Box 5). Three years later, Manuel Barela of Albuquerque claimed that Navajos had taken fourteen of his mules "from a point near the Puerco River" and also some firearms from his herders. He trailed them to "a Navajo camp beyond Cibolleta." Chief Miguelito surrendered the arms, but said that he would have to come in force to recover the animals (Carleton to Kendrick, Albuquerque, February 1, 1856. OIA, NM, LR, Misc. Papers 1856)

Agustin Lacome, resident of Taos Valley, requested permission from Henry Dodge, agent for the Navajos, to trade with them "within the boundaries of the country occupied by the said tribe viz: Tunicha, Chusca, Chey, Carrizos, and San Juan . . . (Lacome to Henrique Dodge, Santa Fe, March 4, 1854. OIA, NM, LR). These were long established homesites of the Indians.

270

When Colonel Washington marched to Navajoland in 1848, he followed a route northwestward from the pueblo of Jemez to the Chaco Canyon:
"After marching over a barren, badly watered, and, in many places, rough
country for eight days, I arrived in the vicinity of the labores or
corn fields of the Navajoes, at Tuna Cha [Tunicha]" (J. M. Washington
to AG, Santa Fe, N. M., September 25, 1849. USAC, NM, IR, Box 456,
514W. Printed in 31 Cong., 1 sess., Sen. Ex. Doc. 1, pp. 111-112.
Serial 549). A decade later, Lt. H. W. Freedley observed that

> There is no good grazing in the bottom lands
> of the Rio Puerco and excepting some on the mesas
> but little on the eastern side of the river. The
> herds belonging to the different towns on the Rio
> Grande are generally grazed on the Western side
> of the Rio Puerco where excellent grazing may be
> obtained (Freedley to Sykes, Los Lunas, April 30,
> 1859. USAC, NM, IR, Box 12, 828/2).

Lt. Freedley's report was supported by a contemporary writer when he   271
described the Puerco Valley in the 1850's as good sheep land, "thousands
of which were seen grazing on every side," also stating that since Navajos
"have confined their depredations to the more southern and western portions of the Territory, the Rio Puerco has become a favorite grazing region
for the rancheros" (Samuel Woodworth Cozzens, The Marvellous Country,
p. 280f. Boston 1891).

The Boundary Line of 1855.

The depredations committed by the Navajos during the early years
of the American occupation led government officials to think of establishing
a boundary line between the two peoples. Major Kendrick in 1853 wrote
that "It is to be regretted that Mexicans place temptation before the
Navajoes by feeding their flocks on grounds belonging to the latter."
He did not in his particular communication define the limits of the
Navajo land holdings (Kendrick to AAAG, Fort Defiance, May 25, 1853.

USAC, NM, LR 1853, K11). In the fall of 1854, Governor David Meriwether
pointed out that it would be difficult to make a map of Navajo land because these and certain other Indians "never have had any specific
boundaries assigned to them, either by treaty or otherwise, and they
claim all the lands not actually occupied by the whites" (Meriwether to
Manypenny, Santa Fe, September 29, 1854. OIA, NM, LR, Misc. Papers
1854). He did send a map to Washington which delimited the Navajo
country as currently understood; but he remarked, "It should be borne
in mind, however, that these Indians claim and roam over a much greater
extent of country than that which I have assigned to them on the map"
(Ibid.).

The first attempt to mark a reservation for the Navajos was
made by the abortive agreement of 1855, negotiated at Black Lake on
July 18. The eastern boundary extended

> up the San Juan to the mouth of the Canada del
> Amarillo /Canyon Largo/; up this Canada to the
> divide between the drainage of the Rio Colorado
> of the West and the Rio Grande; along the divide
> southwesterly to the head of the main branch of the
> Rio Zuni.

The Navajos were to receive a monetary compensation for the cession of
land and removal to the area within the boundary line (OIA, Unperfected
Treaties No. 274A. The National Archives).

In the talks preceding the signing, it was understood that the
reservation boundary included the Sacred Mountain Polonia. When discussing the fourth article, Manuelito remarked

> that the Navajos claimed a much larger country than
> that proposed in the boundary assigned them, and that
> they were in the habit of going to Mount Polonia, and
> another mountain, the name of which is forgotten, to
> worship the spirits of their fathers, and some were loth

272

to give these mountains up; and also that they could not
get salt, unless they were allowed to visit the salt
lake near Zuni and gather it. The Governor then showed
them Park's /Parke/ map of New Mexico, and explained to
them that Mount Polonia was within the proposed reservation, and said he hoped that this one sacred mountain
would be sufficient; he also said he would grant them
the privilege of gathering salt as they desired, and
that he proposed to pay them for all the ceded territory. After some consultation among themselves,
Manuelito said that the boundary was satisfactory
(W. W. H. Davis, Secretary to the Governor, Notes of
a talk between Governor Merewether and the Chiefs,
Headmen, and Captains of the Navajo Indians, held at
Laguna Negra the 16th and 17th of July, 1855, through
the medium of two interpreters. OIA, NM, LR, 1855,
N486).

According to Parke's map, Mount Polonia is the Carrizo Mountain of today

which is a prominent landmark in the northeast corner of Arizona, due

north of Fort Defiance.

To enable you to understand the eastern boundary of
this reservation, refer to Parke's map of New Mexico
which I enclosed to you during the last winter, then
draw a line from the head of the Armarillo to the head
of the Zuni river or creek, which will give you the true
position of the ridge which divides the waters of the
Rio Grande from those of the San Juan, which is a well
defined boundary, well understood by the Indians
(Merivether to Manypenny, Santa Fe, July 27, 1855.
OIA, NM, LS, 2:580).

273

The boundary line of 1855 was approximately the continental

divide. Meriwether was probably correct in stating that it was well

understood by the Indians. The Amarillo was the name for the present-day

Large Canyon, a southeastern tributary of the San Juan River which heads

in the continental divide near the head waters of the Rio Puerco.

Nacimiento Mountain ranges northeast to southwest parallel to the upper

Rio Puerco. The highland extending northward from the mountain had

long been named by New Mexicans the Cuesta Blance or Cuestacita and

also as the Cuestacita de Navajo (Federal Land Office, Santa Fe, New

Mexico. Report 71 (File 83), and Report 73 (File 152)). The term Blanco
refers to the noticable white rock strata that one descends into the San
Juan drainage. Westward of this ridge lay the old Navajo country; that
is, the southeastern tributaries of the San Juan: Largo Canyon,
Blanco Canyon, and Governador Canyon where the Navajos were centered
in the Spanish period of New Mexican history.

The treaty did not eliminate friction between the
Navajos and New Mexicans. In January of 1856, Indians depredated near
the Rio Puerco. The Utes of Tamuche's band were also active and stole
stock (presumably Mexican) west of the Puerco, and "are now living at
the head of the river" (Francisco Tomas C. de Baca, Juez de Pruebas of
Pena Blanca, to W. W. H. Davis, March 7, 1856. OIA, NM, IR); that is,
the headwaters of the Rio Puerco. Some thirty Navajos under Aguila Negra
visited the pueblo of Jemez on June 8, 1856. On the way home they ran
off some cattle at San Isidro, a few miles south of the pueblo. These
Indians "live near the point of Sebolleta Mountain" (Meriwether to Dodge,
Santa Fe, June 17, 1856. OIA, NM, Agency Letters 1856).

Public agitation developed for further limiting the recognized
territory of the Navajos: "New limits should be established for the
Navajos, so as to give more room for our citizens to graze their stock"
(Santa Fe Weekly Gazette, October 18, 1856. Clipping in Miguel A.
Otero to Robert McClelland, Secretary of the Interior, Washington, D. C.,
December 5, 1856. OIA, NM, IR, 014/1856). "There is no necessity for
those Indians to have grazing grounds east of their settlements, for they
have far better pasture lands west of them, and where there will be no
interference from any quarter" (Ibid.). This argument implies that the

274

"settlements" of the Navajo lay west of the boundary line established by the abortive treaty of Red Lake. This would not include, of course, the Cebolleta Mountain sites, which lay east of that line.

Depredations continued as in past years. Some Navajos stole sheep from the borders of the Rio Puerco and were overtaken at Chaco Canyon (Julian Tenorio, Notary of the Probate Court of Bernalillo to the Secretary of the Territory. January 13, 1857. OIA, NM, LR, Misc. Spanish docs.). In some instances, a Navajo headman secured the restoration of stolen stock.

In December of 1858, a new agreement was made with some Navajo leaders concerning their eastern boundary. It was marked from Pescado Spring, at the head of the Rio Zuni, in a direct line to Bear Spring which lay to the north on the road from Albuquerque to Fort Defiance; thence in a direct line northeastward to the ruins of Escondido in Chaco Canyon, and from there northwestward to the junction of the Rio Chaco and the San Juan River. The Navajos were not to plant or graze their stock east of this line which was considerably west of the one drawn in 1855. The agreement was signed by Navajo leaders named El Huero, Armijo, Cabesa Colorada, and others. Major E. Backus, Lieut. G. Granger, and S. M. Yost signed for the Government (Articles of Peace, December 25, 1858. OIA, NM, LR 1859, C1885 or J947).

275

S. M. Yost, Agent to the Navajos, opposed the policy of further delimiting their country. He argued to his superior as follows:

> You state that you do not 'want the lands but it is for the effect upon the Indians.' I do not conceive it to be the policy of the Indian Department or the government, to deprive the Indians of lands which can be of no possible benefit to us, but which are of incalculable value to them.

He added that "The Indians themselves have no objection to an eastern
limit. They consider that they have that now" (Yost to J. L. Collins,
Fort Defiance, Dec. 18, 1858. OIA, NM, LR, Agency Letters 1858). Colonel
Bonneville had favored drawing the line as far west as Fort Defiance,
but in the opinion of Superintendent Collins, and correctly so, that
would have deprived the Navajos of much arable land (Collins to
Commissioner J. W. Denver, Jan. 8, 1859. Ibid., C1885).

Yost also took a dim view of the argument that Sandoval should
be treated differently than other Navajos. He was convinced that they
depredated: "he and his band /quoting Collins/ are permitted to remain
where they are, immediately almost on the border of the Rio Grande /?/;
and assume that he and his band have been entirely guiltless of thefts
. . ." (Yost to Collins, Dec. 18, 1858, op. cit.).

276

Article 18 of the agreement of 1858 stipulated that "The Sandoval
band could continue in the occupancy of land as was customary, but that
otherwise they would be considered a part of the Navajo nation" (op.
cit.). This represented a yielding to the Yost-Collins point of
view, and an attempt to clarify their status according to the white
man's notion of political arrangement. However, the treaty was not
ratified by the United States Senate.

Difficulties continued to occur between the Navajos and the New
Mexicans. Enroute westward from Los Lunas in 1859, Lt. Freedley arrived
at Laguna Pueblo where he

> learned that some days previous a number of horses had
> been stolen by the indians, but it was generally thought
> by the Apaches. I could obtain no other information
> regarding the indians at this town, and leaving it, I
> took the trail for Cavero /Cubero/. This road led over

/a/ high rocky mesa, up the side of which it was
quite difficult for the pack mules to climb. About
12 AM I arrived at Cavero where I found large numbers
of indians /Navajo/, although many had left on my
approach. The people here complained bitterly of the
Navajos, and stated that they were continually stealing
the animals, that were grazing near the town, within
the past ten days they had been stealing more frequently, and on a larger scale than at any time since the
treaty with them. I estimated the number of indians in
and around the town at two hundred. These indians were
camped in the Canons of the Sierra San Mateo /or
Cebolleta/ from four to twelve miles from the town.
These were the band of Navajos (late Sandovals) which
formed the peace party during the War last winter and
some of the indians from the west (Caramilla's band
and others) . . . . Many of these indians lounged idly
about the town living upon what they could procure from
the Citizens and upon the refuse of the town. I had
no opportunity to converse with any of the chiefs, and
all apparently /sic/ endeavored to avoid the command. soon
after my arrival nearly all left the town for their
respective camps (Lt. H. W. Freedley to Capt. George
Sykes, Los Lunas, New Mexico, April 30, 1859. USAC, NM,
Box 12, S28/2).

277

Moving eastward over the mountain ridge to the village of

Cebolleta, Freedley listened to complaints from the residents that the

thieving Navajos in their locality came from Tunicha and Chuska. They

lived for a few days with Andres band (late Sandovals)
then returned to their country much better mounted
and equipped than before. They also accuse Andre's
band of a great deal of petty thieving. The
ranchorilla of Andres is I understand about 10
miles from Sebolletta at the foot of the San Mateo
mountain (Ibid.),

presumably Juan Tafoya Canyon.

In February of 1860, the military reported that several camps

of Navajos were near Cubero on the road to Fort Defiance, "presuming

that the same course will be adopted as was done toward Sandoval's

band in the fall of 1858," that is, that they would be given supplies

(O. L. Shepherd to AAAG, Fort Defiance, February 25, 1860. USAC, NM, Box 14, S30).

Open warfare broke out in 1860 between the Navajos on the one hand and the New Mexicans and Pueblo Indians on the other. The military finally stepped in and arranged another understanding with some Navajo leaders. Under article 5, they were not to graze their flocks nor live in the region that lay to the east of Fort Fauntleroy, located at Bear Springs. Any Navajos found east of the Tunicha and Chuska valley or to the south and east of Zuni Pueblo would be regarded and treated as robbers. The only exception made was in favor of the friendly Navajos under Po-Ha Conta (successor to Sandoval who had recently died), living in the neighborhood of Cubero and Cebolleta (L. L. Rich AAG, General Orders No. 14, by Lieut. Col. E. R. S. Canby, Fort Fauntleroy, February 19, 1861. USAC, NM, Box 14, C 32 and C 32/1).

278

Friction with the eastside Navajos continued about as usual until they were rounded up by orders of General J. H. Carleton and moved to the Bosque Redondo, on the Pecos River, in 1863. The General had trouble, of course, keeping his wards in their new home, and did not always succeed.

> At 6 o'clock this afternoon two Indians of the Pueblo of Laguna came in here, and reported that they had seen the day before yesterday in the Canon Juan Tafolla 30 Navajo Indians all well armed with fire-arms. They had 3 pack animals and 3 women along with them. The Navajoes told them that they had escaped from the Reservation at the Bosque Redondo and that other of their tribe were following them in parties of 15 to 25, and that they also would arrive at the above mentioned place this night (Jose Francisco Arragon to C. O., Fort Wingate, San Mateo, September 12, 1865. War Dept., RG98, NM, IR, FM M97/1865 enclo. Cited in Pl. Ex. 374, Dock, 229, Navajo).

NAVAJO NORTHERN FRONTIER

The interlocking relationship between Navajos and Utes during the Mexican regime continued after 1846. The tendency prevailed among American officials to regard the San Juan River as the boundary line between these two peoples. The former were sometimes referred to as the Upper and the Lower San Juan Navajos, but the distinction was not clear geographically speaking.

From the listening post of Abiquiu, Major L. R. Graham reported in April of 1851 that a large body of Navajos were on the Upper San Juan with their families and stock.

> They can be reached from this Post by easy marches
> in eight or ten days, the grass is good during the
> month of May--on the entire route--and an abundance
> of good water with the exception of thirty five
> miles, the longest stretch without water.

They were reported by a Ute Chief named Tamuchi as having been at peace for a long time and were even anxious to get the Utes to assist them in a war against other Navajos (Graham to AAAG, Abiquiu, April 1, 1851. United States Army Command, New Mexico, Letters Received, Box 2. AAAG to Col. D. T. Chandler at Cebolleta, Santa Fe, April 17, 1851. Ibid., Letters Sent, vol. 7, p. 93. Old Book 4).

279

When reporting on the status of Chief Sandoval of the Cebolleta Mountain Region, who was at odds with his kinsmen, Capt. Chandler stated that Sandoval

> seems to consider that portion of the tribe living
> beyond the San Juan as not being concerned. in
> stealing his cattle, I am induced to believe he is
> not as hostile to them unless we make it his interest
> to be so (Chandler to AAAG, Cebolleta, April 23, 1851.
> United States Army Command, New Mexico, Letters Received
> 1851, C37. National Archives. Record Group 98).

At this same time five Navajo chiefs sent runners to Colonel
Chandler at Cebolleta that they wanted peace. They had received information that an expedition was on foot against them. In reality, there
was no such expedition yet planned, but from the same informants it was
learned that Navajos had planted on both sides of the San Juan that
spring (Chandler to AAAG, Cebolleta, April 19, 1851. _Ibid._, C37).
The planting fields lay along the valley from the present-day town of
Fruitland, New Mexico, to the neighborhood of Blanco. These Indians
were probably the group referred to as the Upper San Juan Navajos. The
following month, traders reported that a large number of Navajos with
families and flocks were living in the Ute country (L. P. Graham to
AAAG, Abiquiu, May 6, 1851. _Ibid._, G 10); or, as Superintendent
Calhoun reported,

280

> The Navajos have, or are removing from 'Cheille'
> to the Rio San Juan, and pitching their lodges
> upon both sides of the river. Upon the north
> side of the river they must mix with the Utahs
> (Gov. J. S. Calhoun to Lea, Santa Fe, May 4,
> 1851. (The Official Correspondence of James S.
> Calhoun, Ed. by Annie Heloise Abel. Washington,
> 1915. p. 342)).

In the light of information furnished by informants who were
familiar with Navajoland, Lt. Parke reported in 1851 that cornfields were
scattered along the San Juan Valley at intervals of one or two miles
from the mouth of Canada del Ojo Amarillo /Largo Canyon/. There were
cornfields also along the rivers on the north side of the San Juan,
although this statement should not be taken literally. Along the easter
side of the Chuska Range, "Cornfields are stretched along at intervals
being more numerous as we approach the San Juan. It is said that

Archalette [Archuleta], Miguelito, Rayatano [Cayetano] Jose Largo and
other rich Navajoes plant in the vicinity and north of the Cerros de
los Ojos Calientes." (John G. Parke to Col. John Munroe, Santa Fe,
March 7, 1851. USAC, NM, IR, Box 3. The Cerros de los Ojos Calientes
are known today as Bennett Peak).

In June, Chandler reported that the Lower San Juan Navajos
were moving southward along both sides of Tunicha Mountain toward the
Zuni road because of the scarcity of grass and were discussing the
question of peace or waging war. The Upper San Juan Navajos were reported as being wealthy and in favor of peace, although they were an outlet for disposing of stolen stock (Chandler to AAAG, Cebolleta, June 2,
1851. Ibid., C 55).

In 1853, the military commander at Fort Defiance, which was
established in 1851 at the mouth of Canyon Bonito in the Chuska Range, 281
demanded that the Navajos bring in a murderer, but they protested their
inability. "Aigle [Aguila=eagle: hence Black Eagle] Negra, the chief
to whose band the murderers of the Mexican belong, has also been in
to day & says that the offenders are beyond the San Juan and does not
think that they will return at present" (Major H. L. Kendrick to AAAG,
Fort Defiance, July 12, 1853. Ibid., IR 1853, K 18. Cf: Kendrick to
Sturgis, Fort Defiance, June 14, 1853. Ibid., IR, Box 5).

Major Kendrick made a military reconnaissance of the Navajo
country from Fort Defiance to the San Juan in 1853. One detachment
then moved eastward from the junction of the Chaco River and the San
Juan, and Major Kendrick moved down the San Juan to the Rio Chelly
(Chinle Wash). He reported that considerable corn was raised east of

the Chuska range in the Chuska and Tunicha valleys, in Canon Blanco
(Pena Blanca), along the Chelly and in the Canyon of the same name
(Kendrick to AAAG, August 15, 1853. Ibid., IR 1853, K 19). The Canon
Blanco in this description is the Pena Blanca wash that drains into the
Chaco Wash from the east side of the Chuska Range. It is not the
Canon Blanco tributary of the Canon Largo which in turn joins the San
Juan River near the town of Blanco, New Mexico. The latter is one of
the canyons in the southeastern drainage of the San Juan in the area
inhabited by Navajos in the eighteenth century.

In September of 1853, Henry L. Dodge, agent for the Navajos,
escorted a delegation of 100 Indians to Santa Fe.

282

> This delegation is headed by their principal
> Chief Sarcillo Largo (or Long Earrings) and con-
> sists of the head men of the several bands residing
> most remote from our settlements, north of the
> Gela /Gila/ and in the neighbourhood of the Tuna
> Cha /Tunicha/ range of mountains.

Sarcillos Largos admitted that there were bad men among the Navajos,
but not from his group. Meriwether attributed most of the depredating
to Archuleta's band: "This chief and his band together with a few
other Navijos live nearer our settlements and on the border of the
Utahs with whom they associate, and are a bad set of fellows in my
opinion" (Gov. D. Meriwether to George W. Manypenny, Santa Fe,
Sept. 19, 1853. Office of Indian Affairs, New Mexico, Letters
Received 1853, N177. The National Archives. Record Group 75).

Discussing the matter of New Mexicans trading with the Mormons
in Utah Territory, the commentator stated that they crossed the San Juan
River enroute to Great Salt Lake City: "On the south of this stream is
the country of the Navijos; and further down on the same side, are the

villages of the Moquis, built of adobes" (Letter of P. P. Pratt in
Deseret News, November 21, 1853. Clipping in Church of Jesus Christ of
Latter-day Saints, Journal History. Church Archives, Salt Lake City.
Hereafter cited as LDS). Traders from New Mexico had been traveling to
Utah for a half century prior to the arrival of the Mormons. The Old
Spanish Trail crossed the San Juan at a point near the present-day state
boundary where the San Juan river flows into New Mexico, but this does
not preclude a turn-off farther west to reach the Navajos from the north.

The notion that the country south of the San Juan belonged to
the Navajos was illustrated when in May of 1854, Major Kendrick advised
some Navajo leaders that if they allowed the Ute Indians to come
south of the San Juan, and the Utes subsequently claimed the country
as their own, "we shall be at liberty to respect such claim" (Kendrick
to AAG, Laguna, May 23, 1854. USAC, NM, LR 1854, K5).

283

Seeking permission from proper authority to trade with the
Navajos, the petitioner specified the locations of "Tunicha, Chusca,
Cheye, Carrisos, and San Juan" (Agustin Lacome, resident of Taos Valley,
to Henry Dodge, Santa Fe, March 4, 1854. OIA, NM. LR). These were all
well-known Navajo homesites that had been occupied for many generations.
But the notion of a separate band of bad men in association with the
Utes was still stated as a fact: "There is one band of Navajos who
have separated themselves from the remainder of the tribe, and removed
eastward to the neighbourhood of the Utahs and Jicarillas" (Meriwether
to Manypenny, Annual Report, Santa Fe, September 1, 1854. OIA, NM, LR,
Misc. Papers 1854, N294).

The Jicarillas were newcomers who had lived eastward from Taos, New Mexico. During the American period, they became associated also with the land west of the Rio Grande because of the policy adopted by officials in New Mexico.

Pressure from the Plains Indians on northeastern New Mexico, especially the Pawnee in this case, led the Superintendent of Indian Affairs to hold an assembly of Utes at Abiquiu rather than at Taos as originally planned, all for the purpose of distributing annuities. Jicarillas were present because they had long been friendly with the Utes (Greiner to Lane, Report, December, 1852. Ibid., LR). A proposal to move the Jicarillas west of the Rio Grande soon followed on the ground that they were related to some extent with the Utes and that it was time for them to settle down to cultivate the soil. Governor Lane and Chief Chacon selected land on the Rio Puerco of the North, a favorite winter grazing spot for Indians for many years. The Utes opposed their location farther north and the Navajos objected to any movement farther west or south (Steck to Lane, Santa Fe, May 20, 1853. Ibid., LR). The seeming contradiction in the Utes' attitude toward the Jicarillas is not surprising They were no more a single unified group than any other Southwestern Indian tribe, so what one band might be doing at a given moment was not necessarily true of another band.

The migration of a few Jicarillas west of the Rio Grande apparently gave them ideas of grandeur about their portion of the earth's surface.

> A part of this band under their chief Chacon were
> assembled and fed around a farm in the vicinity of
> Abiquiu during the Spring and Summer of 1853. . . .

284

The Jicarillas now claim a region of country of
indefinite space, lying west of the Rio Grande
and on the head of the Chama and Puerco rivers,
but they roam over many other portions of the
Territory. . . (Meriwether, Report, Santa Fe,
September 1, 1854. Ibid., IR, Misc. Papers 1854).

The Capotes continued to wander far afield. On one occasion

they wintered in the San Luis Valley of south-central Colorado:

There are a larger number of indians in the
vicinity of Fort Massachusetts than is common owing
to the fact that a large portion of the Capotes who
live on the borders of the Navajoe country are passing
the winter there (Major George J. H. Blake to AAG,
Cantonment Burgwin, January 19, 1854. USAC, NM, Box
6, 1854).

The Jicarillas again were reported planting their fields west of the Rio

Grande in 1857 along the two streams of Rio del Oso and La Cueva

(Labadi to /Supt./, Abiquiu, May 31, 1857. OIA, NM, Agency Letters

1857).   285

Despite the wanderings of the Capotes and the removal of

Jicarillas to the Abiquiu region, the notion that the San Juan River

was the boundary line between the Utes and Navajos continued to be

affirmed. In the year 1854, another Mormon missionary crossed the

San Juan into Navajoland. He did not specify the site of the crossing,

but had probably traveled the Old Spanish Trail into Colorado and then

turned southward down the valley of La Plata or Las Animas to the San

Juan. He met some Navajos south of the river: "Their great captain

wished us not to go among their towns and villages, as there were some

that could not be controlled, and he did not want to fight us"

(Elder Wm. D. Huntington, Deseret News, December 21, 1854, clipping in

Journal History, same date. LDS).

However, the joint use of the valley of the San Juan and its tributaries is once more illustrated by the report of Lt. Ransom in 1853. He led a detachment from Abiquiu along the familiar trail that crossed the headwaters of the Rio Gallina and the Cuestacita Blanca into Largo Canyon. During a night encampment, a Navajo came in and reported that his people were on the San Juan. Jogging along the south side of that river, a few more Navajos were seen but others fled across the stream in fear of the soldiers. Corn fields were noted on the Las Animas and La Plata and in the lower Tunicha Valley. Ransom observed that a post at the junction of the San Juan and Las Animas would be strategically located for controlling the Utes and Navajos. The site was within thirty miles of Tunicha; it would command the "outlet" to the Utah country and would be within "40 miles of the Utahs /Utes7." (Lt. Rob. Ransom Jr., Report, USAC, NM, IR 1853, R13).

286

In the winter of 1854-1855, trouble was reported between Utes and Jicarillas in the San Juan region. In February, a small group of Navajos assembled at the Jemez Pueblo for a three day feast. Agent Henry L. Dodge was present and worried about the possibility of the Navajos becoming entangled in the Ute-Jicarilla trouble:

> I have sent out runners to all the Navijos /sic7
> living near the Rio San Juan to retire south
> fifty or sixty miles and to make every exertion
> to keep the Utau's from passing the aforesaid
> River which is recognized as the line between
> the two Nations.

The rich Navajos followed this advice, but some of the poor, Dodge feared, would join the Utes (Henry L. Dodge to Meriwether, Jemez, Feb. 13, 1855. OIA, NM, IR, Agency Letters 1855).

It is doubtful that Navajos would be interested in forcing a
Ute band out of the country south of the San Juan, but at any rate there
were some Utes there as reported in February:

> I have the honor to state, that the Navajoes informed
> their agent, Capt. Dodge, while on his way to this
> Post, via Jemez, that "Tamocches band of Capote
> Utahs" with a few Jicarilla Apaches were at the
> ojo del Gallo, a point some 30 miles South of the
> San Juan River, & Somewhere between the Chaco &
> Canon Largo of Parke's Map. It is Said that, in
> all, these Indians number Some 200, of which it
> is believed that a large portion are fighting men
> (Kendrick to AAG, Fort Defiance, February 25, 1855.
> USAC, NM, LR).

In April of 1855,

> the Navajoes report to us that the Utahs, with a
> portion of Jicarillas, in all amounting to nine
> hundred (men, women & children) are at the South
> Western base of the Sierra de la Plata, within
> the Utah country. . . . Some time since five
> Mexicans, from Abiquiu, came to their camp with
> corn for sale to the Utahs, who took their corn &
> slew the Mexicans (Kendrick to AAAG, Ft. Defiance,
> April 16, 1855. USAC, NM, LR, Box 7, K5. RG98. Cf.
> Dodge to Meriwether, Ft. Defiance, April 17, 1855.
> OIA, NM, Agency Letters 1855).

287

Meanwhile the Navajos were planting in their usual haunts of Tunicha and
Canon Blanco (Pena Blanca) in the spring of that year (Dodge to Meriwether,
Tunicha, May 2, 1855. Ibid., LR 1855, N440). Unfortunately for the
Navajo's peace of mind, the Utes

> attacked the Ranches of two rich Navijos living on
> the south side of the Rio San Juan killing them
> both capturing three children and running off one
> hundred head of horses. . . . This has produced a
> panick in all their farming operations for the present
> and caused the rich to flee to the mountains with
> their women children flocks & herds where they have
> concentrated in a body for mutual protection.

The mountain location was not specified, but it was the Chuska Range or Carriso Mountain. The outcome was uncertain, Dodge added, because the Utes were well armed, warlike and lived by the hunt, whereas the Navajos farmed, were poorly armed and unwarlike (Dodge to Manypenny, Santa Fe, June 30, 1855. *Ibid.*, IN 1855, N469).

Steps were now taken to arrange the treaty of July 18, 1855, with the Navajos at Laguna Negra (Black Lake). The terms included a northern boundary line along the south bank of the Rio San Juan from the mouth of the Rio Chelly to the mouth of Canada del Amarillo (Largo Canyon), up this canyon to the divide between the drainage of the Rio Colorado and the Rio Grande, along the divide southwest to the main branch of the Rio Zuni (OIA, Unperfected Treaties, No. 274-A, The National Archives. Abstract in Supt. of Arizona, Special File #146).

288

This same year, a treaty was made with the Capote Utes whereby they ceded all their lands to the United States except for reserved lands with the following boundary:

> Art. 3d.--The Capote Utahs, cede to the United
> States all lands in New Mexico, claimed by them,
> except the reserve hereinafter specified. They
> agree to remove within one year, at their own
> expense, to cultivate the soil etc.

> Art. 4th--Reservation, Beginning on the Rio San Juan at
> the mouth of the Rio de las Animas, thence up the Rio
> de las Animas to the Northern boundary of New Mexico,
> thence East with the Northern boundary of New Mexico
> to the top of the mountain which divides the waters of
> the Rio Grande from those of San Juan, thence south-
> wardly with the top of said dividing ridge or mountain to
> the head of the Amarillo /Largo Canyon/, thence down the
> same to the Rio San Juan, and down that river to the
> beginning (OIA, Ariz. Supt., Special File No. 146, Abstracts
> from the articles of agreement and convention, concluded
> with the Capote band of Utahs, at Abiquiu, New Mexico,
> on the 8th of August, 1855).

Neither treaty was approved by the United States Senate, but they indicate official thought concerning Indian land boundaries.

The excitement over the Utes and Jicarillas quieted down. In November, Lorenzo Labadi, Indian agent at Abiquiu, reported that six of the principal Ute residents "who live in the Datil and Sal Mts., in the country occupied by the Capote tribe," visited him at the agency (Labadi to /Meriwether7, Abiquiu, November 29, 1855. OIA, NM, LR,and Ibid., Agency Letters 1855). The Sal Mountain lay to the northwest of the Datil Mountain (Miera y Pacheco map, op. cit.). The current name is La Plata Mountain. This Datil Mountain is not to be confused with a similarly named range that lies about 60 miles south of Cebolleta Mountain.

Events in the spring and summer of 1856 continued the general picture of Navajo-Ute relations and locations. In March, the Ute band under Chief Tamuche were accused of stealing sheep west of the Puerco River. They were now living on the headwaters of that river ("estan viviendo ahora en el nacimiento." Francisco Tomas C. de Baca to W. W. H. Davis, Pena Blanca, March 7, 1856. OIA, NM, LR, Agency Letters). On the twenty-seventh, a killing and theft of sheep belonging to Antonio Jose Otero and the Romeros took place. The sheep were "taken to Tunicha in the Navajo country." The culprits were sons of rich Navajos and lived with the Capote Utes. Navajo chiefs agreed to pay compensation but could not surrender the killers, and they claimed that any attempt to do so would only provoke civil war (Dodge to Davis, Fort Defiance, April 19, 1856. Ibid., LR 1856, N86. Dodge to Meriwether, Fort Defiance, June 2, 1856. Ibid. N138). The robbery was committed

289

by the son of Narbonna, two sons of Archuleta, and two sons-in-law of
Cayetano: These "thieves" live with the Capotes (Ibid., Agency Letters
1856).

The offer of compensation did not change the American point
of view that the above murderers should be apprehended; especially
since they were "believed to be a renegade band under the chief
Archulete, and associated with the Capote Utahs" (AAG to Kendrick,
June 11, 1856. USAC, NM, LS, Vol. 9, p. 486). The Navajo Chief
Manuelito claimed that there were only twenty-eight bad men who were
friends and relatives of the Capotes, and that the latter should also
be held responsible for the wrongdoers (Dodge to Meriwether, Navajo
Agency, July 13, 1856. OIA, NM, LR 1856, N151).

290

In August, Agent Labadi reported from Abiquiu that Chief
Tamuche and the Navajo Calletano (Cayetano) had visited him. They
stated that the Indians had assembled on the tributaries of the Chama
about eighty miles from the agency in order to receive presents from
Governor Meriwether. The Capote, Tabeguache, and Mohuache (all Utes)
were there and the "Navajos who are gathered within this agency"
(Labadi to Meriwether, Abiquiu, August 7, 1856. Ibid., Agency Letters
1856). On the thirtieth he wrote that "In the beginning of this month
this agency was visited by some 30 Navajos who live in the land of the
Capotes and are recognized as Capotes" (Ibid., August 30. 1856).

The Muache Utes had been lured west of the Rio Grande because
of the possibility of supplies at the Abiquiu agency, but their home
land was essentially the San Luis Valley at the headwaters of the Rio
Grande (C. Carson, Indian Agent at Taos, to Meriwether, December 25, 1856.

OIA, NM, IR, Carson Letters). The Tabeguache Utes in general lived northward and eastward from the Capote region in the San Juan drainage.

The Utes or "renegade" Navajos among the Capotes were not the
only trouble-makers in this year. It was reported in June that a Navajo
war party headed by Jose Largo had left Canyon Blanco (Pena Blanca) to
steal and kill (Dodge to Meriwether, Fort Defiance, June 13, 1856. Ibid.,
Agency Letters 1856). About two weeks later Lt. Carlisle reported that

> I have learned that it is probable that a war
> party had gone from near Canon Blanco towards the
> Settlements, to revenge the death of two Navajoes
> killed by the Mexicans, it is said they may go in
> the direction of Laguna . . . (Lt. J. Howard
> Carlisle to Carleton, Cubero, June 14, 1856. NA,
> RG98. Def. Ex. G79, Navajo Dock. 229).

In September, a few Navajos raided some Capotes within fifteen
miles of Abiquiu. The Capotes planned to retaliate (Labadi to Manypenny,
Abiquiu, September 30, 1856. Ibid., Agency Letters 1856. Labadi to
Meriwether, Abiquiu, October 20, 1856. Ibid.). A similar incident
was reported in February of 1857 as having occurred between the northern
point of the Tunicha Mountain and the mouth of the Chelly on the south
side of the San Juan where the Utes struck deep into Navajo country,
killing eight Navajos. Retaliation brought about the death of five
Utes (Kendrick to AAG, Fort Defiance, February 11, 1857. USAC, NM,
Box 9, Kl. OIA, NM, IR, Misc. Papers 1857).

In January of 1855, a trading license was issued to Bernardo
Sanches et al. to do business with the Capotes in the Datil Mountains
north of the San Juan, the Rio de las Animas, and as far as Canada Larga,
within the limits of the country occupied by the said tribe (OIA, NM,
IR, Misc. Papers 1856). Canada Larga is an eastern tributary of Canyon
Largo. The old wagon road from Abiquiu followed Canada Larga into Canyon

291

Largo. The two together constituted the Amarillo Canyon which was the dividing line between the Navajos and Utes according to the Meriwether treaties. The continental divide near this point was also known as Alto del Utah, or the Ute Heights—a Ute camp ground.

The year following the issuance of the above trading license, or 1857, some Navajos again raided the Capotes on the border of the Abiquiu agency near Los Canones de Ramo, or Rio Puerco of the North (Labadi to Meriwether, Abiquiu, April 7, 1857. OIA, NM, LR, Misc. Spanish docs.). The Utes retaliated. They even attacked as far away as Chief Sandoval's homesite in the region of Cebolleta Mountain (Col. B. L. E. Bonneville to James L. Collins, Albuquerque, January 17, 1858. Ibid., Misc. Files 1858). Another band, crossing the Colorado River below the mouth of the San Juan, were accused of killing the Navajo Chief Pelon at Chelly (Maj. W. T. H. Brooks to AAG, March 20, 1858. USAC, NM, LR 1858, B15). The Utes on this occasion passed the Colorado River at the Crossing of the Fathers and journeyed past the Moqui villages to reach the Canyon de Chelly.

The Navajos in 1858 were wary about returning to their planting fields north of Fort Defiance because of possible Ute attacks (Brooks to AAG, April 4, 1858. Ibid., LR 1858, B20). However, they were soon reported with some skepticism as departing on a raid against their enemy (Brooks to AAG, Fort Defiance, April 28, 1858. USAC, NM, Box 10, B29). In the Summer, the military commander at Fort Defiance judged that the Navajos needed to be punished, and he hoped that every encouragement would be given to "the Utahs of Abiquiu" to repeat their raids (Brooks to AAG, Fort Defiance, July 22, 1858. Ibid., B45), a hope that was

292

realized. When Major Brooks' ultimatum for surrendering the murderer of his servant expired, he undertook to punish the Navajos and Ute warriors joined in for the plunder. The campaign covered the region of the Chuska Range northward to Carriso Mountain.

Lt. Cogswell led a detachment and one of his encampments was in the Pena Blanca (Canyon Blanco) arroyo which runs between Beautiful Mountain and Bennett Peak. He ascended the former (then known as Cayetano Mountain) and flushed out the Navajos who fled to the more northern Carriso Mountain (Lt. M. Cogswell to Major E. Backus, Camp at Rio Pajarito, November 8, 1858. _Ibid._, LR, B77).

In November, a large party of Utes attacked a small band of Navajos on the south side of the San Juan River. Their chief, Cavilliard (Caballado) Mucho, "had the day before sent word to the /Navajo/ chiefs who were holding a _junta_ at Laoyo /La Joya/" that he would surrender stolen stock only on certain conditions. The same informant also stated to Major Brooks

293

> that Cayetano and band (to which the murderer
> belongs) had made peace with the Utahs (confirming
> what I had been before told) on the North side
> of San Juan, & that they were all there at this
> time (S. M. Yost to Collins, Ft. Defiance, Nov. 23,
> 1858. OIA, NM, Agency Letters 1858).

The informant was a wounded Mexican escapee from the Navajos; he also reported that the Utes had attacked the Navajo people under Cavillano (Caballado) Mucho on the San Juan "opposite (north)" Carrizo Mountain (Col. D. S. Miles to AAAG, Fort Defiance, Nov. 23, 1858. USAC, NM, Box 10, M97).

According to the terms of the treaty of peace negotiated with the Navajos in the late fall of 1858, the boundary line on the

north was pin-pointed at the junction of the Rio Chaco (the Tunicha) and
San Juan. The Navajos were to stay west of the line from that point to
the ruins of Escondido in the Chaco Canyon. The initial point was downstream from some of the old planting fields of the Navajos along the
San Juan (Articles of Peace, December 25, 1858. OIA, NM, LR 1859, C1885
and J947). The terms also included a provision that the Navajo nation
would be held responsible for wrongdoers, and that the band that had
crossed the San Juan to the Ute country would be considered as outcasts
and separated from the Navajo nation unless the murderer was surrendered
(Yost to Collins, Fort Defiance, Nov. 20, 1858. OIA, NM, LR, Agency
Letters 1858).

     The treaty was not ratified by the United States Senate, nor
was it effective in determining Navajo land occupancy. In April of 1859,
"Cabeson & some other Copotes [were] sent here to let them have some
hoes. . . . They have crops sowed at the San Juan River" (A. H. Pfeiffer
to James L. Collins, Abiquiu, May 1, 1859. Ibid., Agency Letters 1859).
In the spring of 1859 the Jicarillas moved from the neighborhood of
Abiquiu to east of the Rio Grande (Pfeiffer to Collins, May 1, 1859,
and Pfeiffer to Collins, May 6, 1858. Ibid.). Having traversed the
valley of the San Juan, Major Simonson reported that "On the south side
[of the San Juan River] as far down as Tunicha Arroyo [Chaco Wash] the
bottoms have been graized by sheep and other stock of the Indians. . .
And "At this time the Capote Utahs occupy on Las Animas [River], and
Quietanas [Cayetano] band of Navajos [are] on La Plata" (J. S. Simonson
to Collins, Fort Defiance, July 6, 1859. Ibid., Misc. Papers 1859).
In August, Lieut. Cogswell, a member of the Macomb expedition, reported

294

that the Utes, fearing an inroad of Navajos, had "deserted the Rivers
west of the Rio Peadra /Piedra7," and that "Cayatano is encamped about
48 miles below us on the Rio Las Animas." Also "We heard a rumor that
the Tabawatches & Mouatches were waiting for us on the Dolores, for the
purpose of giving us battle" (/Lieut.7 M. Cogswell to /J. L. Collins7,
Rio Florida, August 4, 1859. Ibid.).

The Rio Piedra is a south flowing tributary of the San Juan
River, joining the parent stream near the Colorado-New Mexico boundary.
The rivers to the west are Los Pinos, Las Animas, and La Plata, all
joining the San Juan south of the boundary. The Rio Dolores is a tributary of the Colorado River, flowing northwestward from La Plata Mountain.

Lieutenant Cogswell wrote his letter on the outward bound leg
of the Macomb expedition. On the return trip, they turned southward
and touched the San Juan about fifty miles upstream from its mouth, and
arrived at Abiquiu by way of Canyon Largo. Captain Macomb did not mention
the presence of Navajos, but remarked that the warm season is short
in the San Juan Valley, otherwise the Navajos would plant more extensively
(John N. Macomb, Report of the Exploring Expedition from Santa Fe, New
Mexico, to the Junction of the Grand and Green rivers of the Great
Colorado of the West, in 1859 . . . , p. 6. Washington, 1876).

Macomb's silence is not surprising in the light of Special
Agent Baker's report after traveling with a scouting party around the
Navajo country; "The Navajos have not planted anything on the river
/San Juan7 this year; the Yutahs have driven them all this side /west7
of the Tunacha mountains. We did not see a Navajo settlement in forty
miles of the San Juan River" (Alexander Baker to Collins, Fort

295

Defiance, August 8, 1859. OIA, NM, LR, Agency Letters 1859. Also Baker's
Annual Report, Sept. 1, 1859. 36 cong., 1 sess., sen. ex. doc. 1, 1:716).

The "driving" of the Navajos did not include those north of the
San Juan because "Cayetano with his main body is on the Rio las Animas.
This is the same river where I left Capt. McCombs expedition & I came
from there in two days" (A. H. Pfeiffer to Collins, Abiquiu Agency,
Nov. 23, 1859. OIA, NM, LR, Agency Letters 1859).

In January of 1860, the Ute Chief Rio Abajo and his band visited
the Abiquiu agency, escorting four New Mexicans from the Uncompagre
country. "As the Mexicans came through the Navajo country, they were
attacked by them" and suffered the loss of one life. Rio Abajo informed
Agent Pfeiffer that a great many Utes wanted to plant on the Rio de las
Animas in the next planting season, and that some of them already had
constructed an irrigation ditch (A. H. Pfeiffer to Collins, Abiquiu,
January 9, 1860. Ibid., Agency Letters 1860).

The Indian's reference to the Navajo country is vague. He came
from the Uncompagre country which lies west of the San Juan Mountains
and north of La Plata Mountains in the southwestern quarter of Colorado.
Moving southward, they were bound to strike the Old Spanish Trail. If
they followed this to Abiquiu, the statement about Navajo country is
unsound. The alternative was to follow down the Rio de las Animas to
the San Juan and pick up the trail that led through Large Canyon.

During the preceding December (1859), a party of Ute Indians,
New Mexicans, and probably a few Pueblos, raided the Navajos in the
Tunicha Valley. Since difficulties again broke out between the military
and the Navajos, the Superintendent of Indian Affairs gave permission for
Colonel Fauntleroy to draw upon the Utes to chastize the Navajos (Collins

296

to A. B. Greenwood, Santa Fe, September 16, 1860. Ibid., IR 1860, C741).
These activities flowered in the general campaign of 1860 under Colonel
E. R. S. Canby against the Navajos, which made the country north of the
San Juan important as a refuge. Meanwhile, other Ute Indians were raid-
ing deep into Navajo country, as far south as Ojo del Gallo in the Mt.
Taylor region (Col. M. Chavez to Commander of Department, Fort Lyon,
November 11, 1861. USAC, NM, Box 14, C246) where Old Fort Wingate was
later located.

In May of 1862, the Navajo Chiefs Armijo, Cayetano and Barboncito
entered the village of Cubero, on the south side of Mt. Taylor, and asked
for peace (Wm. Need to J. L. Collins, Cubero, May 16, 1862. OIA, NM, IR,
Misc. Papers 1862. Letter written by request of Manuel Garcia, Alcalde
of Cubero). Col. Canby was of the opinion that the Navajos should be
dealt with once and for all time by the military in an effort to put an
end to the intermittent marauding that had been going on for generations.
This idea was applied by General James H. Carleton in 1863.

297

When officials negotiated with the Utes and Jicarillas in 1868,
shortly after the Navajos had returned to their home land from the Pecos
Valley, the Utes were reported as claiming ownership of the land with the
following boundaries: the Grand and Green Rivers on the North; the San
Juan on the East; the Colorado River on the West; and as far south as the
Navajo country, including the San Juan and its tributaries. The Jicarillas
claimed the land from the Rio Grande on the East to the San Juan on the
West and, so it was asserted, they would accept a reservation on the
Navajo River, an eastern extension of the Rio San Juan (F.M.N. Arny to Mix,
October 3, 1868. Ibid., IR, A610/1868), crossing and recrossing the state
boundary as it flows westward into the parent stream.

NAVAJO WESTERN FRONTIER

Navajoland extending westward from the Chuska Range is a land of wide mesas intersected by canyons and washes with a few high peaks and some traces of volcanic action. The stream of water flowing from the Canyon de Chelly turns northward along the Chinle Wash, hoping to reach the San Juan River, seventy-five miles distant, before being caught by cornfields or death in the sands. The Head of the Chinle Wash is about twenty-five miles south of the Canyon entrance at the divide between the southwestern drainage of the Chuska Range into the Little Colorado River and this northern flowing tributary of the San Juan. Fort Defiance was (and is) on the east side of the divide about thirty miles airline north of the junction of Black Creek with the Rio Puerco of the West, a tributary of the Little Colorado. About twenty-five miles airline west of the Fort the Pueblo Colorado Wash rolls southwestward toward the Little Colorado, joining forces with Cottonwood Wash before entering the main stream about fifteen miles farther on, and about five miles east of Winslow, Arizona.

Beyond these sites little was known of the country toward the west at the time of the American occupation of the Southwest, but military scouts and government sponsored exploration gradually revealed the geographical features of the country. Moving northward along the Chinle Wash and then turning west, the soldier saw the Mesa Calabasa which was bathed on the west and south by Laguna Creek, or present-day Tyende, as it bends northeastward to empty its water into the San Juan. Tyende is also a current name for Mesa Calabasa. Across the creek to the south lay Black Mesa, or as it was called in the days of the Navajo

298

roundup, Mesa de la Vaca. The low spot between the two mesas which carries the waters of Laguna Creek is Marsh Pass, or La Puerta de la Limita, beyond which the soldier boys did not venture in their pursuit of fleeing Indians. Southward and a little to the west the Hopi folk carried on their centuries old precarious existence.

> In fact, the Moquis, from their complete isolation;
> their timidity and ignorance, which make them the
> prey of the rapacious wild tribes which entirely
> surround them; as well as by their numbers, their
> agricultural habits, the hope of their improvement
> and the important effect which the reaction of
> that improvement would have upon the Utahs,
> Coyoteros, Cosninas, Yavipais, Gilenos, Pinalenos,
> and Navajoes . . . call most loudly for the
> services of a faithful Indian agent (Major H. L.
> Kendrick to Governor Meriwether, Fort Defiance,
> August 22, 1856. Office of Indian Affairs, New
> Mexico, Letters Received, Misc. Papers 1856. Cf:
> Father Morfi's description of their surrounding
> neighbors in the eighteenth century. Supra, p. 4).

The western Ute Indians visited the Hopi villages to trade. 299
Chief Walker was a leader in this relationship, moving out from his home area in southern Utah, passing the Rio Colorado at the Crossing of the Fathers about thrity miles upstream from Lees Ferry. He also contacted the Navajos and Zuni people. However, there is no mention of specific Navajo location in the sources relating to his activities (John D. Lee to Dr. Willard Richards, Parowan, Utah, March 13, 1852. Printed in Deseret News, April 17, 1852. Clipping in Journal History, March 13, 1852. Archives of Church of Jesus Christ of Latter-day Saints, Salt Lake City, Utah. A. W. Babbitt to Editor, Journal History, November 28, 1853. Brigham Young to Luke Lea, Great Salt Lake, September 29, 1852. Office of Indian Affairs, Utah Superintendency, Letters Received 1852/U17. National Archives. The Church archives will be cited as LDS in subsequent notes).

Major Kendrick contended in 1856 that the Hopi villages were "the farthest point west, anywhere near its longitude & east of the Grand Colorado, of which white men have any knowledge" (Kendrick to Meriwether, op. cit.). The Mormons by this time had some knowledge of the region west of these villages through contact with Ute traders to the Hopi and activities of Mormon missionaries, but they did not mention Navajos west of the villages in the late 1850's (George W. Armstrong to Brigham Young, Provo City, Utah, June 30, 1855. OIA, Utah, LR 1855, A 392). Jacob Hamblin visited them in 1858, traveling by way of the Kaibab Mountains and the Crossing of the Fathers, and made no mention of Navajos between the Rio Colorado and the villages (James A. Little, Jacob Hamblin, p. 62ff, 152. Salt Lake City, 1881).

Likewise the Ives Expedition, traveling eastward in 1858, did not meet Navajos west of the Hopi. Lt. Ives crossed the Little Colorado River near present-day Sunset, Arizona, and moved up the east side to Cottonwood Wash. From there he turned northward to Oraibi along a well beaten Indian trail which the Hopi followed to the salt spring on the Little Colorado. The trail today is one of the roads to the villages. Ives also traveled about twenty-five miles to the northwest of the Hopi and then turned back because of the rough trail and lack of water, reporting that the region gave every indication of a waterless desert to the Colorado River. It was not until the expedition had proceeded along the route from the Hopi toward Fort Defiance that they met Navajos, and the first ones were only visitors to the villages. Farther along, at White Rock Spring, they met with numerous Navajos, and another dozen miles brought them into the Pueblo Colorado Wash where "Countless herds of horses and flocks of sheep were grazing upon the plain. The Moquis said that we were entering one of the most thickly populated sections of the Navajo territory" (J. C. Ives, Report upon the Colorado of the West. Washington, 1861. Pt. 1, p. 128; pt. 3, p. 90).

Captain L. Sitgreaves of the Topographical Engineers led an expedition from Zuni to the Colorado River in 1852, following down the Zuni river to the Little Colorado then along that stream to the Falls where they crossed over and turned westward toward the San Francisco Mountains. Sitgreaves did not meet with any Navajos, although the party encountered a few Coyotero Apaches enroute to trade some burres at Zuni. They also met a few Tonto Apaches or Yampai Indians near the San Francisco Mountains. The only mention of Navajos is on the map drawn by the cartographer for the party and they are located in the Chuska Range (Capt. L. Sitgreaves, Report of an Expedition down the Zuni and Colorado Rivers. Washington, 1854).

301

The following year Lt. Whipple led another survey party via Zuni, but following a more direct line toward the Little Colorado. After crossing the continental divide and passing through Zuni, the party camped at Navajo Spring (also known as Agua Caliente) near the Rio Puerco of the West, about fifteen miles west from Jacob's Well (now known as Morgan Well) or forty miles from Zuni. Soon after sunset, "two Navajo Indians rode into camp. They said they were hunters from the Canon de Chelly . . . (A. W. Whipple, Reports of Exploration and Surveys . . . , vol. 3, pt. 1, p. 73). Otherwise, "In passing through the Navajo country the natives have kept quite aloof from us." Relying on the words of a New Mexican who had been held captive by the Navajos

for nine months, Whipple reported that the former captive had "accompanied
a party of one thousand warriors through the Moqui country, and afterwards spent much time among their rancherias in the famous Canon de Chelly"
(Ibid., p. 76). The number of warriors in the party was probably
exaggerated.

The Beale expedition that experimented with camels as beasts
of burden for the western country followed the Whipple route from Zuni
in 1857 and did not sight Navajos westward from the Pueblo to the Little
Colorado (Edward F. Beale, Wagon Road from Fort Defiance to the Colorado
River. 35 cong., 1 sess., hse. ex. doc. 124. 1858).

A trading license was issued to Jarvis Nolan et al. in December,
1853, to trade with Navajos "at the following described places within
the boundaries of the country occupied by the said tribe, viz: Rio San
Juan, Rio Colorado, Chaya, Tounicha, Chusca" (OIA, NM, LR, Misc. Papers
1855). The "Rio Colorado" was the Arroyo Colorado or Red Wash which
enters the Rio San Juan from the South near the Four Corners, heading
between Beautiful Mountain and Carriso Mountain. The reference was
not to the Colorado of the West nor its tributary the Little Colorado.

In January of 1858, "an Indian whose Mother is Navajo &
father is said to be Utah, living in the direction of the Moqui villages,"
visited Fort Defiance on the way home from a conference with Navajo
chiefs as representative of some Ute chiefs who professed to want peace
with the Navajos (Capt. W. J. H. Brooks to AAG, Fort Defiance, Jan. 12,
1858. United States Army Command, New Mexico, Letters Received, Box 10,
B5. The National Archives. Record Group 98). The emissary had traveled
as far away as Salt Lake City, and even carried a certificate of

membership in the Mormon Church. The statement, "living in the direction of the Moqui villages," implies to the east of them and not to the west.

In April of this same year, Navajos ran off a flock of sheep and Capt. Hatch led a detachment from Fort Defiance to the Amarillo or present-day ~~Window Rock~~ St Michaels to recover them. About two miles westward on the road to Hopi, he encountered Chief Manuelito bringing in a few of the woollies (J. P. Hatch to Post Adjutant, Fort Defiance, April 6, 1858. _Ibid._, B19-1). During the war of 1858, launched by Major Brooks, "several families" of Navajos who lived 25 or 30 miles northwest of Zuni Pueblo, petitioned the Zuni folk for permission to live with them during the hostilities. An American, E. T. Buckman, advised against it on the ground that in time of war all Navajos were involved, so the few could not seek asylum from American pursuit. The distance by airline places this site at the Colletas on Black Creek, or at the least on the Rio Puerco.

Some of the Hopi were reported as preparing to join the Navajos in the war, but one Hopi Chief traveled to Zuni looking for a way to remain at peace and not be harmed. One alternative, of course, was to seek a haven at Fort Defiance, but "They cannot go through the Navajos to you /Col. Miles/, so they wished to bring their stock and come and live here" /Zuni/ (E. T. Bucknan to Miles, Zuni, Sept. 9, 1858. _Ibid._, IR, M73/1).

The Hopi Pueblos lie due west of Fort Defiance, of course, so if the peacefully inclined folks could not "go through" the Navajos to reach Fort Defiance, but could travel the well-known route from Hopi to Zuni without risk, then the Navajos were not living southwest of Fort

303

Defiance as far as the region between the Puerco River of the West and
the Rio Zuni. The farthestmost group southwest of Fort Defiance were
at the Colletas in Black Creek Canyon.

During Major Brooks' war, a detachment was sent against the
Navajos at the "Collittas" (Colletas), supposedly the home site of
Sarcillos Largos, but the inhabitants were not taken by surprise--the
foes indulged in a little skirmishing the next day. The military
then moved southwestward through Canyon Chenilly without seeing any
more Indians, but they did find heavy tracks of stock that had moved
through the canyon (Brooks to Lane, Fort Defiance, Sept. 25, 1858.
Ibid., Box 10, N61/1).

Col. Miles led a detachment westward from Fort Defiance to
seek the Indians,

304

> passing Peubla /Puebla7 Colorada, and examining
> the valleys beyond in a south west direction.
> My reconnoisance of this section of country, has
> been satisfactory in making me acquainted with
> the favourite haunts of the enemy, the easiest and
> best route to Calabasha Seirra /Sierra7 and Mesa,
> where he grazes his stock. . . .

He marched westward on the first day, October 18, a distance
of 13½ miles "to the water hole on the Moqui road." Early the next day
the Colonel moved westward and reached Pueblo Colorado at 8 o'clock.
On the following day the detachment marched about five miles west, then
turned southwest to Manuelito's village and "encamped by the principal
corn fields, in a beautiful valley with sufficiency of water and very
good grass." These fields were in the Pueblo Colorado Wash at a site
named Cornfields today. From this place, Capt. Lindsay led a force
southward for 12 miles and

came to a field of corn standing, but found
no water, he then coursed west until he struck
the valley of the encampment /Pueblo Colorado
Wash/, he met with large trails of horses and
sheep, but not recent, saw no Indians, Marched
he supposes 35 miles and arrived at camp about
½ past 6 P. M.

Lt. Lane after marching north for ten miles,
came to a bluff overlooking the valley /Beautiful
Valley or Chinle Wash/ where Pvt. Sweeney was
wounded /northwest of Ganado/ (this connects our
scout with the route of that from Canon de Chelley)
found in the rocks a large pool of water /Pine
Springs/, turned west, then south and then east
to the encampment without seeing an Indian or
any flocks, altho there was recent sign of both.

Capt. McLane marched west and northwest and "met the enemy" (Col. D. S.
Miles to AAAG, Fort Defiance, October 23, 1858. *Ibid.*, Box 10, M75).
Subsequent to this military operation, Miles reported that the Navajos
were seeking peace and as a token of good intentions planned to return
stolen stock. In order to do so, they rounded them up from Canyon de
Chelly, Sierra Calabasha, Pueblo Colorado, Chusca, Tuni Chay, Cerrissa
and Cieniga Juan Icho (Juanico) (Miles to Wilkins, Fort Defiance, Dec. 1,
1858. *Ibid.*, IR 1858, M94. RG98, from Pl. Ex. 200, Docket 229 Navajo),
all well-known sites of Navajo occupancy.

In July of 1859, Captain O. L. Shepherd led a scout into the
western part of Navajoland. Departing from Fort Defiance, the detachment marched 36 miles along the road to the Hopi Pueblos which brought
them to the Pueblo Colorado. On the third day they turned southward for
four miles to "the Rio Pueblitos /Pueblo Colorado Wash/ on which we
encamped the night previous. Water not permanent." The following day,
the troop moved southwest through the canyon of the Rio Pueblitos for
15 miles without finding permanent water. The next march was westward

305

for ten miles "into a large Canada leading West in the direction of the Moqui villages." This is a low depression toward Jadito Wash. There was no trail and again the water was not permanent. The guides "not knowing that section of the country, it was thought best not to pursue this valley any further," so the detachment marched about 15 miles across hilly country without trails to the Ojo de la Jara in Steamboat Canyon on the Hopi road. Turning westward, they reached the first of the villages in about 30 miles.

Capt. Shepherd camped "in front of the two Pueblos of Muchonobe [Mishongnovi] & Chupaulebe" (Shipaulavi) at a pond of rain water. Five miles farther west and southwest of the Pueblo of Shongopove they again encamped at a pond of rain water. A Pueblo guide now led them 15 miles south where they encamped in the unnamed canyon which they had abandoned on turning north to Ojo de la Jara. Twelve miles farther south they "encamped on the southern side of some black & high mesas," a volcanic area called the Hopi Buttes, from which could be seen the Little Colorado River, supposed to be about 20 miles distant. The water was permanent but scarce. Marching E. S. E. about 20 miles, they cut no trails and encamped at a spot where the water was not permanent. Ten miles eastward brought them to the Rio Pueblitos again (Pueblo Colorado). From there a march of 15 miles E. S. E. brought them to another Ojo de la Jara (Tanner Springs in Wide Ruins Wash) on the Zuni-Hopi trail. Marching E. N. E. for 14 miles they arrived at the ruins of Pueblo Grande (Wide Ruins); thence E. S. E. for 4 miles to an encampment at the Agua de Viboras (Rattlesnakes Spring)--water not permanent.

From the Agua Viboras the detachment marched E. S. E. for 15
miles and entered the lower end of the Canon de Calites (Colleta, Black
Creek Canyon). A difficult march of about 23 miles toward the northeast
brought them to permanent water in the upper part of the canyon. The
Captain noted incorrectly that the canyon had never been traveled its
length before. A further march of 16 miles brought them to Fort Defiance.

During the total distance of about 265 miles, they "saw no
Indians along the route except on the Rio Pueblitos /Pueblo Colorad_o_/
the second day out." Near the Hopi villages some two or three Indians
came into camp but they did not live near there.

> At the mouth or lower end of the Canon of the
> Calites, some few came into camp . . . , also
> at the tanks near Pueblo Grande /Wide Ruins/.
> At the last camp in the canon of the Calites,
> some few also came into camp. . . . No flocks of
> sheep were seen on the whole route. At the last
> only 16 miles from the Post a herd of horses were
> seen.

307

> Corn fields were seen on the Rio Pueblitos about
> 30 miles hence, also a few small fields down the canon
> of the Pueblitos on the 4th day out. No fields were
> then discovered till we came to the canon of the
> Pueblo Grande, about 30 miles hence, S. west, thence
> none till we entered the lower end of the Canon
> of the Calites where were extensive fields,
> distant hence about 35 miles, and also in the upper
> Canon of the Calites 16 miles. Some few other
> patches were seen along the way hardly worth
> mentioning. Scarcely a hundred acres in all
> were discovered.

> Evidences were discovered of wintering large
> herds of Horses & flocks of Sheep, in the Canada
> leading west towards Moqui from the lower end of the
> canon of the Rio Pueblitos as well as on the Mesas
> adjoining this canon. Also in the canada /Steamboat/
> of the Ojo de la Jarra near Moqui, and thence
> particularly in the valley reaching from the Ojo
> de la Jarra on the Zuni & Moqui trail, to the

Pueblo Grande, and likewise at the lower end
of the canon of the Calites (Capt. O. L. Shepherd
to J. H. Edson, Fort Defiance, August 7, 1859.
USAC, NM, LR, S44/1).

Capt. Shepherd also reported that

The large mountain lying south west of the Moqui
villages is doubtless the Sierra de Francisco and
is beyond the Rio Colorado Chiquito. Being about
five days journey beyond and the home of the
Coninas indians. I am satisfied that the Navajoes
never go there to secrete themselves or property
(Ibid.).

While Capt. Shepherd was scouting the western Navajo country,

Capt. Walker led a detachment through the region of the Canyon de Chelly:

following the Rio Chelly which after freeing itself from the canon turns due North, for six miles
we passed a succession of fields of growing corn,
some of them containing from forty to sixty acres.
This valley and the lower half of the canon are
probably the most populous portion of the Navajo
country. . . . The last cultivated land we saw
upon the Chelly is almost six miles from the mouth
of the canon, and the Indians informed us that there
was no cultivation lower down, but that the
country is grazed over a good deal in the fall after
the rains have brought up the grama grass upon the
plains. . . . (J. G. Walker to AAG, Camp La Hoya
near Fort Defiance, August 3, 1859. Ibid., Box 12,
S44/2).

A year after the Shepherd reconnaissance, or the fall of 1860,

Col. E. R. S. Canby launched a campaign against the Navajos. Moving

westward from the Rio Grande Valley toward the enemy country, he soon

reported that

The information derived from the spies, the
wounded Navajoes and friendly Utes all point to
the conclusion that the Navajoes have been driven
by the operations of Maj. Sibley's command & my
own from their haunts in the Chusca and Tunicha
mountains and are flying to the West with the
Sierra Limita as their ultimate destination.

Toward that point the next operations of the
campaign will be directed in the hope of in-
flicting a decisive blow (E. R. S. Canby to AAG,
Camp near Fort Defiance, October 4, 1860. USAC,
NM, IR, Box 13, C39).

This same season, the Mormon missionary Jacob Hamblin made another trip
to New Mexico. Two day's travel by a crooked trail from the Colorado
River enroute to the Hopi, or 30 to 40 miles west of the village, he met
four Navajos. One of his party, George A. Smith, Jr., was killed by
them. All told about forty Navajos collected at the place bent on
mischief (Little, Hamblin, p. 71f). The Missionaries had traveled
about 100 miles before experiencing this tragedy at the hand of the
"large company" of Navajos who had fled "from their own country for safety"
because of the war waged against them by the United States (Deseret News.
Clipping in Journal History, November 2, 1860. LDS. George A. Smith to
Amasa M. Lyman, Great Salt Lake City, Nov. 29, 1860. Ibid., Nov. 29).   309

Col. Canby's comment as of October 19 supports the Mormon
report that the Navajos were so far west because of military pressure:
"I have the honor to report," Canby wrote, "that our operations since
leaving Fort Defiance have been attended with no important result
except that of driving the Indians to the West and South-west." "We
are now moving in the direction of Puerta Limita with reasonable hopes
of success" (Canby to AAG, Camp on Arroyo 16 miles below mouth of Canon
de Chelly, October 19, 1860. USAC, NM, IR, Box 13, C49/1).

The reasonable hopes of the Colonel rested with Captain H. H.
Sibley who was entrusted with the scout to the westward of Canyon de
Chelly. From the site known as Ewell's Hay camp, or La Hoya, which was
twelve miles north of Fort Defiance, or the present-day Sawmill, the

command moved southwestward some 27 miles to the familiar Pueblo Colorado in the neighborhood of Ganado, "represented by the guides as a favorite haunt of the Indians, and affording excellent water and pasturage." A night march on October 11 was made by a detachment towards the west and north in the direction of some lakes at the head of Pine Springs Wash where it was hoped the Navajos would be taken by surprise. The following morning, the main command moved to the mouth of the Canon Cito Trigo (Pine Springs Wash); "The country traversed, especially in descending from the 'Mesa Colorado' /Ganado Mesa into Beautiful Valley/ is much broken and essentially a 'mal pais' devoid of herbage or trees and the surface covered with petrified forest trees." On the 13th, the country was examined west to some lakes "distant about eight miles towards the base of the 'Mesa de la Vaca' /Black Mountain/. . . ." The grass around the lakes had been entirely consumed by the Indians' stock. Returning to the mouth of the Canon Cito Trigo, the troops encamped in some corn fields already harvested.

Moving northward toward the Canyon de Chelly for a distance of about 8 miles, camp was made at a waterhole. The following day they reached the mouth of the Canyon and awaited the column under command of Col. Canby. The combined force continued the route northward along Chelly Creek (Chinle Wash) from the Canyon, marching twelve miles the first day; the second day, distance unrecorded, they encamped near the red sandstone formation known as La Ventana (Window Rock); the third day they covered 21 miles, passing enroute the permanent water called La Encina Gorda (near Rock Point), not to mention some Indian inscription on the rocks near the trail, and then made camp. The following day, the

310

route turned from the Chelly Creek westward; the column ascended a mesa
and traveled over rough country for six miles to the "'Cienega Boneta,'
/Laguna Creek or Dennehotso/ a deep rock crested gorge, carpeted with
luxurient /sic/ grass and watered from Springs hidden under the cavernous
sides, tributaries of the San Juan." Capt. Sibley now made

> a night march Southward to the middle point
> of the Mesa de la Vaca, distant some 35 miles;
> to ascend to mesa /Black Mesa/ at this point
> and by a south and westerly course to enter
> the 'Puerta de las Lemetas' /Marsh Pass/ near
> some old Pueblo ruins noticed by Capt. Walker
> Mounted Rifles in his reconnauicence of 1859
> (Capt. N. H. Sibley to AAG, Ewell's Bay Camp,
> Nov. 12, 1860. Ibid., IR, C53/4).

The Old Pueblo ruin is

> known by the name "Ruin A" or "Tecolote"
> (the Mexican-Spanish for ground-owl, from
> Nahuatl tecolotl). It was known to white men
> many years ago and was visited by prospectors,
> relic hunters and soldiers. It was also
> indicated on the United States Engineers' map
> of 1877. Here Lieutenant Bell, 3rd Infantry,
> U. S. A., (probably William Hemphill Bell)
> carved his name, with the date, 1859 (Albert B.
> Reagan in El Palacio, 22:536. June 18, 1927).

311

This site is near the west entrance to Marsh Pass.

At dawn, the soldiers located and attacked Delgadito's band
with their considerable herds of horses and sheep. Since the land to
the south and west was unknown as to water resources, Capt. Sibley
returned to his point of departure. They marched to the Chelly Cito,
"a stream of fine water /Laguna Creek/ rising near the mouth of the
Puerta de las Limetas, and flowing north to the San Juan. . . ."
Moving southward along this canyon until it narrowed with vertical sides,
the detachment turned up a side canyon and in four miles distance

joined the main command. After several days, the column marched back to
the Chelly Creek (Chinle Wash) and Canyon (Sibley to AAG. op. cit.).

In Colonel Canby's summary of the operations, after reaching
the point farthest west,

> The command remained four days for the purpose
> of resting the animals and examining the Canon
> Limita and Puerta Limita and the adjacent Sierra.
> These examinations showed that the Navajoes with
> immense herds and flocks had fled to the South
> and West, in the general direction of the Moqui
> villages and the Sierra de los Ladrones, and after
> ascending the Sierra had broken up into small
> parties and dispersed themselves in different
> directions. As there was no water known to any
> of our guides within sixty miles, it was as im-
> possible as it would have been fruitless to attempt
> any further pursuit. . . .

Aside from the destruction of some Navajo livestock,

312

> The attendant and not less important result
> is that of driving the Indians from their homes
> and grazing grounds into the most desolate and
> repulsive country that I have ever seen, and
> where from the statements of captured Indians
> great numbers of their horses and sheep have
> perished from hunger and thirst.

He then planned to operate against "the winter grazing grounds of the
Navajoes" (Canby to AAG, Ewell's Hay Camp, November 8, 1860. USAC,
NM, Box 13, C49. RG98).

Additional campaigns against the Navajos to the southwest in
the late fall and early winter of 1860 furnished additional information
on Indian occupancy of that region. Capt. L. McLaws moved southward
from Fort Defiance on November 18 for a distance of nine miles and
camped "at the Amarillo" (St. Michaels). The following day he moved
along the base of the "Callitas Mountain" /Defiance Plateau/ on the
Zuni road about ten miles, finding a corn field and some springs.

arther along the Callitis [Colletas] Valley [Black Creek] he camped at
Callitis" Springs [Willow Springs]. There were numerous Navajos in
he vicinity who made a request for peace, but the Captain was not there
n a peaceful mission and had no authority for such negotiation. Continuing along the Zuni road through a thickly wooded pass in the hills,
the column descended into the valley of the Puerco River of the West
[near Lupton] where Capt. McLaws tried, without success, to bring on a
fight with the numerous Navajos. He then continued along the river in
a leisurely way from the late afternoon of November 21 until the
forenoon of the 23rd when they "found water in abundance, where an old
and well beaten trail crossed the river. . . ." Crossing at this point,
[Sanders] they moved ten miles downstream and struck Carriso Creek and
a mile farther on the Almagre where camp was made.

313

From camp on the Almagre, Capt. McLaws moved to "Navajoe
Springs," a watering place also known as Agua Caliente and, in the Navajo
language, as Tu-si-to. There was abundant evidence of grazing in the
vicinity, and of trails leading to the south. Lieut. Plummer was sent
along Beal's wagon road to Jacobs Well (Ojo Redondo, or Ojo del Chi)
which lay about nine miles to the east while McLaws followed the
trails to the south. The latter, after traveling twelve or fifteen
miles, found that the trail did not turn east toward Jacobs Well as
hoped for, but continued south

> into a country about which no one knew anything.
> There was no beaten trail, nothing to indicate
> that this was any great thoroughfare used for
> passing between points, but, the tracks indicated
> to me that the animals had been herded over the
> Country, gradually moving along to the South and
> East, and I believe to some watering place between

the Colorado Chiquito and Ojo Navajoe or Caliente,
or perhaps to the Colorado itself. I think this
because there were no evidence at Ojo Caliente
that the Indians had made any stay there, no
huts; not even a sign of a fire. The Indians
while there were merely passing along to occupy
a place previously selected somewhere in the
splended grazing country. I could see before
me from the summit of the Sierra Singes-tin.

Capt. McLaws further reported that

The Indian women prisoners /Navajo7, the Mexican
"Jesus" and the Navajoe boy from Fort Defiance,
all knew the water called Ojo Caliente (Nav Spring)
and the country around but none would acknowledge
having heard even of the Colorado Chiquito; and
after my arrival at that river they said they
knew nothing of its existence, which is additional
evidence that the bands whose tracks were at
Ojo Caliente have some intermediate place of
resort between there and the river, because both
"Jesus" and the women, we afterwards discovered,
belonged to those bands. . . .

314

Lt. Plummer returned to Navajo Springs, reporting signs but
not Indians enroute to Jacobs Well. A night scout southward along the
mountain revealed no signs of Navajos. McLaws now moved westward along
Beal's road about three miles; turning to the left, down the Puerco,
he crossed the river "within two miles." Following down stream, they
traveled all told about 20 miles and camped "in a place indicated by
'Jesus,' our other guides admitting their ignorance of the country."
These other guides were "Mexicans" and also Juan Chi, a Navajo from
Cebolleta, and Juan Chiquito from Fort Defiance.

This camp site was on the grazing grounds for Navajo stock.
For eight or nine miles the Puerco was lined with cottonwood trees.
Water was found in numerous holes in the river bed and the grazing was
good away from the water. Tracks were seen of stock that had wandered

back and forth to the stream, but no distinct sign of a trail approaching
or leaving the neighborhood. Leaving the cottonwood locality, the detachment moved downstream toward the Little Colorado. As the Colorado was
approached, "all tracks except of Antelope which were very numerous,
entirely disappeared"; and for five miles above the junction (two miles
east of Holbrook) there were "no signs of the river [Little Colorado]
here ever having been visited by Indians or indeed by any person or
animal but Antelopes and rabbits."

After failing to find the Zuni River, to the south Capt. McLaws
returned down the Little Colorado for some distance, struck across the
country to the Rio Puerco and finally followed Lithodendron Wash,
noticing numerous tracks of stock. Turning from the Wash, the detachment followed a direct route to Ojo Caliente, distant some eighteen
miles. The next day the troop "nooned" at Jacobs Well. Picking up
Beal's road, they returned to base camp by way of Zuni Pueblo (Lt. L.
McLaws to AAAG, Camp at West Spring near Fort Fauntleroy, December 16,
1860. USAC, NM, LR, Box 14, C12).

315

The information derived from the series of scouts led Col.
Canby to certain conclusions; namely,

> that the country on the upper Colorado Chiquito
> is not now and has not recently been occupied
> by the Navajoes, and that there are no trails
> leading eastward from that now.

> Abundant evidence was found by Capt. McLaws
> of recent occupation and in considerable numbers,
> on the Puerco; the lower Collites; the Ojo de Jesus
> and Navajo Springs. The trail from the last
> mentioned place leading to the South and West.
> This scout and information derived from other
> sources shows that considerable numbers of the

> Navajoes (divided into small parties) are
> now wintering on the Puerco, the lower Collites
> and the Pueblitos or Torrejon.

He planned to operate with small detachments to convince these scattered

folk that they and their kinsmen must learn to live at peace (Canby to

AAG, Fort Fauntleroy, Dec. 11, 1860. *Ibid.*, Box 13, C57).

> Nearly two weeks later the Colonel reported

> that information derived from the Navajoes
> recently captured, and from the delegations
> that have visited this post and Fort Defiance
> to ask for peace, indicates that the great
> body of the wealthy Navajos with their flocks
> and herds are now in the vicinity of the San
> Francisco mountains. This information derived from
> different sources is confirmed by our own obser-
> vations. . . .

> The operations that are now in progress have
> for their object a thorough examination of the
> country west of this place embracing the Navajo
> wintering grounds on the Puerco, the Torrejon
> and Pueblo Grande and north, the Chusca Mountains
> and valley and the broken range bordering that
> valley on the south and east (Canby to AAG, Fort
> Fauntleroy, Dec. 24, 1860. *Ibid.*, Box 14, C2).

316

On the 14th of December, Lt. Stith surprised a camp of Navajos on the

Rio Puerco about thirty miles southwest of Fort Fauntleroy (Canby to

AAG, Jan. 6, 1861. *Ibid.*, C11), or near the junction with Black Creek.

The upshot of Canby's operations was a treaty signed at Fort

Fauntleroy whereby "The Navajo Chiefs shall immediately collect their

people and establish them in the country west of Fort Fauntleroy, and

until it is otherwise stipulated, none of them will be allowed to live

or graze their flocks in the country east of that post" (*Ibid.*, C32/1).

Col. Canby's assertion that the Navajos were in the vicinity

of the San Francisco Mountains with their flocks is vague. When Jacob

Hamblin again explored south of the Colorado in 1862, he traveled past
the north side of these mountains enroute to the Moqui villages and did
not report any Navajos (Little, Jacob Hamblin, p. 85). The following
year he visited the Coninas deep in their canyon on the south side of
the Colorado and then pushed on to the Moqui without encountering Navajos
until he saw a few visiting in the villages. On the return trip he
explored the south and east side of the San Francisco Mountains without
mentioning these Indians, although he did meet some Pi-Utes--and lost
his horses to the Hualapais (Excerpt from his journal in Journal History,
May 13, 1863, p. 8. LDS).

Many years later, the western range of the Navajos was attested
by "An old Navajo, now living at Tuba City, /who/ said that when the
Carson campaign began /1863/ his family lived near Keams Canyon, and
they were the farthest west of the Navajo." In fear of the American
soldiers, some of them fled as far as Cataract Canyon and made their
first contact with the Havasupai Folk (Katharine Bartlett, "Why the
Navajo came to Arizona." Museum of Northern Arizona, Notes, 5:31.
Dec., 1932). This was far to the northwest of the San Francisco Mountains and west of the Grand Canyon.

317

With the cessation of hostilities by Col. Canby, and the
withdrawal of the troops from Fort Fauntleroy at Bear Springs, the Navajos
reoccupied their planting grounds at that site. When Col. Carson arrived
in the summer of 1863 for another campaign against these people, he
found wheat growing and appropriated about 40,000 pounds for the mules.

Moving westward from Fort Defiance in July, Carson found Navajos
in their usual haunts in the valley of the Pueblo Colorado. From a captured

Pah-Ute woman, he learned that Navajos with large herds were at a pond
of water about thirty-five miles to the west (Jadito Wash) of the Pueblo
Colorado, but they had fled before he reached that point and could not
be overtaken without crossing a waterless stretch of ninety miles (Col. C.
Carson to AAG, Pueblo Colorado, July 24, 1863. Department of Justice,
Correspondence of the Navajo Campaign). The following month, the Colonel
led a detachment southward from Fort Defiance to a point about fifteen
miles from Zuni Pueblo; turning westward he marched about twenty-five
miles toward Hopi. The following day, shortly after leaving camp, the
troops destroyed about 12 acres of corn, then traveled about fifteen
miles and camped for a few hours. A night march brought them at ten
A. M. to "a Canon a little west of Moqui." Here the Ute allies took
two women and three children prisoners, and Capt. Birney's Company capture
some stock. From this initial camp site, he marched about three miles
farther west to a spring in the canyon. Then "an Oribi /Oraibi/
Indian brought me news that a party of Navajoes, with large herds had
passed their village twelve miles distant." After pursuing them for
25 miles, Carson returned to his canyon camp. At another spring about
twelve miles west of Hopi, the soldiers destroyed about an acre of corn.
From his camp, Carson headed for the base of operations on the Pueblo
Colorado. While enroute, somewhere along the march he destroyed "about
50 acres of corn." "From all I could learn from the Moqui Indians," he
reported, "and the captives taken, the majority of the Navajoes, with
their herds are at the Little Red River /Little Colorado/, and this is
confirmed by my own observation" (Carson to AAG, Camp on the Pueblo
Colorado, August 19, 1863. Ibid.). After a scout around the Canyon de
Chelly, Carson was able to report:

318

"In summing up the results of the last month's Scout I congratulate myself on having gained one very important point viz: a knowledge of where the Navajos have fled with their stock, and where I am certain to find them" (August 31, 1863. Ibid.).

In October of 1863, the Colonel operated once more to the southwest of Fort Defiance. Moving toward the pueblo of Zuni, he marched over the familiar trail by way of Jacobs Well to the Little Colorado. Mountains to the south and east of the line of march were scouted without finding any Navajos, and likewise to the northwest. The Zuni allies, however, picked up about fifty head of sheep and goats. Carson sent Capt. Pfeiffer with a detachment on a night march down the river: "At the Rapids they saw and pursued seven Navajoes with about fifteen horses, but owing to the broken down condition of our Horses, the Indians escaped."

319

On the 25th, he commenced the return march "on the River," presumably from the point "85 miles from where the California Road first strikes it /near Navajo Springs/." Having traveled fifteen miles on the 27th (the second day), Carson led a detachment to scout the country on a more direct route between the river and Fort Canby. They arrived on the 30th at Camp Four of the previous scout when enroute to Hopi, or a distance of about sixty miles north of the Little Colorado. In the final report of this campaign, Carson wrote that "I examined the River thoroughly a distance of 85 miles from where the California Road first strikes it, and am satisfied that no Indians have been on the River within this distance since last spring, excepting this party of seven seen by Captain Pfeiffer" (Carson to AAG, October 5, 1863. Ibid.).

Col. Carson once more campaigned toward the west in November of 1863 and found some Navajos while enroute to the Hopi villages. From that point he marched 65 miles with only one halt of two hours and arrived at a stream of water, tributary to the Little Colorado River, at 2 A. M. He captured one Navajo boy, 7 horses, destroyed an encampment and one Navajo man voluntarily surrendered. The following day, the 25th, stock was found in the canyon of the Little Colorado. The animals were rounded up, but the five herders escaped by clambering up the steep sides of the canyon.

> From this place /he reported/ to where the
> Navajoes went is three days without water, as I
> am informed by a Mexican boy taken captive some
> time since by the Navajoes, and recaptured by
> Capt. McCabe. This my animals could not stand,
> and I was reluctantly obliged to let them go
> unmolested. Our camp of this day is about
> Twenty-five miles Southwest /Southeast?/ of the
> San Francisco Mountains.

320

From this camp he returned by "a different route," but on neither route, going or coming, was water to be found for a distance of 50 miles (Carson to Cutler, Fort Canby, December 6, 1863. Ibid.). Carson had earlier reported that the Hopi were surrounded by Navajos (Carson to AAG, Fort Canby, October 19, 1863. Ibid.).

After three more months of scouting during the winter, Capt. A. Carey, commander-in-chief during Carson's absence, reported that

> I am now satisfied that nearly all the Indians of
> this Nation north and West of the Rio Colorado
> Chiquito have surrendered themselves; but I also
> believe that there are still a large number of
> wealthy Navajoes South of that River in the
> Apache Country (Carey to AAG, Fort Canby, March 20,
> 1864. Ibid.).

Colonel Carson agreed with his subordinate, although he used
slightly different wording: "that nearly, if not all, the Indians now
remaining are wealthy and are living South-East and South-West of the
Little Colorado at the first intersection of the 'Beale Road,' and in
the Apache country." Nearly all of the Navajos "north and west of the
Rio Colorado Chiquito," he believed, "have surrendered themselves; but
I also believe that there are still a large number of wealthy Navajoes
South of that River in the Apache Country."

> the Herds reported as seen by my Spies on my
> last visit to the Little Colorado, December 6,
> 1863, comprise nearly all of the Navajo Stock
> North-West of the San Francisco Mountains.
> That the owners on discovering my command crossed
> a Desert of four days march to the 'Colorado Grande,'
> or Colorado of the West; and that many of the
> people died of thirst in crossing (Carson to
> AAG, Fort Canby, March 20, 1864. Ibid.).

In April, a detachment of troops was in the field for "protection
to the Navajoes en route from South of Red River /Little Colorado/
against attacks from the Pueblo Indians or the Apaches" (Carson to
Carleton, Fort Canby, April 10, 1864. Ibid.). The policy of total
war was forcing the bulk of the Navajos to accept the Carleton plan
of removal to the Pecos River Valley, although a few recalcitrants
remained at large.

In the summer of 1865, a volunteer expedition encountered
"at or near the San Franziscko Mts about two hundreds warriors, Navajos
& Apaches combined" and seized their stock (Shaw to AAG, July 24,
1865. USAC, Fort Wingate, Letters Sent, vol. 16). The Zuni Indians
took a hand in the game of running down their old enemies and

321

encountered a small group on the Rio Puerco of the West (Shaw to Cutter, August 8, 1865. Ibid., vol. 17).

The Carson campaign forced some Navajos so far west of their usual haunts that they crossed the Colorado River into Utah on raids against the beef cattle and horse herds of the Mormon colonists (George A. Smith to Daniel H. Well, Toquerville, Feb. 19, 1866. Journal History). They were also reported as being "very mad" (James G. Bleak to Erastus Snow, St. George, April 2, 1866. Ibid. Cf: Little, Hamblin, p. 99f and Deseret News, 18:89, in Journal History, March 24, 1869. LDS), and who would say nay.

The Utah Indians added to the terror of the Navajos by striking at them south of the Colorado River. Caballado Chino's band on the Mesa de la Vaca was attacked and in January of 1866 he surrendered at Fort Wingate for transportation to the Bosque Redondo, having come "from the other side of the Moqui Villages" (Capt. E. Butler to AAG at Santa Fe, Fort Wingate, Jan. 18, 1866. USAC, Fort Wingate, Letters Sent). The following summer other recalcitrants yielded to hunger and came in from the Mesa de la Vaca and Mesa Calabasa (Capt. E. Butler to Maj. Cyrus H. De Forrest, Fort Wingate, July 28, 1866. Ibid., vol. 16). Thus, after three years of pressure, the bulk of the Navajos accepted the plan for their removal to the valley of the Pecos River.

NAVAJO SOUTHERN BOUNDARY

The southern limit of Navajo land occupancy was roughly the Rio San Jose from east of Laguna Pueblo westward into the northern part of the Zuni Mountain, but their holdings were precarious because of competition from New Mexican, Pueblo and harrassment from their southern Apache kinsmen. This situation was illustrated for the new ruler of New Mexico the year following the entry of General Kearny by a petition from the Cubero folks for permission to abandon part of their holdings for lack of water and settle on the Rio San Jose; a further reason advanced was the insecurity in their present location, "that being a frontier much harrassed by the depredations of the ungrateful Navajo tribe . . ." (Federal Land Office, File 79. Santa Fe, New Mexico). The land they asked for "has been occupied only by the said Navajo Indians, to the notorious injury of the settlements adjacent thereto . . . ," and they could serve as "a great check to the Navajos who occupy it under the pretext of peace. . . ." Their petition was approved by Prefect Francisco Sarracino on the legal advice of the United States Attorney that the land was open for settlement since it was a part of the public domain and Navajo occupancy did not represent ownership (Ibid.).

323

The controversy over land was revealed in the communication of John R. Tulles a few years later when he informed the newly appointed governor of New Mexico about a dispute with the Laguna folks:

> It appears that the Navajos have possessed and
> cultivated the lands on which they now live for at
> least one hundred years, but never had held any
> grant from the Mexican government. A Laguna Indian

at one time having planted on a portion of these
lands, the whole pueblo, emboldened by this
example, and knowing that the Navajos held no
written title, have called in question the
validity of the claim of the Navajos to the
lands occupied by them (Tulles to James S. Calhoun,
May 4, 1851. 32 cong., 1 sess., hse. ex. doc. 2,
p. 457. Serial 636. Docket 229-Navajo-p. 70).

The notion of a southern limit to the Navajo homeland was
further revealed when Governor Calhoun offered military advice to his
civilian superior: "Military stations ought to be established at
Tunicha, and the Canon of Cheille, in the Navajo country, at or near
Jemez, Zunia and Laguna . . ." (Calhoun to Commissioner Medill, Santa
Fe, October 1, 1849. Annual Report, p. 1001. 31 Cong., 1 sess., Sen.
Ex. Doc. 1. Serial 550). The three pueblos mentioned were historically
and actually the frontier outposts for Spanish relations with Navajos
living to the west and north of these points.

324

Calhoun was also the first Indian agent for New Mexico and
commented along this line when preparing a sketch map in 1849 to locate
agencies for the various tribes under his jurisdiction:

Zuni /he wrote/ is completely isolated, Laguna
and Acoma outposts, are supposed to be the
nearest settlements to it--on the East--on the
West, the Moquies may be found perhaps 100 miles
distant--on the north they /the Zuni/ have the
Navajoes--and on the South, the Apaches (Abel,
Official Correspondence, map insert).

The military soon became a major reportorial service on this
subject as illustrated by Major H. L. Kendrick, post commander at
Fort Defiance:

I am informed that Mexicans from the Rio Grande,
and that vicinity, are again grazing their sheep
in the Navajoe Country, and have been herding
them even to the west of Zuni, one hundred and

sixty miles from their homes, and more than one
hundred miles beyond the extreme frontier town.
I am told that a short time since there were Mexican
flocks in the Sierra de Zuni, between the Gallena
and Inscription Rock, and it is supposed that they
are there now. I am further informed that the
Indians, both Zunis & Navajoes, are very much displeased at this encroachment on their lands, and
have maltreated some of their herders. If these
flocks are grazed there much longer a loss of
some or all of them, at an early date, may safely
be predicted (Kendrick to Gov. D. Meriwether, Feb. 10,
1854. United States Army Command, New Mexico,
Letters Received, Box 6. Record Group 98. The
National Archives).

The following December, Major Kendrick sent a letter to several

sheep owners complaining that they were grazing sheep near Inscription

Rock, which lies on the southwest side of the Zuni Mountains, and far

into the Navajo country (Kendrick to Ramon Luna, et al. Fort Defiance,

Dec. 18, 1854. Office of Indian Affairs, New Mexico, Letters Received,

Misc. Papers 1854. Record Group 75. The National Archives). A year

325

later, a Navajo killed an Isleta Indian who was acting as head shepherd

for Juan Chaves of Sabinal: "the Navajo was hunting in the mountain

near the blue watters /sic/ on horseback . . ." (Agent Henry L. Dodge,

to Act. Gov. W. W. H. Davis, Navajo Agency, Dec. 26, 1855. Ibid.,

Agency Letters 1855).

Enroute to Bear Spring where New Fort Wingate was later

established, Major Kendrick met Delgadito, a prominent Navajo leader

who professed to be at peace. The Major reported that "The principal

man at this time living in the vicinity of Bear Spring, whose people

have been ill-disposed, declares himself anxious to plant in that

quarter & correspondingly anxious to preserve the Peace" (Kendrick to

AAG, Fort Defiance, Feb. 25, 1856. USAC, NM, Box 8, K2). Several

months later "immense numbers of Indians" were at Bear and Carriso Spring
(Kendrick to AAG, Fort Defiance, June 13, 1856. Ibid., K9), the latter
being located a few miles to the east of Bear.

After a visit to Zuni Pueblo in the summer of 1856, Major
Kendrick reported to Gov. Meriwether that

> The largest and best planting grounds of
> these Indians /Zuni/ are at La Nutria & the
> Pescado, each some 16 miles /northeast and east/
> from the Pueblo at present occupied. These
> grounds have been in their possession for many
> years, probably during the entire existence of the
> Pueblo itself, and their continued possession of
> both of them is of vital importance to the main-
> tenance of that community; without them it would
> be inevitably and utterly ruined.
>
> I do not know by what other title than pos-
> session these lands are held, nor have I legal
> knowledge enough to know whether that be good
> against the Navajoes, under the treaty of Laguna
> Negra (Kendrick to Meriwether, Fort Defiance, Aug 22,
> 1856. OIA, NM, LR, Misc. Papers 1856).

326

The Rio Pescado is a western flowing stream, draining the
southwest side of the Zuni Mountains, that provides a major water supply
for Zuni Pueblo. The Rio Nutrias joins this stream from the north. The
Inscription Rock that Major Kendrick believed to lie in Navajo country
lies about twelve miles airline to the southeast of the Rio Pescado.

For the next two years the situation in regard to the Navajos
remained about as usual. Agent Dodge reported that "A very large
majority of the Nation lives at this time upon the road between this
/Fort Defiance/ and the Blue waters . . ." (H. L. Dodge to Meriwether,
Fort Defiance, Nov. 4, 1856. Ibid., Agency Letters 1856); disputes
with New Mexicans over grazing land continued (Col. Bonneville to AAG,
Feb. 28, 1857. USAC, NM, Letters Sent, vol. 10, p. 89), and Es-kit-i-la,

a Mogollon Apache chief, sought to recover some captive children from Sandoval's band of Navajos with the assistance of Agent Michael Steck of the Southern Apache Agency (Michael Steck to Harley, Navajo Agent, Apache Agency, Jan. 10, 1858. Steck Papers, University of New Mexico).

In the late summer of 1858, Major Brooks launched a campaign against the Navajos to teach them to respect and abide by the white man's concept of lawful behavior. Capt. McLane attacked a party of Indians at Bear Springs: "8 or 10 Indians were killed; a number of their houses were destroyed, their blankets and cooking utensils captured . . ." etc. (Capt. George McLane to Lt. Col. D. S. Miles, Fort Defiance, Sept. 2, 1858. USAC, NM, LR, Box 10, M48).

A newsy letter written at Los Lunas, about twenty miles south of Albuquerque, informed Col. Bonneville that a large number of Navajo Indians were on the Rio Puerco of the East and in the mountains as far down as the village of Lemitar, about sixty miles south of Albuquerque.

327

> The Mexicans say that Gordo, a brother of
> Zarcillo Largo, and Nack-ath-lan, are among them.
> I recognised Jose Pilon and Vincente as rich men
> I have often seen at Fort Defiance. I counted
> within the space of two miles Seventeen different
> herds of sheep, and about four hundred head of
> horses. I also saw a number of clouds of dust in
> the mountains which the Indians informed me was
> caused by herds of sheep (Lt. J. I. G. Whistler to
> AAG, Nov. 1, 1858. Ibid., W25).

These southern ranging Navajos were probably keeping out of the way of Major Brooks' soldiers.

The years 1859 and 1860 were also troubled ones for Navajos and New Mexicans. A party of five Navajos drove off a small flock of sheep from the Rio Puerco Valley about twenty miles west of Los Lunas in the month of June. They were pursued to Zuni Mountain where the

sheep were recovered but the Indians escaped without harm (Capt. Geo
Sykes to AAAG, Los Lunas, June 6, 1859. OIA, NM, LR, Misc. Papers 1859).
In August they stole stock from the Zuni folk and escaped into the northern
mountains (Agent Alexander Baker to Collins, Fort Defiance, Aug. 14, 1859.
Ibid., Agency Papers).

The impact of Major Brooks' war is reflected in the report
of Lieut. John D. Wilkins:

> Last winter it was frequently reported that
> the Navajoes had driven large numbers of their
> animals sixty miles south of Zuni, also to the
> waters of the Chiriquito /Little/ Colorado, and
> on the northern slope of the 'Sierra Blanco'
> /southwest of Zuni/. Others represented that
> they were hid to the north and northwest of Moqui,
> and that Cuyatona's band took refuge to the north of
> the San Juan (AAAG to Major J. S. Simonson, Santa
> Fe, Aug. 14, 1859. 36 cong., 1 sess., sen. ex.
> doc. 2, pp. 335-336. Serial 1024).

328

Agent Steck, enroute to his Southern Apache agency, learned at the village
of Tome, some twenty-five miles south of Albuquerque, that Navajos had
stolen 20,000 head of sheep (an over estimate) and had driven them into
the Jornada which lay to the south. He also reported that Capt. Manuel
Chavez had had a fight with sixty Navajos about thirty miles west of
Fort Craig (Steck to Collins, Apache Agency, March 1, 1860. OIA, NM,
LR, Agency Letters 1860), a post near the north end of the Jornada.
And again in March of 1860 Steck reported that a band of Navajos were
as far south as the Jornada and were even accused of having killed some
one in the Organ Mountain to the east of Dona Ana in the Mesilla Valley
(Steck to Collins, Apache Agency, March 5, 1860. Ibid.). The Navajos of
course were also sometimes killed. Leading men such as Gordo, brother of

Sarcillos Largos, was reported as having been killed near the village of
Cubero; and Huero Miles, Mariano and Sarcillos Largos came to untimely
deaths.

Navajos did not always go south merely to escape the boys in
blue; they also had designs on their kinsmen as Agent Steck attested:

> The Navajoes about two months ago /September,
> 1860/ visited the Coyotero Country killing two
> warriors. They /Apaches/ immediately retaliated,
> following the party to their camp west of the Mogollon
> Mountain, and within one days ride of the Moqui vilages
> attacked the camp at dawn in the morning completely
> routing the Navajoes killing on the ground forty-
> four men and women and capturing fifteen children
> and seventy five cattle and horses (Steck to Collins,
> Las Cruces, New Mexico, November 26, 1860. Ibid.).

These troubles ended in an uneasy truce, but difficulties soon
developed again and evolved into the Canby campaign. In January of 1861,
Navajos ran off some mules from Blue Water and were trailed to a nearby   329
canyon in the Zuni Mountains, or about forty-five miles southeast of
Fort Fauntleroy. The pursuers discovered that the culprits had already
been attacked, probably by Zuni warriors (Canby to AAG, Fort Fauntleroy,
Feb. 4, 1861. USAC, NM, IR, Box 14, C23). Another truce was soon
negotiated whereby the principal men of the Navajos agreed to control
their bad people, a task that they had repeatedly claimed lay outside
their power. There was also a provision that "Until it is otherwise
stipulated the Navajoes will not be permitted to live to to graze
their flocks east of this post and any that may be found east of the
Chuska & Tun /i/ cha valleys and in the country to the South and east
of Zuni will be regarded and treated as robbers" (Canby, General Orders
No. 14, Fort Fauntleroy, Feb. 19, 1861. Ibid., C32). This accomplished,

Col. Canby next laid plans to destroy "the ⫽Navajo⫽ Ladrones (associated
with the Coyotero and Mimbres Apaches) that live in the neighborhood of
the Rita Quimado, the head waters of the Colorado Chiquito and the Sierra
de Latalis ⫽Datils?⫽" (Canby to AAG, Fort Fauntleroy, Feb. 19, 1861.
Ibid.). A "roving band (about 200) of Navajoes" were also seen with
kindred spirits among the Mescaleros encamped in the Organ Mountain
near Fort Fillmore in May of 1861 (Stevenson to AAG, Fort Stanton,
May 17, 1861. Ibid., Box 15, S31).

In June of 1862, a party of eighty Navajos were attacked by
troops under Lt. Gerald Russell: "I found them in one of the largest
Besques I ever saw in this country, and had to advance through a swamp
to get at them" (Russell to Capt. G. W. Howland, Bosque, Cerro Cabello,
June 18, 1862. Ibid., Box 18). The postal address and the description
of the country places the location of this fight in the region of the
present-day Caballo Reservoir on the Rio Grande just below Elephant
Butte Dam. The Jornada lies east of the Reservoir. The commonly known
Bosque del Apaches lies farther upstream above the Dam.

In July of 1863, three Navajo leaders, Barboncito, Delgadito
and Sarracino, arrived at Fort Wingate. When informed that they must
move to a new home at the Bosque Redondo, Barboncito replied that "they
(the peace party) cannot leave their country nor prevail upon others to
do so, that they are entirely separated from the ladrones, and they will
neither leave their country nor join the others. . . . " These Navajos
had come "from beyond Zuni" (Col. J. Francisco Chaves, post commander,
to AAG, Fort Wingate, July 9, 1863. USAC, Fort Wingate, Letters Sent,
RG98).

330

Two months later General Carleton passed along a report

> that there is a spring called Ojo de Cibolo,
> about fifteen miles west of Limitar, where the
> Navajoes drive their stolen cattle and 'jerk' the
> flesh at their leisure. Cannot you make arrange-
> ments /he asked Col. Rigg/ for a party of resolute
> men from your command to be stationed there for,
> say, thirty days, and kill every Navajo and Apache
> they can find? (Carleton to Rigg, Santa Fe, Aug. 4,
> 1863. 39 cong., 2 sess., sen. rept. 156, p.123.
> Serial 1279).

And again, a few days later, he claimed that "These Indians sometimes go as low or lower than Fort Thorn. As you are aware, they are a branch of the Apache family, talk the same language, and are said now to be mixed with predatory bands of the Apaches" (Carleton to Brig. Gen. Joseph R. West, Santa Fe, Aug. 7, 1863. Ibid., p. 127). Fort Thorn was near the southern end of the Jornada and on the west side of the Rio Grande.

331

Kit Carson, campaigning west of Fort Defiance, was visited by Little Foot who claimed to have come from the salines southwest of Zuni, heading for the Chusca Valley where his people lived, and had planned for their emigration because of poverty (Carson to Cutler, Pueblo, Colorado, Aug. 31, 1863. Department of Justice, Carson Papers, Washington, D. C.).

The "salines" might have been the salt lake that lies about forty-five miles airline due south of the Zuni Pueblo. The Rito Quemado is to the southeast of the lake. Carson also "ascertained that a large party of Navajos are on Salt River near the San Francisco Mts. among the Appachees, and within easy striking distance of the Pimo villages" (Ibid.). The area indicated was the land of the Coyotero Apaches. On an occasional map the White Mountains of east-central Arizona are marked San Francisco Mountains.

In the month of October, 1863, the post commander of Fort Wingate
led a scout southward for a distance of about 100 miles to a Navajo ranche
in the vicinity of the Datil Mountains, only to find that it had been
attacked two days before by Zuni warriors who had killed the chief,
Barboncito, with sixteen others, captured forty-four squaws and children
and about 1,000 sheep. He also reported seeing another detachment of
Navajos heading northward with a band of horses and sheep. The post
commander then moved south and west by way of the Little Colorado and
Venado Spring to Jacobs Well where he destroyed fields of corn, water
melons and pumpkins. From there the detachment returned to Fort Wingate
where the leader reported: "In the large scope of country over which I
have travelled during the past month, every evidence tends to show that
in that section they /Navajos/ have no longer permanent abiding places,
but are fleeing from one part to another, in a continual state of fear"
(Post Commander to AAG, Fort Wingate, Oct. 6, 1863. USAC, Fort Wingate,
Letters Sent, vol. 16).

332

Sordo (brother to Barboncito), Delgadito and Pedro Sarracino
who belonged to Barboncito's group arrived at Fort Wingate shortly after
this campaign to ask for peace in behalf of their people. They promised
to live up to the terms that had been agreed upon at one time, namely,
to subdue their own wrongdoers and if necessary to aid the military to
overcome them. Meanwhile they asked permission for their people to locate
on "la Gallina" (Capt. Rafael Chacon to General, Fuerte Wingate, Octubre 18
1863. USAC, Fort Wingate, Letters Sent, RG98). The Carleton policy required them, of course, to move to the Bosque Redondo, so there was little
chance that their request for locating on the Gallinas would be granted.

Meanwhile, Capt. Chacon issued a circular addressed to the residents of Cubero, Cebolleta, Laguna, Acoma, Rito and Paguate, advising them that they must cease any movements against the Barboncito band located on the Rito Quemado and thereabouts because of the proposition that had been forwarded to General Carleton as outlined above (Capt. Rafael Chacon, Fuerte Wingate, Octo. 18, 1863. Ibid.).

The following year, in January, Lt. Sanches of the New Mexico Volunteers led a scouting party to the south and reported "many Indians in the dattil mountains these are situated about 15 miles from & south east of El Rita Quemado. . . ." Sordo was killed. (Capt. Julius C. Shaw to AAG, Fort Wingate, Jan. 12, 1864. Ibid.). At this time, Capt. Shaw issued "particular instructions about siezing /sic/ every Navajoe man, woman & child in the towns of Cubero, Laguna, & El Rita" to be sent along with others to the Bosque Redondo (Ibid.). Delgadito also came in with some forty-nine Indians, and then set forth again to search for his own family "in the vicinity of the Rita Quemado and to bring in the family of Sordo his brother . . ." (Ibid.).

333

In September, Apaches were suspected of stealing stock from the Navajos encamped near Fort Wingate and Captain Montoya was sent in pursuit of the marauders: "after travelling between fifty and sixty miles /he/ met some other Navajos that reported the Apaches as having returned to the White Mountains" (Maj. E. W. Eaton to AAG. Fort Wingate, Sept. 29, 1864. USAC, Letters Sent by Subsistence Officers).

Navajos ran off some stock from Lemitar in the Rio Grande Valley in late 1864 or early 1865. Some of the sheep were recovered by the military and a squaw was captured who stated that the culprits were not

escapees from the Bosque Redondo, and that they had been living near the
Hopi villages. In the fall of 1864, they "had started in the direction
of 'Rito Quemado' and 'Cierra del Mangos' . . . stopping at different places
for a time and then moving on again"; furthermore, eight Apaches and eight
Navajos had committed the theft of stock (Maj E. W. Eaton to AAG. Fort
Wingate, Jan. 11, 1865. USAC, Fort Wingate, Letters Sent).

Manuelito was one of the hold-outs. Emissaries were sent out
in the winter to induce him to surrender and move to the Bosque Redondo,
but he refused, claiming that he would plant crops at the Canyon Bonito.
However, he gave information regarding the location of other Navajos:
a small band had been near the headwaters of the Little Colorado,
but were then "below the road that crosses to Fort Whipple. . . .
There has recently come from the 'Conino Mts.' three ranchitos, say
thirty souls. . . . This party are on their way to the Post. Another
group of about forty were at the Quelites /Colletas/ about twenty
miles from Fort Canby" (Maj. E. W. Eaton, post Commander, to AAG, Fort
Wingate, February 9, 1865. Ibid.). A Navajo was sent to the Little
Colorado by way of the Hopi villages in an effort to find Manuelito
and persuade him to surrender (Maj. Julius C. Shaw, Post Commander, to
AAG. Fort Wingate, April 1, 1865. Ibid., Letters Sent, vol. 16).

The army was more successful in locating this band than the
messenger of peace. In the summer of 1865 a pursuit party caught them
"at the Ojo del Mal-Pais about 75 miles South west of the old Fort
Canby, N. M. . . . /where/ they came upon the Camp of Manuelito and
party, they were encamped in deep ravine the descent into which was
very difficult" (Lt. Col. Julius C. Shaw, Post Commander, to Capt. H. B.

334

Carey, Fort Wingate, July 10, 1865. Ibid.). But their days were numbered
when not only the boys in blue but also their ancient enemies, the New
Mexicans and Utes, struck them on the Little Colorado (Capt. E. Butler
to AAG at Santa Fe, Fort Wingate, Jan. 18, 1866. USAC, Ibid.).

Following a raid by Navajos in the late winter of 1866, Capt.
Hodt led a punitive expedition against them. On

> the third day he crossed the Sierra del Datyl.
> . . . The Fourth day he came on the Indians--
> about fifty in number. . . . Capt. Hodt says
> the Indians were mixed--Navajos & Apaches--
> the majority he thinks being Apaches, the
> Indian who was killed . . . was an Apache. The
> Indians were striking for the Sierra Blanco
> (Capt. E. Butler to Maj. C. H. DeForrest, Fort
> Wingate, March 29, 1866. Ibid.).

Manuelito's band had fled as far south as the Sierra Escudilla
which lies southwest of the Datil Mts. The son of Tu-su-ni-nes reported that "Manuelito, Barboncito & Ganada Blanco are in the Sierra
del Escudilla. There are many Apaches with them." He also claimed that
"Manuelito & the two other chiefs desire to surrender & may come into
this Post, but Barboncito wishes to go to the Bosque by a trail to the
Southward of the Sierra del Datyl /Datil7, as he as well as his companions are afraid of the Moqui's and Zuni's" (Capt. E. Butler to Maj.
Cyrus H. DeForrest, Fort Wingate, July 28, 1866. Ibid., vol. 16).

The informant on the whole was correct. A son of El Ciejo
with twenty-eight other Navajos surrendered at Fort Wingate in August.
El Ciejo reported that "he met the Apaches who attacked our herd /the
army's7 at Los Romanzas, when they were about to start on that Stealing
expedition & also on their return from it." Also, El Ciejo believed that
"the Navajoes who are Still with the Apaches will come in and give

335

themselves up" (Butler to DeForrest. Fort Wingate, Aug. 21, 1866.
Ibid.). Manuelito did surrender in September with twenty-three others.
They had come "from the head waters of the Colorado Chiquito. . . . He
confirms the statement that Ganado Blanco is on his way to the Bosque
by a southern trail" (Butler to DeForrest. Fort Wingate, Sept. 2,
1866. Ibid.). A few probably held out to the bitter end and never
went to the Bosque Redondo.

Lieut. K. F. Leggett led a scout from Fort McRae in August
of 1868 westward to the village of La Canada Alamosa in the canyon of
the same name. There he picked up the trail of some Navajos which he
followed up the Canada to a point thirty miles northwest of the Hot
Springs. But more important than this was his description of the Hot
Springs:

336

> The indications at Ojo Caliente are that it is
> the great thoroughfare of the Indians and the great
> abundance of grass and wood and water here, make it a
> most desirable place for a post. The nearest water
> to it being the Ojo Luera, sixty miles distant where
> I believe the Navajoes have a rancheria (Leggett to
> Post Adjt., Fort McRae, August 21, 1868. USAC, NM,
> Fort McRae, Letters Sent, vol. 11).

This region had long been the route of travel for southern Apaches and
a temporary reservation for them was established at Ojo Caliente in
1870.